Dan Pelton leverages his extensive expertise as a clinical psychologist and his firsthand experience with burnout while serving on the front lines in Afghanistan to deliver a unique and compelling perspective on resilience. Combining profound insights with a masterful integration of scientific rigor and systems thinking, he challenges traditional approaches and presents innovative strategies for cultivating healthier, more engaging organizational cultures. This is an essential read for executives, talent management consultants, and anyone committed to creating a transformative, human-centric workplace.

–**GEORGE W. WATTS, MS, EdD,** CHAIRMAN, TOP LINE TALENT;
COAUTHOR OF *BECOMING A STRATEGIC LEADER: CAPITALIZE ON THE POWER OF YOUR PERSONALITY*

Dan Pelton taps into a wealth of experience to address the core challenges of today's workplace. In *Rethinking Employee Resilience*, he presents 10 actionable rules that empower you to navigate your career with confidence and adaptability in an ever-changing world.

–**MICHAEL P. LEITER, PhD,** PROFESSOR EMERITUS, ACADIA UNIVERSITY, WOLFVILLE, NS, CANADA

RETHINKING
EMPLOYEE
RESILIENCE

RETHINKING
EMPLOYEE
RESILIENCE

WHY OUR CURRENT APPROACH TO WORKER BURNOUT IS FAILING, AND HOW TO FIX IT

DAN PELTON, PHD

AMERICAN PSYCHOLOGICAL ASSOCIATION

Published by
American Psychological Association
750 First Street, NE
Washington, DC 20002
https://www.apa.org

Order Department
https://www.apa.org/pubs/books
order@apa.org

Typeset in Charter and Interstate by Circle Graphics, Inc., Reisterstown, MD

Printer: Sheridan Books, Chelsea, MI
Cover Designer: Mark Karis

Library of Congress Cataloging-in-Publication Data

Names: Pelton, Dan, author.
Title: Rethinking employee resilience : why our current approach to worker burnout is failing, and how to fix it / by Dan Pelton.
Description: Washington, DC : American Psychological Association, [2025] | Includes bibliographical references and index.
Identifiers: LCCN 2024045845 (print) | LCCN 2024045846 (ebook) | ISBN 9781433844126 (paperback) | ISBN 9781433844133 (ebook)
Subjects: LCSH: Burn out (Psychology) | Burn out (Psychology)--Prevention. | Job stress. | Quality of work life. | Resilience (Personality trait)
Classification: LCC BF481 .P45 2025 (print) | LCC BF481 (ebook) | DDC 158.7/2--dc23/eng/20241218
LC record available at https://lccn.loc.gov/2024045845
LC ebook record available at https://lccn.loc.gov/2024045846

https://doi.org/10.1037/0000454-000

Printed in the United States of America

10 9 8 7 6 5 4 3 2 1

In the initial stages of my career, my employee ID was P988U. This book is dedicated to employee P988V and the numerous other nameless, faceless employee contributors for whom its message is intended.

Contents

Preface

Why did you pick up this book? Well, if it's not just a time killer, my bet is that, like me, you're captivated by the allure of *resilience*. It's the buzzword of the moment, some would argue a bit worn out, but still raising eyebrows, especially in the aftermath of the COVID-19 pandemic. We're drawn to tales of triumph over adversity, stories that spark hope and make us believe every challenge can be conquered. But let's ditch the Hollywood sheen. Resilience stories aren't polished; they're gritty, dirty, and born from the ashes of suffering. In fact, adversity is the often-overlooked heartbeat of resilience. I can't unravel every mystery, but I will share insights into burnout and resilience forged in my own battles.

Keep in mind, as you turn these pages, that I am a clinical psychologist. My tour as an Army brigade psychologist in Afghanistan in 2011 deeply influenced my views on burnout. The day we deployed remains etched in my memory: farewells whispered to family, a dizzying series of international stops, and a grueling week of training in Kyrgyzstan.

One memory is particularly striking: Our flight into Afghan airspace. We were tightly packed, shoulder to shoulder, in the expansive interior of a C-17, the cabin lights dimmed to shadows. Clad in Kevlar and guided by the faint, eerie red glow of headlamps to evade detection from hostile forces below, a palpable tension filled the air. Landing in the darkness, the weight of imminent danger and responsibility settled on my shoulders as I assumed the role of the sole clinical psychologist for 18 bases and outposts.

Almost immediately upon arrival at our base, I began seeing patients. The issues they faced were familiar—depression, anxiety, work stress—but here, the stakes were unmistakably higher. The complexity of many cases required round-the-clock attention. I navigated this surreal landscape in an environment in which the lines between vigilance and exhaustion often blurred. Amidst this chaos, the unyielding spirit and raw humanity of the soldiers were profoundly inspiring.

Around 2 months into the deployment, I felt an overwhelming sense of isolation. As the sole psychologist on a vast base, responsible for soldiers across 17 other bases, the weight of responsibility grew. The absence of professional colleagues exacerbated feelings of solitude. My natural reaction was to turn inward, relying on training. Only later did I recognize the mounting pressures—incessant grind, isolation, self-reliance—as precursors to my own experience of burnout.

By January 2011, the toll manifested in migraines—these were no ordinary headaches but rather the monstrous kind the world isn't familiar with. Enter *status migrainosus*, a rare condition in which a migraine theoretically lasts more than 72 hours. For me, over the years, it's not a theoretical 72 hours; we're talking months and months and months on end, including this present moment as I write this book. Treatment options were limited and often ineffective, leaving endurance as my only recourse. Intermittent ordinary headaches offered brief respite from this relentless condition, which persisted for 4 months during my deployment.

As these challenges persisted, daily tasks transformed into battles, with the lingering effects of burnout. Burnout fueled a growing cynicism and detachment, eroding my empathy—the cornerstone of my profession. It was a bitter irony: The very efforts to support and heal were the same ones depleting my ability to do so.

How do you provide therapy for emotional pain when you, as a therapist, are also suffering, both physically and emotionally? The irony is stark: Both forms of pain are invisible. Yet the necessity for self-care and perseverance remains constant. So I continued, propelled not by choice but by necessity.

In the months that followed, my sessions with soldiers uncovered a common theme: Overwhelming demands led to their relentless exhaustion. They were not just fatigued; they were experiencing deep-seated burnout, exacerbated by the military's ingrained culture. Yet amidst this struggle, I saw flashes of hope. I recognized that systemic issues were contributing to burnout and that even small changes in leadership approaches and team interactions could significantly alleviate it. This revelation was pivotal: Burnout is not just a personal battle but one deeply intertwined with the organizational culture and ethos. True resilience involves more than just personal recovery; it requires a supportive environment that fosters and sustains it.

Throughout this period, I had a front-row seat into the challenges faced by other soldiers even as I tested my own limits, only to learn the importance of pausing and allowing myself time to recuperate. While resilience is often described as the ability to "bounce back," that definition doesn't capture the full experience of enduring adversity. Rather, the concept of endurance is crucial—not sought after, but necessary. Pain and suffering serve as constant reminders of our vulnerability and dependence, concepts often at odds with our broad cultural narrative of individualism and the perpetual pursuit of being consistently at one's best. But coming to terms with this—admitting that we are both vulnerable and dependent on others during adversity—is freeing and authentic. It's what helps me, and others I have counseled, put one foot in front of the other to endure and become more resilient.

Perhaps endurance is a thought experiment for you. I've been forced to challenge a deeply held belief that if I can't find a reason for pain and suffering, there must not be one. Acknowledging this vulnerability broke through the denial in which I lived and allowed me to fully appreciate my susceptibility to stress, burnout, and anxiety. I'm not invincible, as it turns out. Life's unpredictability has served as a poignant reminder for me that my world can be disrupted suddenly and without warning. And it can happen to you too. Endurance reminds us not to be caught off guard or overwhelmed by our own fragility.

In the pursuit of endurance, I've found solace in embracing the present moment, steering away from the shadows of the past and the uncertainties of the future. Author Timothy Keller (2013) noted that in face of seemingly untenable adversity, we are to "walk, to grieve and weep, to trust and pray, to think, thank, and love, and to hope" (p. 237). These simple practices, often overlooked or minimized, transform from mere survival tools into essential elements of a resilient and enduring journey.

A recurring theme of this book is the importance of focusing on what can be controlled and yielding what cannot. Often, the tendency is to minimize or overlook what can be controlled while worrying about elements beyond our influence. Initially, this inverted perspective posed challenges in navigating obstacles effectively. However, through gained wisdom, I've come to recognize the harmful nature of this inverted perspective.

Resilience, to me, is not about suppressing our true emotional state; rather, it's about possessing the wisdom to discern when to forge ahead and when to yield. Despite the hurdles, I cling to hope, anchoring myself in what provides meaning for me. I wish the same for you—knowing what grounds you and gives you meaning and the things that can anchor you and offer hope within the storm. Through this lens, I am propelled to unpack what it means to be resilient and, more broadly, what organizations can do to harness workforce resilience.

Acknowledgments

Writing a book on adversity while facing it myself—well, that was something I never quite anticipated. What started as a theoretical exercise quickly became personal, as the principles I was writing about took root in my own life.

I've written at length in this book about the power of community and support, and my strongest pillar is at home: my wife, Courtnee. You always had the right words at just the right time, balancing encouragement with challenge so effortlessly. You helped me breathe life into abstract ideas, and you did it all with such grace. You're the steady force behind everything we do, and I love you not just for that, but for all that you are.

To my children, Elliana and Eva—though you think I'm writing a children's book, the way your faces light up when I talk about my work gives me so much encouragement. You've both said you want to be writers when you grow up, and I have to believe that all my hours "going click-clack" at the keyboard left a positive mark on you. That brings me immense joy.

Mom and Dad, Marilyn and Steve—you are my guides. When I need wisdom or encouragement, I turn to you first. Your discernment, your knack for cutting through the noise and offering sound advice, are gifts I hope to pass on to my own children someday. Thank you for everything.

To my family back in Western New York—you didn't flinch when I told you I was writing a book. Instead, you asked the sharp, thoughtful questions that made me rethink and refine my ideas. And while we may be separated by miles, your support feels like it's always right here with me.

A special thanks to my friend and fellow psychologist, Paul El-Meouchy, who planted the seed that grew into this book. Paul, it was you who pushed me to present on workforce resilience at a conference, and that's where it all began. Thank you, my friend and lifelong colleague.

I'm also grateful to Lauren McGroarty, Kelsey Brock, and Ali Muckle. Lauren, you shaped my thinking on culture; Kelsey, your wealth of knowledge helped challenge my approach to resilient leadership; and Ali, your invaluable insights on organizational change were indispensable. I couldn't have done it without this incredible brain trust.

To my colleagues at Deloitte Consulting—Mike Gelles, Lynda Boggs, Pat Nealon, Michael de Leon—thank you for your boundless enthusiasm when I mentioned writing this book in my "free time." Your encouragement meant the world to me.

Lastly, to the team at APA—Jennika Baines, none of this would be possible without you. When my vision for this book was blurry, you had clarity. Your passion for this topic fueled my own, and your support throughout the entire process has been unwavering. Thank you for being my advocate and my champion.

And finally, to all the patients I've worked with in clinical settings and the leaders I've coached—you are the living proof that resilience is born in adversity. You've taught me what it means to endure, to persist, to lean on others, and to emerge on the other side with grace and strength. I am profoundly grateful to have been just a small part of your journeys.

RETHINKING
EMPLOYEE
RESILIENCE

INTRODUCTION

The greatest obstacle to discovery is not ignorance—it is the illusion of knowledge.

—Daniel Boorstin

Humans instinctively crave stability, certainty, and comfort. Our familiar beliefs serve as guiding lights through the unknown, even though in reality they may be merely illusions of control. Occasionally, our cherished assumptions turn out to be more fiction than fact. This book explores the insights that can be unlocked through unconventional approaches to accepted wisdom. It is about acknowledging our intellectual boundaries and challenging our preconceptions about burnout and resilience.

Now, let's clarify what this book is not.

This book is not a self-help book. There are plenty out there, but this is not one of them. In fact, I believe my profession (mental health) has created a disservice to the public by emboldening the self-help industry in its assertions that burnout is solely a personal problem that requires a personal solution. It is not. Like the canary who unwittingly flies into the coal mine to

https://doi.org/10.1037/0000454-001
Rethinking Employee Resilience: Why Our Current Approach to Worker Burnout Is Failing, and How to Fix It, by D. Pelton

confirm, through its death, that deadly toxins are present in the environment, the workforce is at risk for exposure to harm that, without intentional investment, will continue to severely compromise employee health. In the absence of codified workforce norms or strategies to minimize the mental health burden on the workforce, employees will continue to be at mental health risk, even at risk for early and untimely death.

I hope I have your attention. If not, I'll restate it in another way: We don't blame the canary for dying, so why are we blaming the workforce for burnout?

To truly rethink employee resilience, we must first understand its components. At its core sits burnout—a syndrome identified by the World Health Organization (2024) as stemming from chronic workplace stress. Manifesting as exhaustion, increased mental distance from one's job or feelings of negativism or cynicism related to one's job, and reduced professional efficacy, these symptoms are not just troubling. They are cries for help that signal deeper systemic problems.

Contrary to common belief, high engagement at work doesn't always prevent burnout and can, in fact, exacerbate it. Although often viewed as the ultimate goal for HR and business leaders, high engagement without adequate support can paradoxically lead to burnout. This counterintuitive insight drives the need to reconsider our strategies.

Noting the lack of a formal framework for workforce resilience, I introduce a new model that integrates optimizing engagement with robust protections against burnout. I argue that achieving this balance is the key to defining and activating workforce resilience. *Rethinking Employee Resilience* disrupts established notions surrounding burnout by creating new truths about resilience. It's only by questioning the status quo that we uncover innovative solutions.

In Part I of this book, I argue that addressing workforce burnout demands the bravery to contest prevailing yet flawed ideas about well-being. I urge you to acknowledge and identify any resistance you might feel toward reevaluating your beliefs on burnout or resilience. All people, at one time or another, experience these resistances. They could stem from a desire for control or perfection, a need for approval, or fear of change. Resistance might also emerge from emotional discomfort such as anxiety, concerns about others' perceptions, or a reluctance to accept loss. Then I tackle three prevalent wellness myths that shape our subsequent strategies: the misconceptions that (a) burnout isn't all that serious; (b) the responsibility for burnout rests solely with the individual, not the organization; and (c) employee engagement is the ultimate measure of a happy and healthy workforce.

In Part II, I discuss new truths about resilience by deconstructing old ones. This discussion emphasizes the necessity to distinguish between individual, workforce, and organizational resilience. I argue for a shift toward systemic workforce solutions for burnout and disengagement, rather than limiting focus to individual remedies. I introduce an operational definition of *workforce resilience*, highlighting how preventing burnout and creating optimal engagement conditions can significantly enhance a company's bottom line. The transformative journey continues with a deep dive into the job demands–resources model. This model, balancing job demands with available resources, is flexible across 12 work-related dimensions that I have identified. These dimensions pave the way for *cultural fulcrums*—performance management, analytics, job crafting, and strategic communications. When aligned with company values and practices, these four levers become pivotal in steering the organizational culture toward enhanced well-being and performance.

Part III, the concluding chapters of the book, addresses several fundamental principles. These are designed to empower all employees—from the CEO to the newest team member—to foster a culture of workforce resilience. This dynamic exploration reveals how these practices animate every level of the organizational hierarchy. This section culminates with use cases, offering diverse on-ramps tailored to organizations of all sizes.

Throughout the book, I present a series of questions for you to consider. Although you might not be able to answer them all, do try. These questions are designed to tap into your psychological processes, to help you think and, ultimately, change or modify your behavior. I find that addressing such questions not only aids us to understand ourselves better but also links psychological insights to our day-to-day work.

Rethinking Employee Resilience invites you on an exhilarating journey, weaving through the rich tapestry of psychological theory, personality frameworks, and job design principles. I present best practices, consider shifts in organizational culture, and challenge long-held orthodoxies with a sprinkle of ill-timed jokes and exploration of grassroots change, all while maintaining a healthy dose of skepticism toward surface appearances.

In today's world where burnout is becoming more common, this book serves as an urgent call to action. It compels organizations to evolve beyond the confines of boardrooms, extending deep into every cubicle and workstation. By understanding and realigning the deeply ingrained dynamics of the workplace, we possess the power to transform our work environments from places of mere survival to thriving ecosystems. This quest is not solely about enhancing employee satisfaction; it is about safeguarding the future of work, ensuring the survival of organizations, and positioning human resilience at the heart of all progress. As you turn each page, a critical question looms: Will you merely observe from the sidelines, like the majority of your peers, or will you be among the bold 1% who take risks and muster the courage to drive meaningful change?

WHY I WROTE THIS BOOK

As 2020 kicked off, we were graced with the unexpected arrival of a global pandemic. As COVID-19 swept across the world, uncertainty permeated the air, and the workforce felt its weight. At that time, I was 9 years out of the military and had spent nearly all that period at a large management consulting firm. There, I witnessed firsthand the stress and anxiety that gripped our tens of thousands of employees across the globe. And yet, amid this somber backdrop, moments of levity emerged. Top-tier consultants were panic buying ergonomic chairs and squinting at Zoom screens, trying to figure out if Mike from the Analytics Department was frozen or just deep in thought. Throughout it all, I couldn't help but wonder: In the grand scheme of 2020, was being on mute in virtual meetings truly our greatest misstep?

Tapping into my clinical psychology roots, I felt compelled to step in, aiming to be a beacon of hope. I dished out what I believed to be pearls of wisdom on well-being, navigated the maze of burnout, and preached the gospel of resilience. Little did I fathom, those spontaneous TED Talk-esque sessions would define the whirlwind adventure of my next 3 years. Week after week, my calendar brimmed with speaking engagements. It wasn't just my firm; clients and external organizations also sought advice on fostering what they termed "workforce resilience." Like any diligent consultant, I turned to Google and a vast array of Amazon books for answers. To my surprise, the pickings were slim. I found ample content on individual and organizational resilience—how people and companies weather hardships. Yet very little focused on the collective well-being of an organization's people.

Undeterred, I pressed on. Conversations continued, despite my initial doubts. Each week, fueled by tales from my deployment, I found firmer ground. My voice grew stronger. I plunged into the systemic issues driving burnout, engaging leaders, running workshops, and absorbing lessons from countless encounters. A trend emerged. Prepandemic, burnout research often wore a "health care" badge; resilience, a "military" one. My unique cross-section of experiences in both fields bolstered my confidence.

Writing this book forced me to scrutinize my beliefs about burnout and resilience. My military background exposed me to the institutional roots of burnout, yet those memories had faded over time. Then came 2020—everyone's favorite year. Watching many flounder in unsupportive environments jolted me awake. I had too often promoted quick self-help fixes, unwittingly reinforcing the myth of burnout as a lone battle.

Through this journey of self-reexamination, I started by scrutinizing our employee well-being initiatives. I aimed to understand why current efforts fell short and how we might devise a more effective approach that tackles the root causes of burnout and disengagement. It quickly became clear: The corporate wellness movement largely treats burnout and stress as personal issues needing individual solutions. However, perks like yoga classes, nap pods, and ping pong tables barely scratch the surface of the deep-seated mental health challenges in the workforce.

Now, as I pen the final words of this book, I've played dual roles: observer and participant in the arena of burnout. My determination is clear: to advocate for a profound transformation in how organizations cultivate health and well-being. Through these pages, my goal extends beyond sharing insights. I aim to provoke you into recognizing, questioning, and ultimately reshaping the structures that support or undermine workforce resilience.

PART **I** RETHINKING BURNOUT

1 CHALLENGING THE STATUS QUO

Rethinking Mental Health Wisdom

What important truth do very few people agree with you on?

—Peter Thiel, *Zero to One*, p. 5

This chapter-opening question is a favorite that entrepreneur, billionaire venture capitalist, and polarizing figure Peter Thiel asks of all prospective job candidates (Thiel & Masters, 2014). Interviewees likely receive it with wide eyes and sweaty palms, quickly wracking their brains for a response that's thoughtful, compelling, and for the truly daring, a bit provocative. Answering such a question not only demands critical thinking on the spot but also the courage to challenge widely held beliefs.

Thiel has likely used this question with thousands of candidates, looking for those who are willing to publicly challenge conventional wisdom. Having the type of courage to challenge agreed-upon knowledge and share a belief that is likely unpopular, in his estimation, is rarer than genius (Thiel & Masters, 2014). He will commonly hear answers such as "Our education system is broken and urgently needs to be fixed." Thiel notes that this is a "bad answer" because although it may be true, it's a widely accepted belief.

https://doi.org/10.1037/0000454-002
Rethinking Employee Resilience: Why Our Current Approach to Worker Burnout Is Failing, and How to Fix It, by D. Pelton

He asserts that people must challenge their assumptions, as doing so will help to break free from the trapping of conventional thinking and help foster innovation. For instance, in the context of education, it is important to consider whether the current approach is fundamentally flawed and/or whether new models of education have not yet been considered. If a candidate offered him the very controversial assertion, "Our education system can only be fixed by eliminating property tax-based public education," that response would certainly draw his attention.

To truly innovate, Thiel asserts that people must look beyond the present and challenge the status quo (Thiel & Masters, 2014). Duplicating efforts of visionaries like Steve Jobs or Bill Gates is easy because it requires merely building upon their foundations, working with what already exists. True innovation, in contrast, stems from the creation of something entirely new and groundbreaking—taking a lead from nothing to something, or as Thiel describes it, as going from zero to one. His contrarian question is meant to stoke thoughtfulness, courage, and risk taking and ferret out candidates who have the potential to generate new ideas and solutions from those who are prone to regurgitate conventional patterns.

In Chapter 1, I confront the need to challenge established norms to fuel innovation and transformation in mental health and wellness. I argue for rejecting conformity and cultivating diverse perspectives to overcome innate biases and enhance organizational thinking. The chapter includes a critical examination of the transition of the wellness industry toward evidence-backed strategies, including the integration of AI and digital tools in therapy. Highlighting the mismatch between rising wellness investments and the prevalence of burnout, I call for a deeper understanding of burnout as a systemic issue, pushing for significant shifts in both thought and practice.

REVISITING MENTAL HEALTH PROBLEMS, SOLUTIONS, AND OUTCOMES

To stoke the fire a bit more, let's revisit the contrarian question. Imagine that you're waiting to meet with Peter Thiel to discuss a potential role in his wellness startup, and you're feeling confident. You've done your research; you know the latest digital therapeutics, market trends, and all the competitive details. But then Thiel asks you the question, "What important truth about mental health and well-being do very few people agree with you on?" You stumble and try to throw some graphs and pie charts at him, but it's clear you're not prepared for this question. Later, you bump into a friend who's also applying for the job, and you share the question. Your friend, now a quivering mess, recognizes how ill prepared they are for the interview, but at least they have time. They consider whether Thiel's question is more than just a curveball but rather a window into a mindset that could transform the industry.

Let's think through how we might answer this question. First, let's start by questioning conventional truths about mental health and wellness. It's no secret that our nation is facing significant mental health challenges, a situation exacerbated by what has been identified as the loneliness epidemic (U.S. Department of Health and Human Services, 2023). These challenges include, at minimum, limited access to mental health services, health inequity, stigma reduction, mental illness among the homeless population, substance use and addiction, and suicide.

Next, think about solutions that have been offered to address these problems and the effectiveness of each solution. Conventional approaches to address these problems are outlined in Table 1.1. So far, so good—clean problems with clean (and effective) solutions.

Now let's talk outcomes, but not without considering the fine print. Each statement in the outcomes column deserves a footnote to clarify that the associated solutions work, with a few conditions. Take, for instance, the

TABLE 1.1. Conventional Approaches to Solving Health Care Challenges

Problem	Conventional solution	Outcomes
Access to mental health services	Increase funding, reduce cost, increase number of professionals	Effective for improving mental health outcomes
Health equity	Ensure all have access to affordable, quality health care	Can reduce disparities in health outcomes
Stigma reduction	Education and awareness, reducing negative attitudes	Can increase awareness and reduce negative attitudes
Mental illness among the homeless population	Housing-first models, support services for mental health	Can reduce homelessness and improve mental health outcomes
Substance use and addiction	Prevention, treatment, recovery support programs	Some interventions have been shown to be effective
Suicide	Increase access to crisis hotlines, training programs	Can reduce suicide rates

conventional belief that public health campaigns and education are game changers in transforming attitudes toward mental health, leading to increased treatment engagement. Surprisingly, and against common wisdom, empirical evidence doesn't wholeheartedly back this up. In a report by the RAND Corporation (Acosta et al., 2014), the notion that stigma hinders treatment seeking was unsupported. While there's no shortage of studies on immediate outcomes such as changing attitudes and intentions, the big question remains unanswered—does reducing stigma truly result in sustained improvements in therapeutic initiation and long-term engagement, the supposed keys to tackling mental illness rates?

Before hitching our wagon to public health campaigns as the panacea for treatment engagement, it's crucial to face the reality that this approach might not be as effective as it seems. It's time to challenge our assumptions, open our minds, and explore alternative solutions that can genuinely boost treatment seeking and engagement. After all, questioning the status quo is the first step toward making real strides in tackling the formidable issue of mental health stigma.

This isn't just theoretical musing. Prestigious publications like *The Wall Street Journal* and *The New Yorker* are already on the case, suggesting that overcoming persistent challenges such as mental health issues and homelessness may require bold, innovative solutions. Imagine integrating AI into psychotherapy or reevaluating the role of asylums in modern society. Provocative headlines such as "It's Time To Bring Back Asylums" (Oshinsky, 2023) and "Can A.I. Treat Mental Illness?" (Khullar, 2023) not only capture attention but also provoke thought. And if those aren't startling enough, consider that the U.S. Food and Drug Administration recently approved the first prescription video game for treating attention-deficit/hyperactivity disorder, signaling a new era in which technology significantly intersects with mental health interventions (Office of the Commissioner, 2020). This series of developments underscores a growing trend: Conventional approaches are being challenged, and perhaps rightfully so, as we navigate the complexities of mental health solutions in the 21st century.

For a clinician, the thought of reviving asylums, trading hard-earned expertise for chatty bots, or prescribing video games for mental health might trigger a healthy dose of skepticism. However, before we dismiss these innovations outright, it's worth asking a crucial question: Is this skepticism rooted in deeply ingrained beliefs, such as the fear that technology threatens the future of our profession, or are we genuinely concerned about the effectiveness and ethics of these groundbreaking approaches?

Let's probe a bit deeper with our beliefs. We can apply the same rubric—problem, solution, effectiveness—to the broad wellness movement to help deepen our thinking. To begin, consider some data and financial trends.

- Data Insights
  - In a survey of workplace burnout (Deloitte, 2015), 77% of respondents reported having experienced burnout in their current job.
  - Additionally, 91% said stress affects their work quality, 83% said burnout affects their relationships, and 66% admitted to skipping meals because of stress or being too busy (Deloitte, 2015).
  - Workforce burnout has reportedly increased since the peak of the pandemic (Aflac, n.d.).
- Financial Trends
  - Worldwide, the corporate wellness market was valued at 54.1 billion U.S. dollars in 2021 and is estimated to be valued at more than 93 billion U.S. dollars by 2028 (Statista, n.d.).
  - The self-improvement market, encompassing tools for personal growth and self-improvement without professional intervention, saw 5.6% year-over-year growth, anticipating a market size of $13.2B in 2022 (Uţă, 2019).

In a nutshell, even as spending on wellness climbs, burnout rates also rise, revealing a perplexing contradiction: Greater investments in well-being don't necessarily equate to healthier employees. Moreover, given the spike in corporate wellness investments and the booming self-help sector, we might infer that

- the rise in workforce stress-related problems, including burnout, signals a lack of effective self-help practices;
- the underlying expectation is that employees are solely responsible for self-care; and
- embracing the right self-help strategies can be the antidote to burnout and workplace stress.

While many people agree that tackling workplace stress (problem) goes beyond merely relying on self-help strategies (conventional solution), the realization that current solutions might be skimming the surface of the issue (outcomes) is growing. It's time to critically evaluate the impact of self-help approaches on corporate wellness. But beyond that, a more pressing and intricate question looms: How can systemic approaches authentically cultivate a culture of wellness?

WELLNESS: MORE THAN JUST A TREND

The wellness industry, promising enhanced physical and mental well-being through exercise, nutrition, and self-care, elicits mixed reactions. Some advocate for wellness initiatives as essential to healthier living, while critics argue they exploit vulnerable consumers with costly and ineffective solutions. To understand the complexity, we must examine the data more closely and uncover the nuanced story beneath the surface.

After navigating a global pandemic and binge watching some impressive TV marathons that showcased the latest and greatest innovations in wellness, it's evident: Wellness is much more than a hot new fitness buzz or an exotic tea cleanse. At its heart, it's about holistic practices and choices aimed at enhancing overall well-being. Forget just munching on quinoa salads or sipping mysterious green juices; wellness encompasses everything from functional training and nutrition to the rise of meditation apps. And the numbers love a good wellness story:

- Wellness sector growth is projected at 8.6% average annual growth, with the wellness economy reaching $8.5 trillion in 2027 (Global Wellness Institute, n.d.).

- Corporate wellness sector projected market share is estimated at $138.1 billion by 2031 (Transparency Market Research, n.d.).

- mHealth Apps funding in 2020: Nearly $1.2 billion (Mercom Capital Group, 2024).

- Mental wellness apps have an expected revenue in 2022 of almost 500 million U.S. dollars (Auxier et al., 2021).

As investment in the wellness sector surges, it's clear that this movement isn't just a top-down initiative. Despite the challenges of the pandemic, there's an unmistakable, worldwide emphasis on well-being. Key data points underscore its significance in the corporate world:

- A report of trends in human capital (Deloitte, 2020) suggested that 80% of surveyed participants recognized well-being as crucial for organizational success (Deloitte, 2020).

- 91% of surveyed employees reported setting well-being goals (S. Hatfield et al., 2022).

- 75% of all surveyed employees and 89% of the C-suite considered well-being a top priority (S. Hatfield et al., 2022).

- 87% of surveyed employees reported having access to mental well-being resources (S. Hatfield et al., 2022).

- More than 77% of employers surveyed viewed wellness programs as vital in reducing health care costs (Miller, 2010).

Collectively, these findings emphasize that the commitment to well-being is both organizational and personal, and underline the essential role of comprehensive wellness programs in today's corporate culture.

FROM INTENTION TO IMPLEMENTATION: WHERE WELLNESS PROGRAMS FALL SHORT

In her influential book, *The Burnout Epidemic,* journalist and author Jennifer Moss (2021) sheds light on the complexities of the wellness movement. While there's undeniable enthusiasm and momentum supporting wellness, Moss emphasized a need for informed skepticism. She asserted, "It's critical that organizations ensure that the programming is well executed, not just well intended" (Moss, 2021, p. 126). This sentiment is especially poignant considering many efficacy reports are often sponsored by program vendors.

Nevertheless, several robust empirical studies provide insights into the impact of these programs, and tension within the wellness sector becomes even more apparent when looking at recent scientific investigations. For example, in a randomized controlled trial, researchers examined the claims surrounding workplace wellness (Song & Baicker, 2019). In this study of 30,000+ employees, some wellness behaviors saw an uptick, but vital health and employment metrics stayed stagnant. Clinical markers, including body mass index and blood pressure, didn't significantly change. Furthermore, the impact of the program was minimal on the 27 self-reported health behaviors, 10 clinical health markers, and 38 spending measures. Benefits such as reduced absenteeism and enhanced job tenure were not evident.

This sentiment of skepticism is further amplified by the findings of Mattke et al. (2013). While many employers are confident in these programs as cost-saving measures, the study revealed two key insights: (a) Only half of the employers had formally evaluated their program's effects, and (b) just 2% saw tangible savings. Further, a study of the lifestyle management program at PepsiCo (Caloyeras et al., 2014), which exemplifies traditional wellness initiatives promoting healthy habits, showed no clear return on investment, particularly concerning health care costs. While absenteeism showed a minor dip, the data overall suggest that workplace wellness programs might not deliver the expected outcomes. Although it's not accurate to dismiss all wellness programs as ineffective, Moss's (2021) argument underscores the need to move beyond mere intentions. Rather, when possible, we must invest in robust research designs and outcomes that can validate our efforts.

The effectiveness of the wellness industry is a topic of much debate when it comes to mental health. Notably, more than half of American employers surveyed reported offering mindfulness training (Keng et al., 2011), which, when used clinically, can have a demonstrable impact on mental health. However, it's not just about offering these programs; it's also about how they're applied, particularly outside of a clinical context. Some studies underscore the benefits of mindfulness in the workplace and highlight a concerning trend: Many practices in the industry are self-centered. For instance, breath-based meditation techniques can be beneficial, but there's a catch. By effectively reducing feelings of guilt, they can unintentionally decrease the motivation to rectify past mistakes or make amends (Cameron & Hafenbrack, 2022).

Now, this perspective is not all doom and gloom. As in other industries, the wellness industry might be constrained in its creative problem solving, to Thiel and Masters's (2014) point, because of a lack of courage to test unconventional thinking. People often believe in an idea, witness a surge in its popularity, and then seize the opportunity to capitalize on this momentum.

The wellness movement undeniably offers promising tools, potentially equipping individuals with the means and assurances to better manage their health. However, blindly accepting its effectiveness without scrutiny may perpetuate harmful myths, such as blaming employees for their burnout. Furthermore, the tendency to increase hype without sufficient evidence may undermine its credibility.

FROM CLINICAL OBSERVATION TO WORKPLACE EPIDEMIC: TRACING THE EVOLUTION OF BURNOUT

Part I of this book addresses the concept of burnout in detail, including challenges to traditional perspectives surrounding it. Let's start with confronting the burnout monster.

While the pandemic has cast a stark light on workplace burnout, this malaise is far from a modern phenomenon—it was first clinically described in the early 1970s by Freudenberger (1974). At its heart, burnout manifests from prolonged work-related stress and is characterized by persistent exhaustion, a growing negativity or cynicism toward one's job, and a noticeable decline in professional efficacy (Maslach, 1993). The World Health Organization (2024) defined *workplace burnout* specifically as an occupational syndrome resulting from chronic, unmanaged workplace stress.

We can better understand burnout through some vivid metaphors. Picture this: You're diligently working at your laptop in your home office. Unseen, yet perilous, are invisible carcinogens swirling in the air—silent but deadly threats to your health. Everything appears normal, yet something feels distinctly off, the danger hidden yet palpable. Next, shift this image to the bustling floor of the New York Stock Exchange. Imagine yourself slumped at your desk, overwhelmed and immobilized by chaos. Around you, the world moves at a frenetic pace. Your coworker taps your shoulder, urgently, unaware of the turmoil churning inside you. You open your mouth to speak, but words fail to capture your profound fatigue. Finally, envision yourself adrift in the ocean, clinging to a life preserver. You are alone, surrounded by the immense sea, menaced by lurking threats and the occasional dive-bombing seagull. The isolation is profound, the silence overwhelming, as waves of loneliness and despair wash over you. You are trapped in this watery expanse, helplessly bobbing in the swells, a stark metaphor for the feelings of isolation and helplessness that burnout engenders. These scenarios, while metaphorical, underscore the insidious and often invisible nature of burnout, illustrating how it can permeate various aspects of our lives, often without clear or immediate solutions.

Recent studies provide empirical evidence that reflects these metaphors and offer a striking quantification of the repercussions of burnout. According to leading research surveyed by the American Psychological Association (2023), the effects on individuals and organizations are alarmingly concrete:

- Employees with burnout have a 57% increased risk of workplace absence greater than 2 weeks due to illness.

- Employees with burnout have a 180% risk of developing depressive disorders.

- Employees with burnout have an 84% increased risk of Type 2 diabetes and have a 40% increased risk of hypertension.

- Burnout can have a negative impact on essential cognitive processes such as short-term memory and attention, which are vital for day-to-day work activities.

As for recovery, naturalistic studies indicate that the recuperation period spans from 1 to 3 years (Bernier, 1998). Some researchers even question the feasibility of full recovery from burnout (Hakanen & Bakker, 2017).

Ironically, while burnout is now a buzzword, understanding of the phenomenon seems more clouded than before. It's emerged from the shadows: More people are familiar with the term, yet it's largely untested and oversimplified. The prevailing notion is that burnout is just part and parcel of the modern work experience—an individual's predicament that might be alleviated if they were merely more passionate or engaged with their job.

HOW NONCONFORMITY FUELS WORKPLACE INNOVATION

Navigating the challenges of today's work environment demands a willingness to question conventional wisdom and explore unpopular ideas, fostering a culture that prevents burnout and boosts engagement. This approach isn't merely about being contrarian; such a strategy is an evidence-based method for fostering innovation and resilience, as seen in Asch's (1955) classic study on social conformity. Asch's findings showed that group pressure often leads people to make incorrect choices, even when they know the right answer, with 75% conforming to majority opinions at least once. Similarly, Eurich (2018) found that although a staggering 95% of individuals report believing they possess self-awareness, the empirical reality exposed a stark discord: Only a scant 10% to 15% were genuinely self-aware. This finding highlights the inclination to embrace falsehoods, especially about ourselves.

What drives this tendency toward conformity? Studies suggest that individuals who resist conformity and possess traits such as high self-esteem, self-control, and a tolerance for ambiguity are more likely to challenge societal norms and foster innovation (Crutchfield, 1955; Tainaka et al., 2014). Consequently, companies seeking to build a resilient and engaged workforce should foster environments that promote diverse perspectives—precursors to nonconformity—and encourage the questioning of entrenched norms. With this context in mind, Part I of this book closely examines, and dismantles, three commonly held beliefs about burnout, as outlined in Table 1.2.

The first pervasive myth is deeply ingrained in our culture: the belief that burnout isn't all that serious. What on earth—who believes that? Unfortunately, some in the popular press treat burnout as a farce, or a minor issue that can be easily overcome with simple solutions, such as motivation techniques, time management strategies, or simple self-help activities. Some even suggest that burnout may in fact be good for your health and well-being. Take a look at a few headlines:

- "Not Everyone Is Buying the 'Millennial Burnout' Fad" (Houlis, 2019)
- "The 4 Surprising Benefits of Burnout" (Clarke, 2020)
- "Self-Care Tips to Fight Burnout and Compassion Fatigue" (Washington Psychological Wellness, n.d.)
- "4 Steps to Beating Burnout" (Valcour, 2016)

TABLE 1.2. Traditional Versus Unorthodox Thinking

Traditional thinking	Unorthodox thinking
Burnout isn't all that serious.	Prolonged stress from burnout can have fatal consequences (see Chapter 2).
The burden of burnout falls on you, not your organization.	The burden of burnout falls on the organization (see Chapter 3).
Employee engagement is the cornerstone for a happy and healthy workforce.	High engagement can be a catalyst to high burnout (see Chapter 4).

This type of sensationalized, hyperbolic, and self-referential language trivializes the health implications of burnout, which can further enable a toxic work culture that values overwork. It also puts the burden of responsibility on the individual to solve what may be an organizational problem.

And it's not just in the press. I recently had a conversation with a senior executive about mental health-related challenges she was observing in some of her teams. I suggested that perhaps she should speak more in depth with the team about some of the factors driving their burnout. She responded by questioning whether burnout remains a relevant topic, noting that it was particularly pertinent during the pandemic and suggesting that it might be time to move on. I understood her frustration, that it seemed some teams were having a challenging time adjusting to the new postpandemic rhythm and pace of work. But explaining away or minimalizing burnout just perpetuates the problem.

Chapter 2 examines the true health consequences of burnout and evaluate whether conventional wisdom may be wrong. Although some believe that burnout is a minor issue that can be easily overcome, data suggest the opposite: Burnout poses a risk to your survival.

CHAPTER SUMMARY

- Challenging established norms is crucial for progress as it fosters innovation, drives transformation, and breaks down complacency.

- Conformity stands in direct opposition to autonomous thinking. Despite the innate inclination to conform, it is imperative for organizations to intentionally cultivate a diversity of perspectives and ideas to counteract this predisposition.

- The holistic wellness industry stands to gain significantly from increased scrutiny, promoting a transition from ineffective or untested approaches to evidence-informed strategies.

- Burnout is a reaction to prolonged work-related stress, manifesting in persistent exhaustion, heightened negativity or cynicism toward one's job, and decreased professional efficacy.

- The field of therapy is not immune to the necessity for critical examination and innovation. A transition toward AI and digital tools is needed to challenge the limitations of human-only interventions.

- A critical reevaluation of existing strategies is vital to address the clear disparity between the rise in wellness investment and the surging rates of burnout.

- The postpandemic era has popularized the term "burnout," yet the understanding of burnout lacks depth, and burnout is often addressed as just a personal issue.

- Debunking common myths and managing burnout requires shifting responsibility from individuals to organizations.

CHAPTER QUESTIONS

- What important truth do very few people agree with me on?

- Is my skepticism rooted in deeply ingrained beliefs and emotions, such as the fear that technology threatens the future of our profession, or am I genuinely concerned about the effectiveness and ethics of these groundbreaking approaches?

- Have I ever intentionally or unintentionally put the burden of burnout on someone else, for example a colleague or fellow employee, to solve their own burnout? Why or why not?

- Consider the following burnout metaphors, discussed in the chapter: deadly carcinogens jeopardizing your health when working from home; exasperation as you slump across your desk in the New York Stock Exchange; isolated and alone in a vast ocean. Do any of them resonate? If not, what metaphor does resonate?

2 GRAVE GAPS IN BURNOUT PERCEPTION

I'd rather be dead than sing 'Satisfaction' when I'm 45.

—Mick Jagger, The Jaggers, 1975, para. 8

Mick Jagger, the charismatic and age-defying front man of The Rolling Stones, cheekily quipped in 1971, "I'd rather be dead than sing 'Satisfaction' when I'm 45" (Jerome, 1975, para 8). At the spry age of 31 and a decade into performing the hit, his jest hinted at the grind of rock 'n' roll, yet he'd encore that very song countless times over the next half century, solidifying his legendary status in the rock pantheon.

Interpreting Jagger's quote can lead to various conclusions—did he exude rockstar cockiness, face a midlife crisis early, or just need a long vacation? After all, even rockstars aren't immune to burnout in the glitzy yet grueling showbiz world. Neil Diamond, another rock legend, put it aptly: "When you're on a merry-go-round, you miss a lot of the scenery" (A-Z Quotes, n.d.).

If Jagger truly experienced burnout at the age of 31, he is not alone. Many people, when immersed in seemingly intractable emotional and physical

https://doi.org/10.1037/0000454-003
Rethinking Employee Resilience: Why Our Current Approach to Worker Burnout Is Failing, and How to Fix It, by D. Pelton

exhaustion, might find comfort in thinking about death. As an Army psychologist, I saw my fair share of weary soldiers, particularly on the battlefield. The more accurately I could capture the patient's sentiment, the quicker and more accurately I could offer support. I frequently encountered soldiers who turned to morbid ruminations for temporary relief, without any intention of taking their own lives. They were simply in such psychological pain and distress that they sought any thought that could provide some respite. Similarly, those experiencing burnout may engage in similar coping mechanisms (thinking about death) as a temporary escape. However, it is crucial to treat any visible signs of suicidal ideation with utmost seriousness and immediate attention.

In this chapter, burnout is redefined as a critical health issue, debunking the myth of "good burnout" and emphasizing its severe impacts on mental and physical health. I explore how work-induced stress, a leading cause of death in the United States, leads to cognitive decline and structural brain changes, and I detail the effects of nonverbal overload and frequent context switching on cognitive load, which exacerbate mental exhaustion and diminish work quality (McGregor, 2018). Finally, I advocate practical measures such as incorporating breaks and meditation to mitigate burnout and enhance overall well-being.

AMERICAN KAROSHI

In America, when we think of workplace hazards, we might picture unsafe construction sites, miners exposed to toxic substances, or people slipping on an icy sidewalk while on the job. While physical hazards typically come to mind, the harm inflicted by a hostile social work atmosphere often goes overlooked. Many people underestimate the strains of work, often viewing them as trivial nuisances or challenges only for those lacking resilience. This perspective dangerously ignores the significant toll these pressures can take on an employee's overall well-being.

A stark reflection of this issue can be observed in Japan, a country deeply familiar with the tragic phenomenon known as *karoshi*—literally translated as "death from overwork." Recognized since the 1970s, karoshi has claimed hundreds of lives in recent years, and sadly, the rest of the world isn't far behind (Dickinson, 2023). The first report on karoshi in Japan (Agence France-Presse, 2016) indicated that 12.5% of British employees work more than 50 hours weekly but in Japan, the figure is almost double, 22.3%. Although official figures record an average of 400 overwork-related deaths in Japan annually, some researchers estimate the number could be as high as 20,000 (Carney, 2015).

In a global context, working 55+ hours a week contributed to 745,000 global deaths from stroke and heart disease, representing a 29% increase since 2000 (World Health Organization, 2021). An approximate 9% of the worldwide population, equating to 488 million people, likely faced these exhaustive work conditions. In this study, such extensive work hours were associated with a risk of ischemic heart disease and stroke, contributing to significant global mortality and disability.

Despite these alarming figures from Japan, it's crucial to acknowledge that the United States isn't exempt from similar threats. In fact, a recent meta-analysis indicates that work-related stress and associated outcomes is the fifth leading cause of death in the United States (McGregor, 2018). This isn't attributed to physically taxing jobs but rather to contextually driven work factors such as high job demands, low job control, long working hours, and low social support.

The term "American karoshi" has emerged (Schulte, 2022), capturing the essence of overwork and its tragic consequences in the United States. While this construct may not be a direct parallel to Japan's karoshi, the underlying causes are strikingly similar. Rooted in a culture of individualism, people in the United States often glamorize burnout and glorify relentless labor. Companies might proffer superficial remedies such as nap pods or meditation apps yet simultaneously elevate extreme dedication to one's job as an almost holy commitment.

The burnout arising from these factors isn't just a sign of fatigue; it's a profound exhaustion—emotionally, mentally, and physically. When left unchecked, it doesn't merely lead to decreased productivity; it has lethal consequences. The American burnout orthodoxy, that burnout isn't all that serious, poses a risk to survival if left unchallenged. Overlooking or downplaying burnout could lead to the gravest consequence: working ourselves to death.

BURNOUT AND THE BRAIN

Overwork is a recognized health hazard in many cultures, as in Japan. It can lead to increased cardiovascular risks, such as heart attacks and strokes, and the deep effects of burnout on the brain are particularly alarming. "Burnout" isn't just an overused term in hushed tones around the workplace cooler; its effects on people's brains are both tangible and concerning. At the heart of this condition is stress, which not only muddies immediate decision-making capabilities but can also leave lasting scars on neurological structure and function.

When under the influence of stress, the brain releases a flood of neuro-transmitters, particularly dopamine and norepinephrine. In an overabundance, these chemicals can obstruct the operations of the prefrontal cortex (PFC), which acts as the primary hub for decision making and complex problem solving. Imagine an air traffic control room at a bustling airport: Screens display critical flight paths, controllers guide aircraft with precision, and every communication is crucial to maintaining order in the skies. But when the brain is overwhelmed, it's like radar blurs and communication lines cross, and the once-seamless coordination turns chaotic. That's effectively what happens when the PFC gets flooded and overwhelmed with stress. This inundation doesn't merely hinder on-the-spot decision making; it affects our overall cognitive function.

Research offers additional insight into this phenomenon, suggesting that enduring chronic and uncontrollable stress results in marked deterioration of the PFC (Woo et al., 2021). This part of the brain, so vital for governing our thoughts, actions, and emotions, undergoes a stark transformation under stress. The PFC is instrumental in shaping a person's goals, directly impacting the ability to think abstractly and retain working memories, yet the release of excessive stress hormones can effectively disrupt these connections, leading to severe cognitive impairment. It's a wake-up call that repeated and unchecked stress can threaten both mental well-being and the very structure of the brain.

The link between burnout and changes in the brain is sharply illustrated by a study conducted at the Karolinska Institute in Sweden (Golkar et al., 2014). Two distinct groups were compared, 40 individuals experiencing burnout (attributed to prolonged workweeks of 60 to 70 hours for several years) and 70 healthy controls. Although both groups had similar reactions to neutral or strong emotional triggers, their responses diverged significantly when asked to suppress reactions to negative events. Those with burnout found it particularly challenging to regulate these negative emotions, and their heightened startle response signified their compromised ability to handle stressful emotions. This vulnerability is consistent with familiar burnout symptoms, including a tendency to overreact and a pronounced negativity bias.

The findings didn't end there. Using brain scans, Golkar et al. (2014) discovered pronounced differences in the amygdala, an essential brain region for emotional reactions. Individuals with burnout exhibited enlarged amygdalae, and even more concerning, they had weakened neural connections to regions such as the anterior cingulate cortex (ACC), which is involved in processing emotional distress. This diminished connectivity suggests that burnout has the potential to seriously diminish how the brain processes and handles emotion.

Another key finding was the weakened bond between the amygdala and the medial prefrontal cortex (mPFC; Golkar et al., 2014). The mPFC plays a pivotal role in executive functions, aiding in impulse control and long-term planning. These findings can be summarized in a relatable analogy: Imagine the alarm system of the brain is constantly triggered, even by minor stressors, and the mechanisms designed to shut it off are malfunctioning.

However, amidst this concerning landscape is a glimmer of hope. The brain is a remarkably resilient organ. Another study (Savic et al., 2018) illuminated the brain's incredible capacity for resilience, revealing that appropriate interventions, notably cognitive therapy, can reverse burnout-induced brain damage, such as cortical thinning and amygdala enlargement. These neurologic alterations corresponded with individuals' perceived stress levels but, encouragingly, showed reversibility post-therapy. This study bolsters the understanding that consistent, everyday stress results in specific yet amendable changes in brain networks. However, it's crucial to note that such recovery necessitates an environment that fosters healing. Continual immersion in toxic work settings could inhibit this restoration, emphasizing the need to view and tackle burnout as a systemic issue that can lead to severe consequences for the workforce. If the importance of burnout is overlooked, we risk severe consequences, including threats to survival reminiscent of conditions like karoshi.

But there's more to this narrative. Beyond these overt dangers lies a subtler yet pervasive threat: the insidious stress that festers in the backdrop of daily toil. This everyday strain, though less overt, has a profound cumulative impact on our health. The next section of the chapter covers these covert manifestations of burnout and stress, exploring how the daily grind can stealthily erode health, well-being, and longevity.

THE RELENTLESS PACE OF THE DIGITAL DAY

My wife and I, both working as clinical psychologists in business, have been taken aback by how frenzied our days have become in this postpandemic, work-from-home world. It's a whirlwind of back-to-back meetings, nonstop commitments, kid drop-off and pick-up, and barely a moment in between to catch our breath.

To cope, we've started a simple end-of-day tradition that's practically radical in its simplicity. At dinner time, typically after a glass of wine, I ask my wife, "What did you do at work today?"; she asks the same. I know, revolutionary. And we're psychologists. Often, instead of a crisp answer, we're met with a vacant stare or a prolonged "ummm," not from a memory lapse but from sheer overload. It's like trying to recall the plot of one movie while watching three others. The sea of faces, tasks, and talks merge into a blur, and I often resort to pulling out my phone and glancing at my calendar, trying to piece together the day.

This isn't just my story. It's a common narrative in the postpandemic workforce, and I've heard it from thousands of people. With the rise of remote work, employees' days are now populated with back-to-back video conferences. Many people have transformed homes into offices, but in the process, many have lost the pockets of respite that came naturally while driving to work or simply transitioning between meetings or tasks in a physical workspace. This process is known colloquially as taking *microbreaks*, and the evidence in its favor is compelling. Studies show that microbreaks not only boost performance and productivity (Albulescu et al., 2022) but, by bolstering satisfaction and overall well-being, also act as safeguards against the emotional exhaustion that often leads to burnout (Hunter & Wu, 2016).

The pandemic didn't just alter where people work; it reshaped how many people work. Without a clear roadmap for navigating this new reality, workers are at risk of burnout and significant health repercussions.

ZOOMING INTO FATIGUE

After the postpandemic rise in remote working, videoconferencing platforms, such as Zoom, have experienced unprecedented growth. These platforms have become essential tools for remote connections, but they've also unveiled a unique type of exhaustion, commonly known as *Zoom fatigue*. And yes, the research is just as concerning as the name suggests.

In a pivotal study (L. Schwartz et al., 2022), researchers examined how the brain connects (i.e., *brain synchrony*) while people are speaking face to face and while using technology. When people spoke in person, researchers identified nine significant cross-brain links, especially in areas involved in cognitive and emotional processes. Notably, the right frontal region appeared to play a role in synchronizing emotional and social cues between participants. Yet when people communicated via technology, the connections were far fewer, especially on the right side of the brain, which is involved in interpreting social cues. Though the interactions looked similar from the outside, the disparity in brain activity was undeniable. This research suggests that the brain may work harder to connect with others during virtual interactions, potentially contributing to the fatigue many people feel.

Further research has explored this phenomenon. Bailenson (2021) identified four primary culprits of so-called Zoom fatigue, all rooted in nonverbal overload. Topping the list is the intense and sustained close-up eye contact characteristic of video calls, which forces an interpersonal distance (around 5 inches) typically reserved for one's closest relationships (typically under 24 inches; Hall, 1966). In essence, daily videoconferences can sometimes feel like being confined in a small space with your boss, where every movement and expression is magnified. It's a unique kind of awkwardness, especially when trying to navigate the nuances of virtual communication, like remembering if you're on mute.

Second, videoconferencing heightens cognitive load. Because facial cues are limited and exaggerated gestures are needed during digital interactions, they are more mentally taxing than face-to-face chats (Jiang, 2020). Furthermore, studies show people speak 15% louder on video calls (Croes et al., 2019), which adds to the daily mental strain. For example, not only are you in a confined space with your boss, but now he's speaking loudly about that "hilarious" email he sent.

Third, the continuous self-view feature is like an all-day mirror, increasing self-awareness and potentially amplifying stress and negative emotions. For example, being in close quarters with your boss who is constantly seeking validation and making frequent comments about appearances can significantly heighten your stress and fatigue.

Finally, the confined visual frame restricts our natural inclination to move. Unlike in-person meetings where pacing or gesturing can boost creativity and engagement, videoconferencing feels like wanting to stretch but being restricted by the tight space—and yes, that includes your boss standing too close. This lack of physical freedom not only hampers cognitive performance and overall well-being but also forces our brains to exert extra effort to catch every nonverbal cue, amplifying our exhaustion.

But Zoom fatigue isn't merely a mental strain; its physical toll is equally concerning. In response to a survey by Rump and Brandt (2020), 30% of the people who reported Zoom fatigue suffered from headaches, 28% experienced back pain, 23% had visual disturbances, and 14% battled insomnia. Such symptoms often correlate with physiological changes such as elevated cortisol levels (Melamed et al., 1999) and may be linked to chronic stress, mood disorders, disrupted sleep, weight gain, and a weakened immune response. There is even growing debate about classifying Zoom fatigue as a stress-related disorder in upcoming diagnostic criteria (e.g., K. Anderson & Looi, 2020).

Furthermore, when people's brains are fatigued, they often take shortcuts in decision making (Riedl, 2022). Individuals fatigued from videoconferencing might prioritize heuristic processing (Chaiken & Eagly, 1983), relying on shortcuts in decision making rather than in-depth analysis. Ferran and Watts (2008) highlighted something similar, noting that video seminar attendees were influenced more by a speaker's likability than by content quality. Essentially, this situation is like a C-suite making pivotal business choices based on someone's likability rather than on the strength of their argument. While such biases may already exist, the broad economic implications could be significant if this trend becomes prevailing.

Using Zoom, Skype, Microsoft Teams, Google Meets, and other technologies is not the issue; in fact, videoconferencing offers many benefits, including positive health outcomes from enabling people to work virtually from nearly any location. However, it is crucial for workplaces to foster a culture that not only monitors teleconferencing frequency but also understands its nuanced impact on employees. Unchecked overuse of videoconferencing platforms can lead to burnout, and prolonged burnout poses a genuine threat to well-being and, ultimately, survival.

THE HIDDEN COSTS OF CONTEXT SHIFTING

In addition to the health implications of prolonged videoconferencing, it's vital to consider other facets of digital work habits. At first glance, the newfound ability to multitask in the digital era seems commendable. However, lurking beneath the surface is an insidious productivity killer: context switching. The American Psychological Association (2006) noted that context switching, even if it appears seamless, can cost as much as 40% of someone's productive time.

Let me paint a picture that might resonate with you. You're at work, deep into a critical task—maybe you're crafting an important report, managing patient care, or teaching a room full of eager students. Your focus is razor-sharp, but suddenly your phone buzzes. It's a text from a loved one, urgent and impossible to ignore. You quickly step away to find a quiet spot and start dealing with the issue. Just as you're getting a handle on it, a coworker appears, hovering nearby. They need something, and they need it now. "Hey, can you approve this real quick?" they ask, urgency in their voice. You glance at the document, give a hurried nod, and sign off, barely processing what you've approved. After you complete your call, you head back to what you were doing before and give a quick computer check, only to find that dreaded instant messenger—the lifeline of your workplace—blinking urgently with 12 new messages. Sound familiar? If so, you have experienced the exhausting reality of context shifting.

Constant mental juggling comes at a price. Each switch carries a cognitive load, causing up to a 20% dip in cognitive capacity (Weinberg, 1991). Data from a survey of more than 15,000 professionals indicate that, between February 2020 and October 2021, workers participated in an average of 25.6 meetings each week, with context switches about five times daily (Reclaim, 2021). This type of switching doesn't only drain time; it also affects our work quality and mental health. With every shift, the brain produces more cortisol, a stress hormone, intensifying feelings of exhaustion. Couple this with the elevated cortisol from extended videoconferencing, and the picture becomes alarming. In one study (Watson & Strayer, 2010), a staggering 97.5% of participants reported that they struggle to multitask effectively. Given that professionals and team workers reported experiencing, on average, nearly 32 interruptions daily (Reclaim, 2022), this constant switching imposes a "toggling tax" that drains energy, reduces efficiency, and hampers the ability to concentrate (Murty et al., 2022). Quantitatively, context switching can consume up to 80% of productive time (Weinberg, 1991), which may significantly affect work quality.

The implications are more severe than just stress. One study suggested that frequent context switching can result in a 10-point decrease in IQ, akin to the effects of missing a night's sleep and more than double the effect of smoking marijuana (Wainwright, 2005). Even more alarming, persistent multitasking has been shown to lead to permanent brain damage, specifically a reduction in the density of the ACC, which is involved in processing empathy as well as cognitive and emotional control (Loh & Kanai, 2014).

FINDING RESPITE IN A DIGITAL ERA

It's clear that human bodies and minds aren't designed for the nonstop digital bombardment, a predicament that only intensified in the midst of the pandemic. Recognizing the critical nature of this issue, the Microsoft Human Factors Lab initiated a comprehensive study to understand the cognitive impacts of relentless virtual meetings (Microsoft WorkLab, 2021). Employing electroencephalogram (EEG) equipment, researchers observed participants in two distinct situations, one in which participants navigated four half-hour meetings consecutively and another in which they had 10-minute meditation breaks between the meetings. The results were telling. In the absence of breaks, participants consistently showed an increase in beta wave activity throughout the day, a direct marker for stress. However, the introduction of meditation breaks halted this trajectory. Rather than a relentless increase, the beta activity plateaued. These findings underline the role even brief rest periods play in mitigating stress.

The researchers also considered the impact of breaks on participants' engagement during meetings. When participants had no breaks, their brainwave patterns indicated a decline in engagement over time (Microsoft WorkLab, 2021). In contrast, when breaks were integrated, participants experienced a marked positive shift in engagement. This finding suggests that the benefits of breaks aren't confined to stress reduction; breaks also play a pivotal role in enhancing focus and overall engagement.

A particularly notable finding was the pronounced increase in stress levels during transitions between continuous meetings. Michael Bohan, senior director of Microsoft's Human Factors Engineering group, hypothesized that "you're coming to the end of the meeting, knowing you have another one coming right up, and you're going to have to switch gears and use your brain to think hard about something else" (Microsoft WorkLab, 2021, p. 8). Brainwave spikes, which are reflective of the cognitive strain of switching contexts or preparing for another task, were notably subdued when meditation breaks were interspersed between sessions.

Microsoft's study highlights a simple yet vital truth: Regular breaks are essential. And it's not just about stepping away from work. It's about allowing ourselves a genuine break, away from screens, even for a few minutes. Without these intervals, we're not merely straying but sprinting toward stress and burnout, which, left unmonitored, can have devastating consequences.

CHAPTER SUMMARY

- Rethinking burnout as a serious issue forms the foundation for prioritizing workplace well-being.

- Acknowledging the severe mental and physical health impacts dispels the notion of "good burnout."

- Work-induced stress, fueled by factors including demanding jobs and extended work hours, stands as the fifth leading cause of death in the United States (McGregor, 2018).

- Prolonged stress from burnout can result in cognitive decline and structural changes in the brain.

- Mental and physical exhaustion arise from nonverbal overload, heightened cognitive load, and persistent self-view.

- Cognitive load, stemming from frequent context switching, affects work quality and mental health, potentially leading to long-term consequences.

- Incorporating breaks, including short meditation intervals, plays a pivotal role in preventing burnout and sustaining overall well-being.

CHAPTER QUESTIONS

- How does my view of hard work and resilience shape my understanding of American karoshi and my definition of success?

- How has Zoom fatigue from digital workspaces affected my stress, and what strategies can I use to mitigate it?

- How often do I context switch? What steps can I take to reduce context switching?

- How could incorporating 5-minute breaks into my routine help mitigate stress and enhance my focus during digital meetings?

- How will my understanding of the health consequences of burnout change my work habits?

3 BURNOUT AND THE ORGANIZATION

A Story of Avoided Responsibility

We have to hammer on the opioid abusers in every way possible. They are the culprits and the problem. They are reckless criminals.

—Richard Sackler

Richard Sackler's chilling words as the former CEO and chairman of Purdue Pharma echo the sentiment of a system refusing to acknowledge its inherent flaws. At the height of the opioid crisis, amidst a storm of accusations, Purdue Pharma—and specifically the Sackler family—consistently externalized blame, directing it at the consumers they had ensnared with their potent drug, OxyContin.

In the mid-1990s, the opioid epidemic exploded, propelled by the aggressive marketing and widespread prescription of OxyContin by Purdue Pharma. This drug, approved by the U.S. Food and Drug Administration, became a harbinger of an unprecedented wave of deaths linked to legal prescription opioids (Feldscher, 2022). From 1999 onward, this crisis resulted in over 200,000 fatalities (Armstrong, 2019). Alarmingly, by 2006, OxyContin alone accounted for an estimated $4.7 billion of Purdue's profits (Armstrong, 2019).

https://doi.org/10.1037/0000454-004
Rethinking Employee Resilience: Why Our Current Approach to Worker Burnout Is Failing, and How to Fix It, by D. Pelton

A 1997 internal memo revealed that Purdue Pharma had capitalized on doctors' misconceptions of OxyContin as less potent than morphine, spurring a prescription surge and an addiction crisis (Armstrong, 2019). Overdoses increased and families suffered while Purdue evaded accountability, focusing on legal defenses. In 2022, Purdue Pharma was ordered to pay $6 billion in restitution and to acknowledge their significant role in the opioid epidemic (Attorney General Press Office, 2022).

The opioid crisis reflects systemic issues beyond just one company's missteps; for example, it highlights broad flaws in workplace culture. Often, organizations place emphasis on individual responsibility, overshadowing bigger structural challenges. Whether it's Purdue Pharma evading blame or workplaces suggesting burnout is an individual's fault, the message is consistent: the person, not the system, is at fault.

Chapter 2 focused primarily on the gravity of burnout, in particular its profound and sometimes life-threatening impact on health. Chapter 3 addresses a pivotal question: Within the context of an organization, whose job is it to address burnout? This chapter details the foundational structures that enable burnout, emphasizing the symbiotic relationship between individuals and their environments. The primary focus is on the concrete measures organizations can and should adopt.

This issue was illuminated during a workshop I attended recently. An attendee asked, "In a toxic work environment, who would burn out faster, an emotionally stable or a fragile person?" Such questions reflect common beliefs that challenges like burnout arise solely from personal dispositions rather than systemic flaws. In response, aiming to shift the focus from individual traits to systemic root causes, I asked, "Which of the two has defined job expectations?" It's essential to be particularly mindful of Peter Thiel's words, "The goal isn't to be contrarian but to uncover the truth" (Thiel & Masters, 2014).

The workshop discussion highlights a frequent oversight—the tendency to favor simple explanations. Often, people attribute challenges to individual factors such as temperament while overlooking the intricate interplay of environmental, structural, and interpersonal factors. Many voices, especially from the self-help realm, place the onus squarely on the individual, arguing that if you're experiencing burnout, the problem—and the solution—lies within you. This attitude sets the stage for the second conventional thinking trap presented in Chapter 1 (see Table 1.2), the assumption that the burden of burnout rests solely on the individual, not the organization. Although individual traits play a role in burnout susceptibility, they're merely a piece of a larger puzzle. I assert that burnout is a reflection more of the organization than of the individual. While certain personalities might be more prone to burnout, it's vital to grasp that vulnerability doesn't equate to culpability.

This chapter provides a deep look into how organizational environments can magnify these inherent susceptibilities. Then, I move from the individual to the organizational to unravel the stark divide between frontline workers and top-tier executives, revealing the blind spots of many leaders when it comes to grasping burnout's widespread impact on their teams. I also spotlight the often overlooked dimensions of pay equity and transparency. These aren't mere Human Resources buzzwords; they significantly shape employee morale, trust in leadership, and overall satisfaction. The chapter concludes with a discussion of the contagious nature of burnout within organizations, as I dissect the ripple effects it can have when it gains a foothold in an organization and begins to spread.

DECODING BURNOUT: THE CRITICAL ROLE OF PERSONALITY

Burnout is frequently dissected in academic circles yet is often misunderstood in a culture that subtly celebrates overwork as a badge of honor. This cultural view is eerily similar to that all-too-familiar interview tactic of presenting a strength when asked about a weakness, for example the timeless "I'm just too dedicated" and the ever-popular "I care so deeply, it's painful."

Let's delve into the essence of burnout, cutting through the cultural noise. At a recent conference, I posed a question: How do you define burnout in a single sentence? The room was filled with uneasy glances until one woman bravely shared, "My experience of burnout felt like running an endless race, and with every mile, an on-looker added a 5-pound weight to my backpack." It was a powerful response. Her words resonated deeply with the group, as she adeptly captured the exhausting, joy-stealing nature of burnout. This quiet battle can, at its worst, be fatal.

While debates linger on culpability and whether responding to burnout is the responsibility of the employer or the employee, a growing body of research suggests that certain personality traits might make some people more vulnerable to burnout than others. Focusing on personality traits is not an attempt to absolve organizations of responsibility but rather is about equipping them to identify and assist those individuals more susceptible to burnout.

Research shows a person's personality can influence how they handle job stress. McCrae and Costa's (1987) five-factor model, a leading framework in personality psychology, pinpoints five key personality traits:

- Agreeableness: fostering harmony and good relations
- Conscientiousness: how organized and dependable you are
- Extraversion: your comfort in social situations
- Neuroticism: how you cope with negative emotions
- Openness: your love for new ideas and experiences

Many studies have explored the links among these traits and burnout without clear consensus, but a recent meta-analysis of 83 studies offered a unified perspective (Angelini, 2023). Simply put, individuals with pronounced neurotic tendencies face a higher risk of burnout. Neuroticism, in essence, is a predisposition to experience negative emotions such as anxiety and sadness, especially in challenging situations. Rather than confronting and processing these emotions, individuals with high levels of neuroticism often avoid or minimize them, making those individuals more prone workplace burnout. If this finding resonates with you, know that you're not alone, as it's estimated that 30% of the global population exhibit neurotic traits (Chamorro-Premuzic, 2022).

Clinically, the implications of neuroticism are stark. Beyond just workplace challenges, neuroticism is associated with a risk of several mental disorders, including depression, anxiety disorders, schizophrenia, eating disorders, and certain personality disorders (Gale et al., 2016). Notably, neuroticism has been pinpointed as the dominant risk factor in behavioral public health (Lahey, 2009). The economic burdens of neuroticism are expected to eclipse the combined costs of major depressive disorder, dysthymia, anxiety disorder, and substance use disorder (Cuijpers et al., 2010).

While neuroticism has some adaptive functions—increased vigilance, preparation, depth of emotion, and more—people high in neuroticism often find it challenging to channel their anxieties into prosocial behavior, particularly when burdened with protracted workplace stress. Consider John, an employee at a bustling tech company, who is known for his dedication and hard work. His sensitive nature makes him prone to anxiety, especially under the pressures of the tech industry. John receives some unexpected feedback from his boss and interprets it as a threat to his position. From that point, every "good morning" or "nice shirt" feels like coded critique. His colleagues notice the change, including his nervousness during presentations and defensiveness when receiving feedback. They express concern, only to be met with John's go-to mantra, "I'm okay." This response, ironically, is the red flag that heightens their worries, as regular conversations become potential distress triggers for John, affecting his mood, sleep, and overall performance. Over time, the stimulating work environment feels increasingly hostile to John. His heightened emotional responses aren't merely personality quirks—they indicate a risk for disorders such as depression and anxiety. And yet, every day, John maintains his facade, burying his feelings and reassuring everyone that everything's just fine.

Understanding the intricate relationships among neuroticism, burnout, and mental health is pivotal for organizations today. Although neuroticism isn't the sole cause of burnout, it heightens one's vulnerability to stress. Addressing burnout doesn't simply lie in acknowledging the issue or placing the onus on individuals like John to find their own coping mechanisms. Instead, it demands a proactive organizational response. Businesses must foster a supportive culture, implementing systems specifically tailored to alleviate stress. Taking such proactive steps is not just beneficial; it's essential for shielding the most vulnerable.

In stark contrast, the other four personality traits emerge as formidable barriers against burnout (Angelini, 2023). Agreeableness not only minimizes workplace conflicts but also allows a person to cultivate a network of supportive colleagues and peers, making it easier for them to navigate professional stresses. For example, Sarah mediates team disputes and strengthens collaborations, creating a stress-reduced workspace. Conscientiousness equips individuals to tackle challenges methodically, reducing feelings of chaos and overwhelm. David, for instance, not only efficiently plans for unexpected deadlines but also allocates resources and communicates clearly, ensuring his team stays calm, organized, and focused. Extraversion serves as a vital conduit to external support networks. Mike, during a tough month, used his natural tendency to connect and communicate to arrange team lunches, bolstering team morale and resilience. Openness endows individuals with a unique blend of curiosity and adaptability, making them more receptive to innovation and change. When her company introduced new software, Naomi didn't hesitate. She actively sought training, embraced the change, and shared her insights, transforming potential disruption into a growth opportunity.

While people can't fundamentally alter their core personality traits, it's essential to understand the interplay of personality with daily work. Instead of expecting organizations to cater to each individual nuance, they should recognize that people with certain personalities may be more vulnerable than others. Embracing unconventional strategies can foster trust and rejuvenation. For example, incentivizing time off (explored further in Chapter 7) shifts the responsibility of preventing burnout away from the individual, especially the most vulnerable, and places it firmly on the organization.

This awareness and subsequent shift in responsibility also raises questions about other impacts of the workplace environment. How does constant pressure mold an employee? Can it bring about transformations in who we are, much like external forces shape and change substances in the natural world?

HOW STRESS REVEALS AND RESHAPES THE WORKFORCE

Many people may fondly recall pop culture icon and superhero Superman transforming a lump of coal into a diamond with a mere squeeze of his hand. While some may argue the "facts"—Superman isn't real, and technically,

coal and diamonds have different chemical compositions and formation processes that make Superman's act implausible—this imagery presents an
intriguing metaphor for professional life: Under intense workplace pressure,
do we metamorphose into different versions of ourselves? Can job-related
stress actually redefine our personalities at the core?

Recent research suggests a resounding yes. Historically, organizational
research viewed personality traits as fixed entities, unaffected by the dynamics
of workplace culture, but Smallfield and Kluemper's (2022) research suggests
that the work environment, especially when it's very stressful, can quickly
influence certain genes. The stress prompts the release of cortisol, the so-called
stress hormone, which provides energy and aids in tissue repair. Over time,
constant stress can elevate and normalize these cortisol levels, affecting the
regulation of stress, mood, and pleasure. Once these new normals are set, they
stay that way unless other external factors come into play.

These scientific findings have tangible repercussions in daily life. In my
professional experience, I've encountered couples, especially during the
onset of the pandemic, attributing increased marital tension to work-related
stressors. The uncertainties of remote work, escalating work demands,
unrealistic expectations, and looming job insecurities have not only influenced individuals' behaviors but also caused relational strain, in part because
personalities are reshaped by relentless stressors.

For individuals (or couples) with neurotic tendencies, who are inherently
more sensitive to stress, the impact is even more profound. Their innate
sensitivity to stress is a double-edged sword: It makes them more attuned
to their environments, and it amplifies their inherent anxieties, plunging
them deeper into neurotic behaviors. Most alarmingly, persistent workplace
stress can alter how DNA is expressed, shifting one's personality toward
heightened neuroticism in just a month (Smallfield & Kluemper, 2022).
And if that weren't bad enough, epigenetic research hints that these stress-
induced changes could be passed down through generations (Nestler, 2016).
If the challenges of Gen Z feel demanding to a manager now, time is of the
essence to reconsider workplace practices. Otherwise, management should
prepare for the even more complex hurdles posed by their malcontent Gen
Beta offspring.

Now, it's not all doom and gloom. Organizations hold the potential to
counteract this trajectory and, ideally, help slow down this sobering her-
itable genetic stress cascade. By deeply understanding how employees perceive and respond to stress, businesses can adapt their practices, helping
employees reframe or mitigate stressors, which can lead to healthier work
environments.

Let's circle back to the story of "I'm okay" John. On the surface, he seemed to handle things well, but internally, stress was taking its toll. His boss repeatedly missed opportunities to address growing concerns for John and for his team. He made no effort to regulate the workload, align tasks, solicit feedback, or acknowledge the escalating anxieties. The boss's failure to set clear boundaries, hold himself accountable, and foster collaboration led to a decline in corporate culture. The boss's bad behavior amplified John's neuroticism to a degree in which, in Smallfield's words, "stresses stop being healthy challenges and become overwhelming, out of our control, or without purpose" (as quoted in Yeo, 2021). Organizations must recognize that personalities can evolve in response to workplace environments. Furthermore, by aligning job roles with individual strengths, organizations can minimize stress and encourage positive challenges. Providing flexibility and the right tools can help prevent adverse personality changes and foster a positive organizational culture.

DECODING THE EXECUTIVE-EMPLOYEE DISCONNECT

Effectively tackling burnout requires viewing it in light of systemic structures and cultural issues, not just individual traits. A notable illustration of the disconnect between executive views and employee experiences can be observed in major corporations; leadership perspectives often differ significantly from the realities faced by employees. For example, in an exposé on working conditions at Amazon (Kantor & Streitfeld, 2015), a former human resources director described the company as a place where "overachievers go to feel bad about themselves." Although Jeff Bezos, Amazon CEO, disputed this depiction, the article underscored a possible chasm between executive perception and employee reality. Amazon's lead recruiter emphasized the company's ambition, while a former marketer noted he frequently saw colleagues cry at their desks.

Such perception gaps between management and staff aren't unique to Amazon in the corporate sphere. Deloitte's research serves as a wake-up call for organizations worldwide (S. Hatfield et al., 2022). In a survey of 2,100 nonexecutive employees and C-suite executives in four countries, an overwhelming 91% of employees reported that they believe their job plays a role in determining their well-being. This sentiment was shared by 97% of the executives. In complex work environments where it's rare to achieve consensus on anything, there's almost universal agreement that work affects everyone's well-being. But here's the catch: While 75% of C-suite executives reported that their jobs benefit their overall well-being (physical, mental, social), a mere 36% of employees said their roles benefit their well-being.

Exploring the perception gap between leaders and nonexecutive employees uncovers unsettling insights. While the majority of C-suite individuals felt that they've fully grasped the challenges presented by the pandemic, that sentiment wasn't reciprocated by the nonexecutive workforce (Hatfield et al., 2022):

- When asked about their perceptions of the impact of the pandemic and the response from their companies, only 47% of the surveyed nonexecutive employees reported that they believed that the executives understand the challenges caused by the pandemic. In contrast, 90% of the C-suite individuals said that they do.

- When asked whether decisions made by executives during the pandemic were in their best interest, 53% of the employees agreed, whereas 88% of the C-suite executives reported that they felt that their decisions were optimal.

- When asked if they felt the executives at their company care about their well-being, 56% of the employees agreed. However, nearly all (91%) of the C-suite individuals said that they believed their employees feel they care.

- When asked about priorities, 68% of the employees and 81% of the C-suite executives said they prioritize improving their well-being over advancing their career.

- When asked about physical well-being, 65% of the employees rated their physical well-being as good or excellent, compared to 89% of the C-suite executives.

- Only 22% of employees reported that C-suite executives were transparent about their well-being, whereas 73% of the C-suite individuals said that they believe they are.

The stark discrepancy in perceptions demands an urgent reevaluation of leadership strategies.

The movie *Barbie* (Gerwig, 2023) portrayed this disconnect in a key scene. The CEO of Mattel, portrayed by comedian Will Ferrell, assures Barbie that he and his all-male board know what's best for her. When Barbie queries the representation of women in leadership, the CEO responds, "We are a company literally made of women. We had a woman CEO in the 90s. And there was another one . . . at some other time. So that's two right there." He ends with a tone-deaf request for Barbie to "Get back in your box!" (46:46).

While cultural references like *Barbie* might elicit chuckles, real-world statistics paint a sobering picture of the disconnect between employees and the C-suite. These numbers represent real individuals with authentic experiences. They also highlight a pervasive issue in work culture: The prevalent "always-on" mindset, excessive work hours, and the blurring lines between professional and personal lives, particularly in remote work environments, are detrimental to employee well-being. Deloitte's research amplifies this concern (cf. Hatfield et al., 2022), showing that 83% of employees and 74% of executives struggle with well-being, primarily because of work demands.

In light of these findings, a recalibration is needed. Burnout reflects organizational blind spots and flaws, not just individual ones. The remedy? Structural and systemic change, which are discussed in detail in Parts 2 and 3 of this book. Leaders must grasp workforce needs and meld organizational aims with employee well-being.

NAVIGATING THE PAY-PURPOSE PARADOX: WHAT TRULY MOTIVATES EMPLOYEES?

The exploration of the evolution of organizational growth and the responsibility for employee wellness makes it clear that a human-centric approach should be at the forefront of company priorities. From this perspective, the objective isn't merely about nurturing employee well-being; it's also about optimizing their performance. This perspective raises a fundamental question: What truly drives an individual's performance? Competitive pay, satisfaction from meaningful work, or both?

I recently facilitated a meeting with senior leaders at a large company. We were trying to figure out the best ways to keep their top managers engaged and loyal. The conversation often swung between the importance of having a meaningful purpose and offering competitive pay. The central question we tackled was how to truly motivate employees in upper management positions.

Our discussions revealed that survey data from the company differed significantly from the executives' views. Salary emerged as the unequivocal driver for both upper management turnover and upward mobility. If pay wasn't competitive and transparent, upper management left for better opportunities. This pay disconnect wasn't unique to this company; industry studies consistently rank salary as a pivotal factor in employee satisfaction (Bersin, 2023b). Yet as discussions progressed, a palpable resistance emerged among the executive team. They seemed almost deliberately to sidestep the conversation on compensation. Why this oversight? A few deeply rooted, but mistaken, assumptions: first, that in the executives' eyes, upper management valued purpose over paycheck; and second, that the managerial journey was a one-way linear path, with the unequivocal goal of becoming an executive. This gap led us to two pressing questions: (a) Why is there such a clear disconnect? and (b) How do the data weigh the balance between pay and purpose?

In delving into the first factor, we identified a prevailing herd or survival mentality among executives, who seemed to believe that the prestige of executive roles would suffice to attract and retain talent while dismissing the significance of competitive pay. This emphasis on the allure of executive prestige brought to mind a sentiment that I now view as misguided, once expressed by a grizzled Army colonel, that the allure of title and status can be more valuable than gold. The data from the company I was working with suggested the contrary. Moreover, external research, particularly a survey of 3,625 full-time workers across the country, revealed that only 7% aimed for a high-ranking senior or C-level position (PR Newswire, 2014). Staff turnover was dismissed; those who left simply weren't cut out for executive roles, or so the narrative went. The belief persisted that a connection to the company mission was motivation enough. The demand for better pay amidst economic downturns wasn't even broached, reflecting the insular executive mindset. In fact, this mindset was preventing others from joining its ranks.

Addressing the second concern, we found that research on pay versus purpose shows mixed results. Some studies (e.g., Deci & Ryan, 2000; Gerhart & Fang, 2014; Pink, 2009) highlight the importance of compensation, while others stress intangible rewards and internal drive. This polarity reflects Herzberg's two-factor theory (see Herzberg et al., 1959), which differentiates basic needs, such as pay and job security, from motivators, including meaningful work and recognition. If these basic needs are not met, dissatisfaction can lead to burnout. However, genuine job satisfaction comes from motivators. So, for companies to motivate their staff effectively, they must offer competitive pay while promoting factors that truly inspire and engage the employees.

Pay discussions often focus on pay as "equitable" and "transparent," sidelining the actual amount. Pay equity, at its core, advocates for equal pay for equal work. Josh Bersin, known for his insights in HR and leadership, found that while 71% of companies see pay equity as vital, 95% struggle to implement it (Bersin, n.d.), and he suggested that pay equity is 13 times more important to employees than the amount of money they receive (Bersin, 2023a). Companies such as Google and BBC have faced reputational damage from overlooking pay equity (Lam et al., 2022), and this oversight can erode trust and foster a culture counter to fairness. Notably, fairness is identified by Leiter and

Maslach (1999) as a primary driver of burnout. It's not merely about the pay; it's the perception of fairness. As Bersin (2023a, para 10) aptly put it, pay inequity essentially communicates to employees that "our company is a political place, and if you're underpaid, you're out of luck."

Imagine finding out a colleague with the same or less experience gets paid 20% more than you for the same job. How would you feel? Would you still be motivated to do your best at work? Would you think the company values you? Such feelings often remain unspoken and cause misunderstandings. Bersin (2023a, para 12) emphasized the importance of pay equity and pay transparency as the foundation of a company's trustworthiness, portraying them as the twin pillars underpinning a company's credibility and advocating for leaders to "communicate, communicate, communicate what we're doing." Pay transparency isn't just about revealing salary figures. It's about explaining why pay decisions are made, detailing pay scales, and promoting open discussions about wages (Lam et al., 2022).

The appeal of transparency is undeniable, with research showing 75% of employees prefer companies known for clear pay practices (Threlkeld, 2021). Payscale's (2018) findings suggest that without such transparency, younger employees are more likely to leave a company within 6 months. About 75% of individuals who say they are skeptical of raise decisions or are given no reasons said they would consider switching jobs. However, only about a third of companies think their pay transparency efforts are excellent or average (HRMorning, 2023).

Organizations must ensure fair pay and transparency, balancing compensation with their mission. While competitive pay is crucial, the clarity behind it matters most. If companies falter here, they risk not only morale—they gamble with their reputation.

FROM WERTHER TO WORK: UNDERSTANDING BURNOUT CONTAGION

In Goethe's (1774/2012) novel *The Sorrows of Young Werther*, the main character, Werther, becomes profoundly infatuated with Charlotte. When he learns she's engaged to someone else, he's consumed by despair. He writes,

> Must it ever be thus—that the source of our happiness must also be the fountain of our misery? The full and ardent sentiment which animated my heart with the love of nature, overwhelming me with a torrent of delight, and which brought all paradise before me, has now become an insupportable torment, a demon which perpetually pursues and harasses me. (Goethe, 1774/2012, p. 52)

He writes that the same emotions that once brought him joy now torment him. His tragic choice to end his life highlights the intense pain of loneliness resulting from his unrequited fixation.

The novel's publication had profound, real-world consequences, creating a ripple effect in the form of imitative suicides across Europe (Lewis, 2021). Disturbing accounts emerged of young men, profoundly affected by Werther's story, dressing in yellow pants and a blue jacket like the protagonist and, with copies of the book nearby, ending their lives. These disturbing trends led to several regions banning the book and a newly coined term, the "Werther effect," to denote the contagious nature of such suicidal behaviors following the book's release (Niederkrotenthaler et al., 2007). The Werther effect is a testament to the powerful impact of media and literature on human emotions and actions, a phenomenon that echoes even in today's society. Moreover, this pattern of media-induced suicide contagion wasn't limited to Goethe's time. Studies indicate that between 1947 and 1968, the publication of suicide incidents in newspapers in Britain and the United States was associated with a notable increase in suicides, especially in areas where the news was distributed (Phillips, 1974).

The principle of emotional contagion further underscores our innate ability to subconsciously mirror the emotions of those around us. Such alignment, often driven by subtle cues like facial expressions and tone, can have both positive and negative ramifications (E. Hatfield et al., 1994). Case in point, negative emotions are often more contagious than positive ones (National Research Council, 1994). Emotional contagion is exemplified in a recent study using AI to evaluate the facial reactions of health care professionals viewing emotional film clips (Neuroscience News, 2023). The results showed a correlation between heightened facial reactivity and increased depression risk, hinting at the potential of AI as an early detection tool in emotion-intensive careers.

Burnout, fundamentally, is a social issue, spreading from person to person. Daily conversations and interactions transfer emotional cues. Engaging with burned-out colleagues increases the risk of feeling similar emotions. For instance, high school teachers who discussed difficult students with fatigued peers began echoing the negative sentiments (Bakker & Schaufeli, 2000). In medical settings such as intensive care units, discussions on burnout are alarm bells: They're often better indicators of overall burnout than other work-related stressors (Bakker et al., 2005). This trend isn't restricted to specific professions; in most workplaces, shared emotions can influence feelings of burnout. Individuals who are deeply connected with their colleagues may be especially likely to feel burnout, in particular if they have looming job security concerns (Petitta & Jiang, 2020). The bottom line? Just as Werther's sentiments echoed far beyond Goethe's pages, conversations about burnout should resonate as early warnings, signaling a need for organizational transformation beyond individual adjustments.

In light of these insights, it is evident that burnout isn't merely a byproduct of individual deficiencies. It's the collective result of a convoluted interplay among individual vulnerabilities, a demanding work environment, leadership discrepancies, financial incentives, and the shared emotions of the workforce. Painting it solely as an individual problem is both reductive and misguided. Instead, recognizing burnout as a multifaceted challenge necessitates a multifaceted response.

Historically, workplace issues have been approached with a binary lens, with distinct lines between the organization and the individual. Common band-aid solutions like "take some time off" or "go sit in that nap pod and get your head right" outsource the problem, dismissively absolving the organization of responsibility. However, burnout blurs these distinctions and is positioned at the intersection of personal vulnerabilities and organizational pressures. Armed with a deep understanding of this relationship, organizations can cultivate an integrated, compassionate, and forward-thinking strategy to tackle it.

CHAPTER SUMMARY

- Burnout is complex and often oversimplified.

- Organizations must take concrete steps to address burnout.

- Neuroticism is associated with vulnerability to burnout and demands proactive organizational efforts.

- Workplace stress can reshape personality, affecting genes and mental health. A supportive culture is needed.

- An executive–employee gap underscores the need for aligned leadership, ensuring harmonized goals, transparent communication, and responsive actions across all organizational levels.

- Pay equity, transparency, and purposeful balance are crucial for employee well-being.

- Burnout is contagious in the workplace and spreading through emotional cues, signaling the need for organizational transformation.

CHAPTER QUESTIONS

- Have I experienced burnout before, and what was that experience like?

- How can I personally champion initiatives to address burnout complexities and promote a healthier workplace environment?

- Amid executive–employee disparities, how do I plan to involve leadership actively to enhance well-being and foster alignment?

- In my daily interactions, how attuned am I to emotional cues, and what specific proactive measures can I take to prevent the spread of burnout?

- Do I possess insight into pay practices at my organization? What concrete steps can I take to advocate for fair pay while encouraging transparent discussions?

4 WHEN EMPLOYEE ENGAGEMENT CRIPPLES THE WORKFORCE

Across the country, our doctors are jumping from hospital rooftops, overdosing in call rooms, and found hanging themselves in hospital chapels. It's medicine's dirty secret.

–Dr. Pamela Wible, *Why Doctors Kill Themselves*, 2:14

The chilling testimony from Dr. Pamela Wible's 2015 TEDMED talk (Wible, 2016) underscores a grim reality many overlook. As she revealed, each year, more than a million Americans lose their doctors to suicide. A deeper dive into the statistics reveals that, every year, 300 to 400 doctors take their own lives (Matheson, n.d.). This number is roughly equivalent to losing an entire midsized medical school graduating class to suicide each year! In 2022, one in 10 doctors contemplated or attempted suicide (Medscape, 2023). Disturbingly, physicians have a suicide rate of 28 to 40 per 100,000—more than double that of the general population. This rate exceeds the rate among military personnel, who are traditionally regarded as being in the most

https://doi.org/10.1037/0000454-005
Rethinking Employee Resilience: Why Our Current Approach to Worker Burnout Is Failing, and How to Fix It, by D. Pelton

high-stress profession. Notably, although female physicians attempt suicide less frequently than the general female population, their completion rate is 2.5 to 4 times higher, on par with male physicians (P. Anderson, 2018). These data are deeply unsettling. Physicians are killing themselves at disturbingly high rates.

A closer examination of this burden also exposes a troubling connection between depression, suicide, and burnout in the medical field (Grassi et al., 2021). While the research on physician suicide is complex, it's hard to ignore how burnout and depression seem to contribute to these tragic outcomes. A survey of 9,100 physicians across 29 specialties revealed that 24% met the criteria for clinical depression (Medscape, 2023). In stark contrast, the National Institute of Mental Health (2023) reported that 8.3% of all individuals over the age of 18 in the United States experienced a depressive episode in 2021. The sentiment of an emergency medicine physician poignantly captures the depth of this anguish: "I have little joy in performing the job that I believe I was born to do. Now, not only am I tired of work—I'm tired of life" (Medscape, 2022). This sobering perspective is but one voice among many, highlighting the pressing need to reevaluate deeply entrenched cultural norms contributing to this crisis.

Such feelings raise questions about the underlying causes of this despair. It's noteworthy that the problem isn't necessarily rooted in a lack of physician dedication or involvement. On the contrary, their deep commitment, in the absence of organizational safeguards, could be a contributing factor to their overwhelming exhaustion and, in some cases, despair. This issue transcends the medical field, challenging the dominant perspective among Human Resources (HR) professionals that mere engagement is an adequate shield against workplace stress and burnout.

In this chapter, we'll delve into the complex relationship between engagement and burnout. Challenging the traditional notion that employee engagement is the sole foundation for workforce well-being, I explore the potential hazards of overreliance on engagement and shed light on the shadows that can cast a detrimental impact on the workforce. Contrary to common belief, engagement and burnout can coexist, and thus we need to reevaluate our understanding of the workplace psyche. Notable studies and real-world examples illustrate the intricate interplay between job demands and resources and their impact on the workforce. Additionally, I address the issue of workload, along with its implications and the broad concept of resilience. These insights collectively reshape our comprehension of employee well-being, burnout, and organizational culture.

NAVIGATING THE ENGAGEMENT PARADOX AND THE RISKS OF "TOO MUCH"

Employee engagement is every HR department's dream and the topic of countless articles boasting titles such as "Employee Engagement: The Holy Grail of Talent Management" (Ramesh, 2018) and the heartwarming "Engaged Employees are Happy Employees" (Owl Labs Staff, 2021). Yet lurking behind these uplifting headlines is a complicated, sometimes murky narrative. Some data paint a picture of enthusiasm and motivation, while others hint at something more somber. Why this dichotomy?

A good starting point is the insights of sociologist Ervin Goffman, a pioneer of social theory from the late 1950s. Goffman viewed daily interactions as theatrical performances. He termed this idea "dramaturgy," suggesting that all people assume roles, adapting their behavior based on social surroundings (Goffman, 1961). Think of it as acting in a play: Sometimes you're deeply engrossed in your character, while at other times you're merely going through the motions. For example, am I going to be the laid-back dad leisurely sipping a vanilla latte at Starbucks or the wild-eyed caffeine fiend drumming my fingers with rising impatience as the old lady ahead unfurls her ancient checkbook, holding up the line. It's all about the scene and the role that the person opts to play. Goffman argued that roles shift fluidly with the social context. Although Goffman's theories were insightful for everyday interactions, they may be less so for workplace settings, where interactions extend over longer periods. The dynamics in the workplace aren't just about fleeting roles; they encompass deep feelings of belonging, autonomy, and long-term interpersonal relationships.

Kahn (1990) built on Goffman's insights, applying them to the workplace context. Regarded as a trailblazer in the field of engagement, Kahn emphasized the equilibrium between an individual's enthusiasm for their work and the autonomy inherent in their job. He posited that engagement arises from the dynamic interaction between an employee's personal commitment to the job and their opportunities for self-expression at work. Engaged employees display profound emotional and mental dedication, so disengagement signals a detachment. Kahn's contributions highlighted the dialectical interplay of these elements, shaping the contemporary understanding of engagement (Leon et al., 2015).

Picture work as a dance. When an employee's energy and their job role are in perfect harmony, they're in the groove—fully engaged and distant from burnout. But if they step out of rhythm, they might feel either the exhaustive weight of burnout or the distance of detachment. Engagement is the feeling of being passionately involved in the dance, while burnout feels like tired legs after dancing too long without a break. Importantly, one doesn't rule out the possibility of the other. This interplay between burnout and engagement is akin to the push and pull in a dance, showcasing this dialectic tension.

The dance rhythm of work is orchestrated by yet another dialectic—the interplay between job demands and resources. Demands are the pressures or challenges at work, whereas resources, such as support from teammates or personal skills, are aids for navigating these challenges. An excess of demands can tip the scale toward burnout, and ample resources can tip the scales toward engagement. However, without a balance against demands, resources can become overwhelming. As discussed later in the chapter, these dynamics play a central role in shaping organizational culture.

Building on Kahn's foundational work, Schaufeli and colleagues (2002) characterized engagement as having three components: vigor (energy and resilience at work), dedication (deep involvement with a sense of significance), and absorption (full engrossment in tasks). Schaufeli et al. emphasized job demands and the role of resources, noting that more engaged employees typically show better performance, lower turnover, fewer absences, and improved well-being, ultimately boosting organizational success. In simple terms, safeguarding against burnout and fostering optimal engagement conditions can have a positive impact on a company's bottom line.

Is there such a thing as too much engagement? Contemporary wisdom would argue otherwise, as being fully immersed in your job—brimming with energy, commitment, and focus—is generally considered a positive thing. Why on earth would we ever want to stifle someone's engagement?

Imagine filling a balloon with water. In the beginning, your green engagement balloon expands beautifully as you slowly pour water into it, swelling and growing more impressive with each drop. But there's a limit. Overfill it, and the pressure mounts until . . . POP! It can't handle any more. As per the conservation of resources theory (essentially the instinct to protect personal resources, our "energy banks"; see Hobfoll, 1989), becoming too consumed by our jobs can make us overextend, potentially causing the metaphorical balloon to burst. Despite good intentions, excessive immersion can sometimes lead to unintended negative outcomes.

Consider Jacinda Ardern, for instance. At age 37, she rose to become New Zealand's youngest female Prime Minister. Recognized for her transformative leadership and audacious decisions like presenting her baby at the United Nations and swiftly closing New Zealand's borders at the onset of the 2020 pandemic, she epitomized dedication (Whiteman, 2023). However, the pressures of leadership, intensified by personal threats and protests, took their toll. In 2023, after 6 years in office, she resigned, stating, "I know what this job takes, and I know that I no longer have enough in the tank to do it justice. It is that simple" (Oliver, 2023). Her words reflect a clear sign of her unwavering commitment as well as an indicator of the likelihood of burnout.

The relationship between engagement and burnout isn't linear: Hyper-engagement might paradoxically exacerbate burnout. This phenomenon mirrors the too-much-of-a-good-thing principle, that even beneficial aspects can become detrimental when overextended (Nerstad et al., 2019). As with the balloon analogy, there's a fine line between an impressive fill and an explosive overfill. To strike the right balance, nurturing engagement while mitigating the risk of burnout, it's crucial to equip ourselves with the necessary resources to counter work-induced stresses.

INSIGHTS ON THE ENGAGED-EXHAUSTED WORKFORCE

Imagine it's the first day of Workforce Psychology 101 at college. In stumbles the psychology professor, the very embodiment of chaos, wearing a fuzzy-elbowed sports jacket that's seen better decades, mysteriously stained with what appears to be relish remnants from a rogue hotdog. His beard, wild and untamed, has become a storage unit for shards of Krispy Kreme donut glaze. His briefcase? Half-open with papers making a desperate bid for freedom. As he attempts to collect himself, he looks up, slightly out of breath, and asks, "Alright class, pop quiz! What percentage of the U.S. workforce do you reckon is burned out?"

As a skeptic, you're convinced the rumpled professor is playing mind games. Is this some sort of reverse psychology trick? In a dilemma, you scribble both 99% and 1% on your paper, weighing the odds of extremes. Just then, ever-eager Sally Jane's hand shoots up into the air like a human antenna, and she confidently declares "50%." The professor, nodding appreciatively, echoes, "Safe bet, Sally. But why 50%?" "Well professor, in a world post-COVID, with the buzz about burnout, the overwhelming tidal wave of new work responsibilities, and the wild west of hybrid working, it just makes sense to me that about half of everyone is just . . . exhausted. I for one, however, am not exhausted," she declares.

With a mischievous grin, the professor takes a dramatic pause, sips from his dented metal coffee mug, and drops the bombshell: "Based on that reasoning, you'd think so. But in reality, the percentage of the workforce that's purely burned out is closer to 2%." You silently shake your head in amused disbelief. Well played, professor. Well played.

In a recent study, researchers explored the interplay between work engagement and burnout in over 1,000 U.S. employees (Moeller et al., 2018). The research addressed the ways in which daily job demands and resources influenced burnout and engagement using the job demands–resources model. The findings suggest that engagement isn't always the savior we perceive it to be.

Let's first repackage the question asked by the whimsically chaotic professor. In your estimation, which of the following choices best describes most workers?

1. High engagement, low burnout
2. High engagement, high burnout
3. Low engagement, low burnout
4. Low engagement, high burnout

Option 4 may not be your first guess, given the nutty professor's response to Sally Jane. However, if your original estimates hovered around 50–60%, you hit the mark—with the added twist that many in this bracket are both engaged and burned out. Here's the detailed breakdown (Moeller et al., 2018):

1. High engagement, low burnout (41.1%)
2. High engagement, high burnout (54.7%)
3. Low engagement, low burnout (2.4%)
4. Low engagement, high burnout (1.8%)

While approximately 2% of the workforce experience burnout devoid of engagement, a much larger cohort of employees are simultaneously engaged and burned out. This dual state likely challenges our conventional image of a burned-out employee.

Figure 4.1 shows the data in a scatterplot. Each data point represents one of the 1,000+ workers who completed the survey. What stands out to you?

The two quadrants on the right indicate the good news. A whopping 95.4% of the employees said they were engaged (Moeller et al., 2018). Yahoo! Of course, the caveat, the not-so-good news, is that over half (54.3%) are both engaged and burned out. Alarmingly, the engaged–exhausted group also has the highest turnover intention. So, while employers might bask in the glory of an engaged workforce, many might be oblivious to the underlying burnout. The engaged-but-burned-out employees might be labeled as silent exiters.

The data also reflect some unconventional insights: The stereotype of people experiencing burnout—deeply exhausted, cynical, and disengaged from their daily tasks—is not as widespread as one might think, with only

FIGURE 4.1. Outcomes Associated With Burnout and Engagement

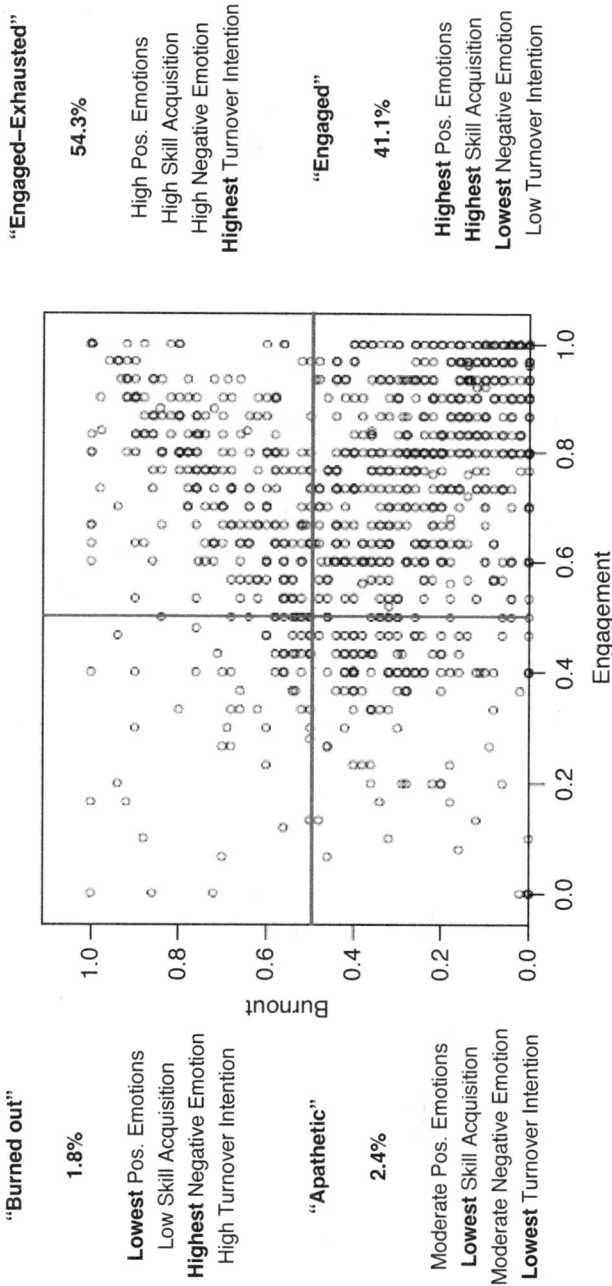

"Burned out"

1.8%

Lowest Pos. Emotions
Low Skill Acquisition
Highest Negative Emotion
High Turnover Intention

"Apathetic"

2.4%

Moderate Pos. Emotions
Lowest Skill Acquisition
Moderate Negative Emotion
Lowest Turnover Intention

"Engaged–Exhausted"

54.3%

High Pos. Emotions
High Skill Acquisition
High Negative Emotion
Highest Turnover Intention

"Engaged"

41.1%

Highest Pos. Emotions
Highest Skill Acquisition
Lowest Negative Emotion
Low Turnover Intention

Note. Data are segmented into quadrants and labels were added. "Moderately engaged–exhausted" and "highly engaged–exhausted" are collapsed into one group in the top right quadrant. Outcomes for each segment are highlighted using bold text for highest/lowest adverse outcomes. Adapted from "Highly Engaged But Burned Out: Intra-individual Profiles in the US Workforce," by J. Moeller, Z. Ivcevic, A. E. White, J. Menges, and M. A. Brackett, 2018, *Open Science Framework* (https://osf.io/preprints/osf/h6qnf). In the public domain.

1.8% of employees falling into this category. It's vital not to conflate burnout with apathy; 2.4% of the employees were characterized as apathetic.

In sum, the U.S. workforce appears to be largely engaged. And many are also burned out. Trying to balance these seemingly contradictory states, as discussed in the exploration of dialectic tension earlier in the chapter, challenges the notion that they are two sides of the same coin. Instead, they might be distinct coins altogether, with each concept carrying unique characteristics or elements absent in the other.

BALANCING JOB RESOURCES AND JOB DEMANDS

If engagement isn't as straightforward as it appears and isn't the panacea HR has long heralded, then how should organizations step up? Two key factors emerge: job resources and job demands. While they may appear similar, they serve different purposes in the context of burnout and engagement. Job resources are the tools, support, and conditions that help an individual perform their role effectively and remain motivated. Conversely, job demands are the stressors and challenges encountered while fulfilling job responsibilities.

Moeller et al. (2018) offered additional clarity on how these two factors impact workplace well-being and productivity. Each of the four groups shown in Figure 4.2 highlights "high" and "low" demands and resources for each of the four groups. For example, some workers high on engagement had low demands and high resources (those in the "engaged" quadrant), whereas others had high demands and high resources (in the "engaged–exhausted" quadrant).

Individuals in the engaged group are bolstered by abundant resources and tempered by manageable demands. However, high resources with low demands doesn't necessarily equate to an engagement magic potion. Imagine possessing every tool at work, but your job is devoid of any stimulating challenge. This scenario evokes memories of my grad school days, moonlighting as a valet at the posh Chateau Marmont in Los Angeles. One night, my part-time actor-turned-temporary-valet boss nonchalantly tossed me the keys to a gleaming Porsche, a prize from Hollywood's elite. Dreaming of an open thrill ride, I found myself instead trapped in the snarl of Sunset Boulevard and then in a dimly lit bar parking lot merely a stone's throw away. With all that horsepower, without a challenge, I might as well have been driving the trusty school-bus yellow Plymouth Reliant from my teenage years. This dilemma—having ample resources without a corresponding

FIGURE 4.2. Job Demands and Resources Associated With Burnout and Engagement

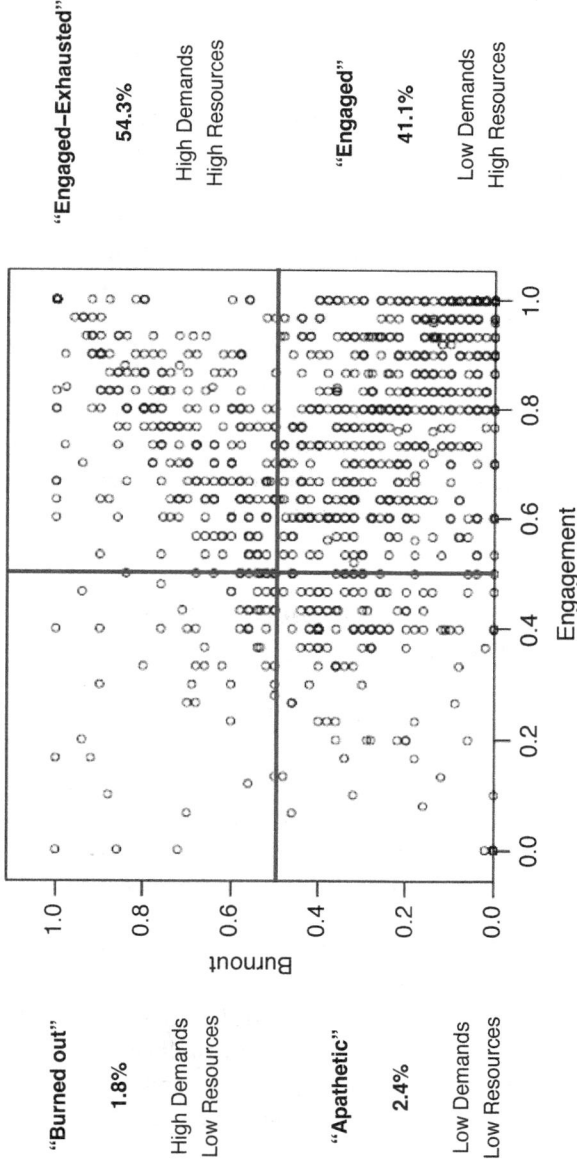

Note. Adapted from "Highly Engaged But Burned Out: Intra-individual Profiles in the US Workforce," by J. Moeller, Z. Ivcevic, A. E. White, J. Menges, and M. A. Brackett, 2018, *Open Science Framework* (https://osf.io/preprints/osf/h6qnf). In the public domain.

challenge—reflects the Yerkes-Dodson principle (Yerkes & Dodson, 1908), which suggests that peak performance hinges on achieving the right level of stress—not too high, nor too low, as both extremes can have an adverse impact on performance. Having an open road for the Porsche would been a good way to strike that balance. Similarly, equilibrium between job resources and demands is essential for optimal engagement and burnout mitigation.

Next, consider the apathetic workers in the lower left quadrant. This group stands out as having the smallest skill acquisition (see Figure 4.1). Intriguingly, these individuals also showcase the least inclination to exit their roles. Demands inherently sharpen competencies and stoke a person's drive. However, these demands require adequate resources to complement them. When this synergy is absent, the scale often tips, with demands driving a person to fatigue rather than motivation. For example, think of an Olympic athlete. Their intense dedication and rigorous training lead to remarkable achievements, but their fervor requires balance. Without the proper mix of challenges and resources such as rest, expert coaching, feedback, and autonomy, they're vulnerable. Too few challenges can dull their edge, while too many without the right support increases the risk of burnout. This balance is the essence of the optimal training zone, where ambition meets the right support system.

UNPACKING WORKLOAD: THE SILENT CONTRIBUTOR TO WORKPLACE BURNOUT

The Moeller et al. (2018) study highlights the nuanced dance between engagement and burnout. High engagement is often praised, but it can sometimes backfire, particularly when commingled with burnout. Organizations need to be vigilant, looking for burnout signs even in their most spirited employees, ensuring they have the right supports. But what are the primary demands and resources that strike the balance, fostering engagement without burnout?

Consider the following example to illustrate a ubiquitous challenge that's become particularly salient postpandemic. You're back in the oversized and dimly lit auditorium with the delightfully disheveled professor. With the first day in the rearview mirror, the class has successfully unpacked the conflicted relationship between burnout and engagement and has been introduced to the intriguing dance between job demands and resources. The professor, swiping a stray donut crumb from his wild beard, pauses to acknowledge that the class, to this point, has been deep in the realm of theory. But what about the practical, real-world stuff? Without missing a beat, he references Leiter and Maslach's (1999) research pinpointing six work environment elements—workload, control, rewards/recognition, community, fairness, and values. Simply put, the Big Six can contribute to burnout in an organization or act as buffers against it.

With a mischievous glint in his eye, he springs another surprise. "Everyone get out your phones. I want you to vote on this question." He flashes the following question on the screen: "Over the past month, which factor has been the primary source of your stress or burnout?" Students, intrigued and slightly amused, hastily punch in their responses. The emerging graph, paints a compelling if not slightly chaotic portrait of students' experience, which, in reality, closely mirrors much of what I have observed within the modern workforce. In fact, Figure 4.3 represents approximations of data not from undergraduates but from a broad spectrum of the workforce I have polled in conferences and other venues over the years. In these diverse groups, I have observed a consistent pattern. Despite careful definitions of all the key terms, the results converge: The primary burnout driver across age, experience, education, race, or ethnicity is workload.

While overwhelming workload is a recurring theme across various sectors, nowhere is it more palpable and distressing than in health care. Even with deep engagement—the enthusiasm, immersion, and dedication health care workers bring to their tasks—the constant and overwhelming workload can lead to feelings of exhaustion and burnout. In a compelling op-ed,

FIGURE 4.3. Over the Past Month, Which Factor Has Been the Primary Source of Your Stress or Burnout?

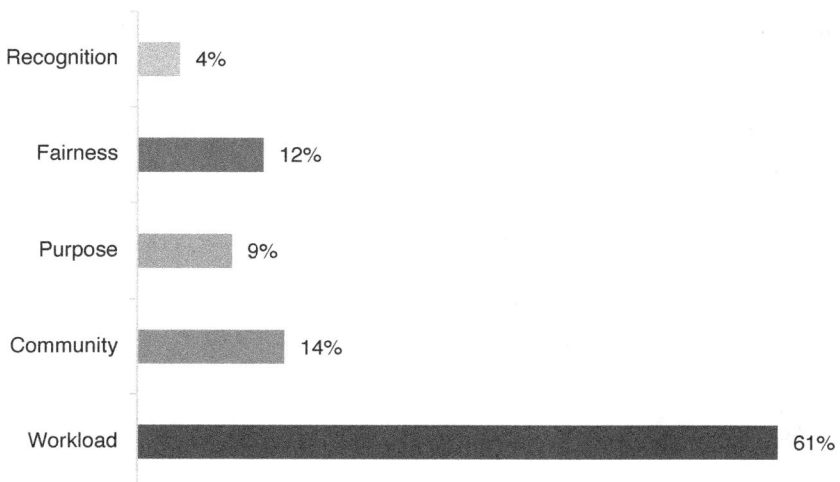

Factor	Percentage
Recognition	4%
Fairness	12%
Purpose	9%
Community	14%
Workload	61%

Ofri (2019) painted a chilling picture of the modern medical landscape. She depicted doctors and nurses, once the pillars of health care, stretched to their limits by a surge of responsibilities. Central to their overextension is the electronic medical record (EMR), which Ofri evocatively described as having "entwined its digital tendrils deep into every facet of patient care." Although EMR offers certain benefits, it has become a relentless taskmaster. Ofri noted that for every hour spent on direct patient care, primary care doctors find themselves trapped in 2 hours of EMR data entry. These burdens, coupled with the myriad other pressures of modern medicine, have ignited a burnout epidemic among health care professionals, compromising both health care professionals and patient safety. Echoing this sentiment, Dr. Christine Sinsky voiced her alarm at the staggering 86 minutes family physicians devote to after-hours administrative tasks, lamenting, "I and other physicians began to wonder if we were spending more time caring for the computer than caring for the patient" (as quoted in Berg, 2017).

Considering your own profession, take a minute to think of your answer to this pressing question: Of the following drivers of burnout—workload, control, rewards/recognition, community, fairness, and value—which one factor can you address to have the most positive impact on your team in the next 30 days? Take a minute to think of your answer.

When I ask this question in conferences, most people respond that they feel confident in addressing recognition (see Figure 4.4), which should not

FIGURE 4.4. Among the Following Drivers of Burnout, Which Factor Can You Address To Maximize Positive Impact on Your Team?

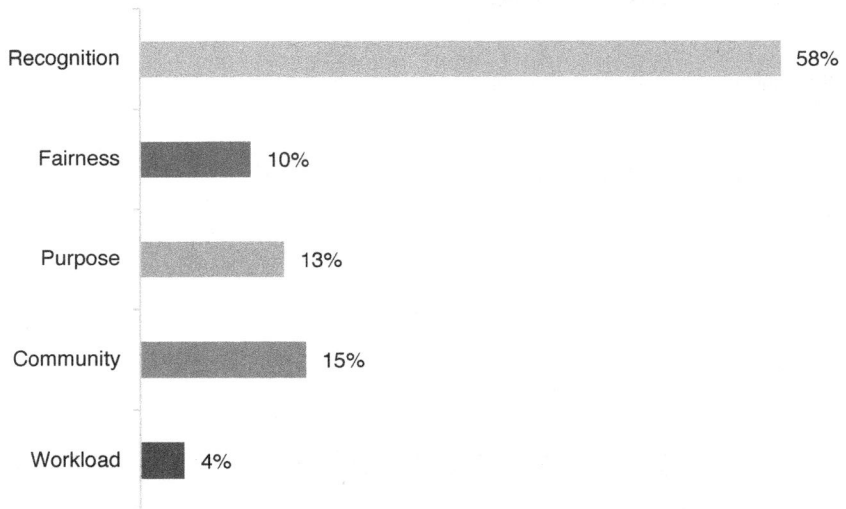

Recognition — 58%
Fairness — 10%
Purpose — 13%
Community — 15%
Workload — 4%

come as a big surprise. After all, it's one of the more actionable items on the list. What's even more interesting is that workload received the fewest votes, suggesting that many seem skeptical about their ability to actually influence (i.e., reduce) workload for their colleagues. This skepticism reflects a troubling reality: Excessive workload doesn't merely increase the risk of burnout—it nearly triples the risk (L. S. Rotenstein et al., 2023). Moreover, overwork doubles the chance that someone decides to leave their job. Given that the question functions a bit like a projective test, the answers might indicate that people view altering their workload as an insurmountable, complex challenge. They might be yearning for recognition, as that is at the top of the list. This sentiment is consistent with human nature—the fundamental need for acknowledgment, even if we sometimes understate our desire for it.

Projective interpretation aside, the results showcase what I call the *burnout conundrum*. Given that workload appears to be a key obstacle, how do organizations tackle it? By lavishing praise and recognition? Instead of addressing the fundamental issue of workload, organizations are inadvertently bolstering a system that continuously fuels burnout through a cycle of intermittent reinforcement.

How, then, do leaders navigate this intricate landscape of burnout and engagement to foster a culture of wellness? One thing is clear: Engagement, while beneficial, reaches its pinnacle only when it is carefully calibrated with other work demands and resources. Workload has surfaced as a dominant factor companies grapple with. The approach to burnout, then, shouldn't be merely symptomatic; it should be systemic. It's not about temporary fixes or isolated interventions; it's about a profound, organizational transformation that addresses the root causes, often insidiously interwoven into the DNA of an organization.

What do we call this process? "Moderating the tension between burnout and engagement, while being equally attuned to demands and resources inherent in the design of a job and, of course, acknowledging employee intrapersonal capacities that weigh in" seems wordy.

During my time in Afghanistan, I consistently noticed a contrast in unit dynamics. Members from cohesive, healthy units exhibited a clear sense of well-being. Their units buzzed with energy—soldiers interacted openly, shared jokes, and appeared genuinely invested in their roles. Such positive environments seemed to act as a buffer against severe mental health challenges. Consequently, these individuals rarely needed therapeutic sessions, and when they did seek help, their recovery was often swift, largely attributable to the secure and supportive environment they returned to. In contrast, members from dysfunctional or toxic units were frequent visitors to my office, and I often found myself embedded within their teams. The atmosphere in such units was unmistakable—conversations were sparse, faces rarely broke into smiles, and a general sense of apathy prevailed. When they sought therapy, the toxic unit culture often dominated our discussions. Regrettably, I encountered many individuals battling these circumstances. It's worth noting that while a positive unit culture doesn't serve as an impenetrable shield against mental illness, it can significantly mitigate its impact. My observations pointed to the value of such a positive culture as a buffer against mental health challenges.

Building on this idea of the protective role of culture, I'm reminded of established research on resilience. Kalisch and colleagues (2017) characterized resilience as "the maintenance or quick recovery of mental health during and after exposure to significant stressors" (p. 2). Notably, this perspective focuses on individual resilience, leaving a research gap regarding collective resilience. Much research looks into attributes that affect personal resilience and the ways in which entire organizations rebound from disruptions such as financial setbacks. However, the resilience of the collective workforce—the individuals that form the organization—remains underexplored. Part 2 of this book is a deeper dive into this less-charted territory, shedding light on the resilience of the collective workforce and its role within organizations.

CHAPTER SUMMARY

- Balancing job demands and resources is essential for optimal engagement and burnout mitigation.

- Research reveals a significant portion of the workforce is simultaneously engaged and burned out.

- Recognizing workload as a primary burnout driver is crucial for effective intervention.

- High levels of engagement do not necessarily translate to low levels of burnout (i.e., the engagement paradox).

- Resilient organizational cultures play a pivotal role in mitigating the impact of burnout.

- The burnout conundrum is that positive reinforcement without workload reduction perpetuates burnout cycles.

CHAPTER QUESTIONS

- How do I distinguish between burnout and apathy in my own experiences or in the experiences of people I manage?

- When I recall a moment of work-related burnout, how do I feel? Did engagement play a role?

- How aligned are job demands and resources in my workplace? Can I spot instances of imbalance?

- How will addressing workload positively impact my (or others') engagement while mitigating burnout?

- Who can I publicly recognize this week?

- How receptive is my organization to systemic changes addressing burnout's root causes? What steps could I take—at the individual or team level—to foster a culture of well-being?

PART **II** RESILIENCE PATHWAYS

5 THE ORGANIZATIONAL PATH TO WORKFORCE RESILIENCE

In times of adversity and change, we really discover who we are and what we're made of.

—Howard Schultz, *Onward*

Born in 1953 in Brooklyn's Canarsie Bayview Housing Projects, Howard D. Schultz's early life was marked by adversity. Although Schultz was raised in a working-class family, his father struggled with low-paying blue-collar jobs and lacked health insurance. This hardship was compounded when his father broke his ankle and could not work, plunging the family into financial crisis. These struggles deeply influenced Schultz, planting a seed of determination not only to succeed but also to ensure he supported those around him in future endeavors (Clifford, 2018).

Moving to Seattle for a sales job, Schultz discovered Starbucks, a local coffee store that ignited his passion for coffee. His vision for Starbucks expanded after a transformative trip to Italy; inspired by Italian café culture, he reimagined Starbucks as a community hub. Despite resistance, Schultz

https://doi.org/10.1037/0000454-006
Rethinking Employee Resilience: Why Our Current Approach to Worker Burnout Is Failing, and How to Fix It, by D. Pelton

was relentless. He founded Il Giornale, an Italian-themed café and by 1987 had acquired Starbucks, setting the stage for a global coffee revolution (Entrepreneur Life, 2023).

Schultz's leadership extended beyond coffee. He was committed to employee welfare, and, driven by memories of his family's struggles, he introduce health benefits and stock options. When the 2008 financial crisis hit, Schultz's approach to adversity was tested. Rather than cut staff, he chose to close stores temporarily and retrain employees, prioritizing long-term integrity over immediate profits. Starbucks lost $6 million in revenue and gained its share of criticism (T. Schwartz, 2011). But instead of looking at short-term profit, Schultz viewed the situation through the lens of company values and long-term goals.

If we were to distill Schultz's journey, the word "resilience" comes to mind. I imagine words and phrases like "tenacity," "perseverance," "overcoming odds," and "hard work" may be apt descriptors for his experience. Interestingly, when I probe groups and ask them to give one word to define resilience, many of these words come up, as do the usual suspects: "bounceback," "endure," "thrive," "overcome," "dedication," "persistence," "grit," and the like. Know what one word has never come up before? Adversity.

Resilience hinges on adversity; there's no recovery without it. Schultz exemplifies resilience, from a challenging upbringing to reshaping the coffee experience and prioritizing employee well-being at Starbucks. He prioritized long-term brand integrity over short-term profits, weathering setbacks and reinforcing the brand's reputation even through controversial decisions he's made, most notably in response to Starbucks' unionization efforts. Enduring hardship builds resilience in individuals, teams, and organizations, as seen in Schultz's early life journey, leading to positive outcomes.

In Part I, I delved deep into dismantling our conventional views of burnout. This effort was essential, revealing burnout as a complex, weighty phenomenon that shapes the discussion profoundly. The same critical analysis applies to resilience—it often gets lost in vague definitions, stumbling into pitfalls similar to those of burnout and the broader wellness movement.

Beginning Part II, the focus in Chapter 5 is on unraveling the misconceptions surrounding resilience. I closely scrutinize its construction and definition, particularly within the realms of individual and organizational resilience. Additionally, I explore the often-overlooked concept of workforce resilience, emphasizing its importance and practical implications. Building on insights gained from the examination of burnout in Part I, I refine resilience principles and introduce a new perspective: Workforce resilience is an organizational solution to an organizational problem. Furthermore,

I integrate various themes discussed throughout the book, such as burnout, engagement, job design, and resilience, to introduce a new model. This model includes four key cultural levers—performance management (PM), job crafting, analytics, and strategic communication—that can mold organizational culture into one characterized by workforce resilience.

In Chapter 6, I explore leadership at every level, highlighting the importance of adaptable resilience qualities in driving organizational change. Introducing a new framework, I discuss these traits among leaders and discuss methods for cascading them across teams and the organization. The chapter also offers practical use cases to demonstrate how these principles can be applied in the daily work environment.

RESILIENCE DEFINED

Let's start with basics: a foundational definition of resilience. Amidst extensive debates in the 1990s, involving both advocates and skeptics scrutinizing the concept, Dr. Raffael Kalisch, research group leader at the Leibniz Institute for Resilience Research, formulated a robust definition: "the maintenance or quick recovery of mental health during and after exposure to significant stressors" (Kalisch et al., 2017, p. 2). While this definition alludes to the "bounce-back" concept, the added details and explicit mention of mental health help to create a more nuanced picture. Notably, the concept also underscores adversity, as discussed at the start of this chapter (and in my story), and emphasizes its role as a prerequisite for resilience.

With a foundational understanding of resilience, let's examine its impact on three key areas: the individual, workforce, and organization. "Workforce" refers to employees collectively (e.g., multiple individual canaries), and "organization" signifies the entire entity (e.g., the coal mine). Let's shift our attention first to the individual and the organizational perspectives of resilience. Both areas have garnered significant scholarly attention. They are deeply rooted in recovering from stressors, yet each exhibits unique characteristics, scope, and outcomes (see Table 5.1).

The literature addressing the connection between individual and organizational resilience is conceptual and sparse (Gröschke et al., 2022). While substantial research emphasizes the multilevel nature of resilience (Williams et al., 2017), there is limited clarity in the interdependencies among individual, workforce, and organizational levels; thus, organizational resilience is not assumed to be simply the sum of individual resilience (Lengnick-Hall et al., 2011). An organization can be resilient even if it has employees with

TABLE 5.1. Contrasting Individual and Organizational Resilience

Aspect	Individual resilience	Organizational resilience
Definition	Capacity of an individual to adapt, recover, and thrive in the face of personal challenges and stressors	Capacity of an organization as a whole to withstand, adapt to, and recover from disruptions, crises, and external challenges while maintaining core functions and integrity
Focus	Personal well-being and psychological capacity of an individual	Overall resilience, adaptability, and continuity of an entire organization
Characteristics	Personal attributes including optimism, adaptability, problem-solving skills, emotional intelligence, and support networks	Organizational strategies, contingency plans, crisis management, resource allocation, and ability to sustain core operations in the face of disruptions
Scope	An individual's psychological and emotional resilience	The resilience and adaptability of the entire organization, including its structure, processes, and ability to withstand external challenges

low resilience because the organizational focus is not on individual well-being but rather on the continuity of the entire entity.

Let's turn our attention to the workforce. Crane (2021) explored how significant occupational stressors such as high workload, organizational changes, and job insecurity affect employee resilience, which is deeply embedded within their socioecological context. Crane emphasized that understanding employee resilience extends beyond traditional job design to include the broad workplace system or ecological context. This expanded perspective considers not only job demands and resources but also the surrounding ecological context and cultural forces, which are pivotal in either supporting or obstructing these elements.

The key takeaway is that connecting individual resilience to organizational resilience requires a deep understanding of the entire workforce and its specific challenges. Investigating the workforce directs us to focus on job design and considering both demands and resources that have an impact on the entire workforce system. A resilient workforce, in this context, focuses on team dynamics, communication, collaboration, and leadership. It can result in short-term improvements such as higher engagement and lower burnout as well as long-term benefits such as job satisfaction, commitment to the organization, and employee retention (see Table 5.2).

Given the significant impact in workforce outcomes overall, there is a clear business imperative to drive workforce resilience. Not only is it an ethical

TABLE 5.2. Demystifying Workforce Resilience

Aspect	Workforce resilience
Definition	An organizational process (job demands and job resources) that shapes workforce culture (engagement and strain pathway) to optimize employee well-being (increase engagement, decrease burnout)
Focus	Organizational job demands/resources
Characteristics	Team dynamics, effective communication, collaboration, adaptability, leadership, and shared goals within a workforce
Scope	Focus on the resilience and teamwork of a group of employees or a specific workforce
Outcome	Increase engagement, decrease burnout (short term); job satisfaction, productivity, recruitment, organizational commitment, retention (long term)

imperative, but it also directly impacts the bottom line. However, organizations aligned with the operationalization of workforce resilience (as defined in Table 5.2) are harder to find than I expected.

While comprehensive studies and definitions on workforce resilience are lacking, organizations such as Aon and the Center for Strategic and International Studies (CSIS) are actively shaping this area. Aon (2022, p. 8) defined a resilient workforce as one that is capable of "withstanding the unpredictability of major events" and emphasized human capital priorities like skill development and value creation. In contrast, CSIS describes workforce resilience as intricately connected to diversity and inclusion, serving as a mechanism to promote security, belonging, and adaptability (Ali & Subah, 2022). Both Aon and CSIS seem to capture the essence of what Crane (2021) envisioned in terms of incorporating the workforce context. However, it's notable that Aon's (2022) description somewhat blurs the lines between workforce with organizational resilience. CSIS's (Ali & Subah, 2022) emphasis on culture is commendable, leaning toward outcomes related to security, belonging, and adaptability. While this distinction is not necessarily incorrect, existing organizational scholarship often highlights the connection between resilience and mental health (cf. Kalisch et al., 2017). Therefore, it might be advantageous for organizations to set explicit goals that focus on mental health or at least touch on the complex issue of burnout when addressing the interplay between job demands and resources.

At the organizational level, when an organization wants to maintain agility during times of change, they might deploy training programs focused on teaching employees how to adapt and remain nimble. While influencing the workforce in this manner is important, organizational strategies and levers designed to foster agility (e.g., cross-functional teams, agile methodologies, digital transformation) may be more effective in achieving the desired outcomes.

THE RESILIENCE DEBATE: A NEW LENS ON CORPORATE CULTURE

The term "resilience" is not without its share of critics. Some may argue that, broadly, resilience is an overused and poorly defined term. Others might contend that it lets organizations off the hook for corporate responsibility amid a stressed or burned-out workforce. Attenberg (2020) described how her understanding of resilience evolved during the pandemic. Initially viewing it as a "work hard; suck it up" mentality, she noted that she now embraces a nuanced view that considers systemic and socially ingrained issues rather than individual problems. Attenberg interviewed skeptics such as Anne Gisleson, who remarked, "It puts the onus on the person to fix things that should be a civic priority." Another, Alison Fensterstock, bluntly stated, "'You're so resilient' is just code for 'You're on your own, sorry.'" Attenberg concluded that reflecting on resilience prompts an examination of its contemporary incarnation, revealing that the prevalent use of the term may conceal a potentially harmful trick involving the manipulation of language against individuals.

Attenberg (2020) raised several valid points. Like burnout and well-being, resilience has succumbed to corporate buzzword status, obscuring its genuine meaning beneath layers of unquantifiable jargon. Organizations, with good intentions, may inadvertently misconstrue resilience, potentially encouraging employees to endure harmful situations in its name. Additionally, organizations may mistakenly perceive resilience as a substitute for comprehensive employee support programs, risking its exploitation and stigmatization. There's concern that resilience is sometimes taught as an unchangeable personality trait, unjustly stigmatizing employees who face adversity. Parul Sehgal succinctly encapsulated these concerns, pointing out that resilience is often reduced to "a doubling down of old bootstrap logic, where your success or failure is attributed to your character" (as quoted in Martin, 2015).

It's troubling to observe how the concept of resilience has been diminished, reduced to a mere buzzword used as flippantly as phrases like "synergizing synergies" and "leveraging paradigm-shifting competencies." This degradation has stripped resilience of its empirical roots, rendering it ineffective in many corporate programs—akin to glaring failures rather than achievements. Building on this critique, it's worth exploring a more contrarian view, as suggested by thinkers like Attenberg (2020) and Sehgal (as cited in Martin, 2015). They have argued that, in U.S. culture, handling of resilience programs has been superficial and negligent. This critique prompts a deeper investigation into what truly constitutes an effective resilience initiative.

Despite these challenges, there's a clear pathway toward improvement. Integrating insights from experts such as Crane (2021) can lead to the adoption of a more refined approach to workforce resilience. This approach involves rethinking job design and workplace systems, which are important for nurturing a supportive culture that genuinely enhances employee well-being.

However, the struggle to perfect this formula is not new; organizations have wrestled with it for decades, striving to create environments where employees not only survive but thrive. This ongoing challenge leads to the question: How does my proposed approach differ? To illustrate, I offer a metaphorical teeter-totter, introduced as Exhibit A. This simple analogy helps to unpack the balance needed to foster true resilience in the workplace.

BALANCING ACTS: NAVIGATING WORKFORCE RESILIENCE IN UNCONVENTIONAL WAYS

On a dreaded middle school March afternoon, my gaze fixated on the forlorn teeter-totter, bathed in the aftermath of a late spring snow. Summoning courage, I approached the aging Ironhorse, perching myself on one end, only to plummet unceremoniously to the ground. Enter Tommy "Mad Dog" Harrison, a horsey-shaped boy, who clumsily occupied the opposite side, ineptly slinging his legs over the top. Then came the "wham" moment, propelling me skyward as I clung to the handle gingerly. I invited three of my slender friends to join, and a delicate equilibrium emerged—a 4-on-1 teeter-totter ballet ensued. As Mad Dog pushed through labored breaths, we ascended; our collective force pushed back, and he descended.

This tenacious teeter-totter battle provides a parallel to a struggle in the workforce—the ongoing tension between job demands and resources. It's a delicate balancing act in which, ideally, the weight and volume of job demands find equilibrium with the weight and volume of available job resources. When this balance falters, and the Mad Dog job demands significantly outweigh job resources, disequilibrium quickly emerges, and, as you might expect, leads to burnout. Without adequate resources to counter the demands, the teeter-totter tips unfavorably. On the flip side, when Mad Dog is in check, resources are in excess and outweigh demands. Sounds appealing, right? A job with minimal demands? Might seem ideal. However, maintaining a balanced equilibrium is vital to sustain motivation and ward off apathy.

The job demands–resources model (JD-R; Demerouti et al., 2001) provides a theoretical lens through which to explore the dynamic relationship between job demands and job resources. It offers a way to look at how these factors affect how employees are doing and feeling about their work. Imagine a scale with job demands on one side and job resources on the other side. When the scale is balanced, the workplace is harmonious. But, as illustrated in Figure 5.1, if the demands of the job become too much and outweigh the resources available, then employees are at risk of burnout (Crane, 2021). Burnout happens when the pressures at work are more than what the job provides to help cope with those pressures.

What constitutes the ideal mix of characters in my middle school analogy, encompassing the right blend of demands and resources to foster a sense of

FIGURE 5.1. The Balancing Act Between Job Demands and Job Resources

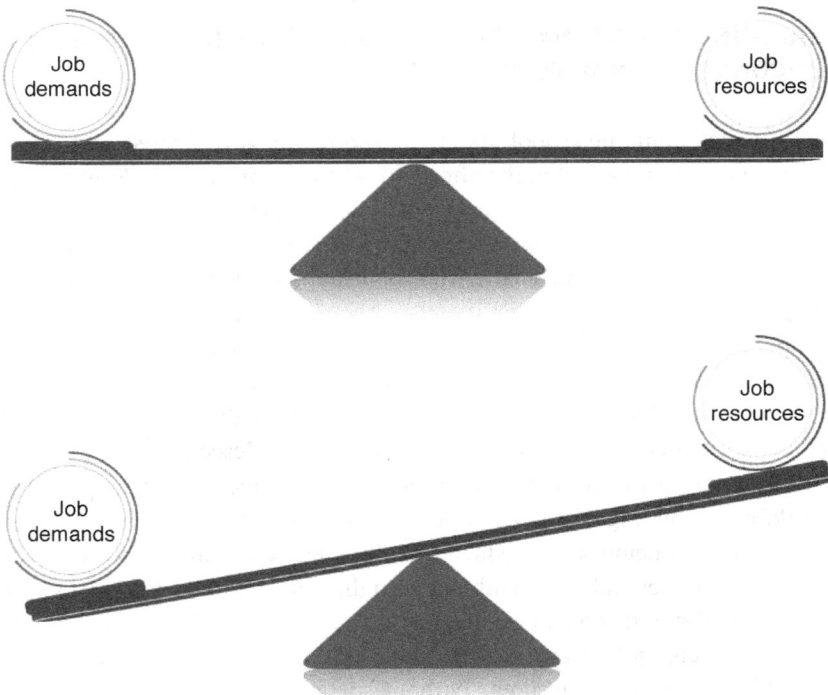

equilibrium or balance? The answer is not as straightforward as it seems. Bakker et al. (2014) highlighted the popularity of the JD-R theory, which has remarkable flexibility. This theory can work well in all sorts of jobs because it can adjust to the unique details and challenges of different workplaces. Bakker et al. (2014, p. 399) emphasized that "meaningful variations in levels of certain specific job demands and resources (such as work pressure, autonomy) can be found in almost every occupational group, other job demands and resources are unique" to specific professions. For instance, physical demands may be more prevalent in law enforcement, whereas cognitive demands may take precedence for scientists and engineers. Thus, there may be some universal and some targeted attributes, depending on the workplace system.

In my experience, I have found 12 institutional job demands and resources to be essential to workforce resilience and ultimately to organizational performance. My audiences generally are relatively homogeneous and consist of diverse professionals such as policymakers, analysts, and business leaders who share common challenges. I draw heavily from Crane's (2021) resilient work systems framework and integrate insights from Maslach's (1993) pioneering literature that identified key organizational factors that contribute to burnout. Additionally, guided by Kahn's (1990) conceptualization of engagement, I place emphasis on both engagement and burnout, which is rare in workplace systems models. With this dual focus, I recognize that resilience is an ongoing, dynamic process that entails both bolstering engagement and curbing burnout.

The workforce resilience model outlined in Figure 5.2 delineates 12 work-related dimensions, comprising six job demands and six job resources. As with Crane's (2021) model, within each dimension are anchors at opposing poles, clearly defining the distinctive characteristics inherent to that dimension. For example, amplifying any of the job demands tends to result in diminished resilience outcomes, particularly through heightened engagement and reduced burnout. Conversely, reducing these demands tends to elevate resilience outcomes. Similarly, enhancing job resources tends to improve resilience outcomes, while diminishing them can lead to decreased outcomes. Purpose, availability, and psychological safety, in particular, align with Kahn's (1990) conceptualization of engagement.

Managing this balance can be tenuous. While each dimension has a strong evidence base, the question remains how to maintain this balance in a dynamic work environment. Figure 5.3 illustrates a balanced scale model, incorporating the 12 institutional factors. However, in my experience, organizations without a clear strategy for shaping organizational culture often prioritize demands over resources, as illustrated in Figure 5.4. This prioritization may involve not only

FIGURE 5.2. Workforce Resilience Model

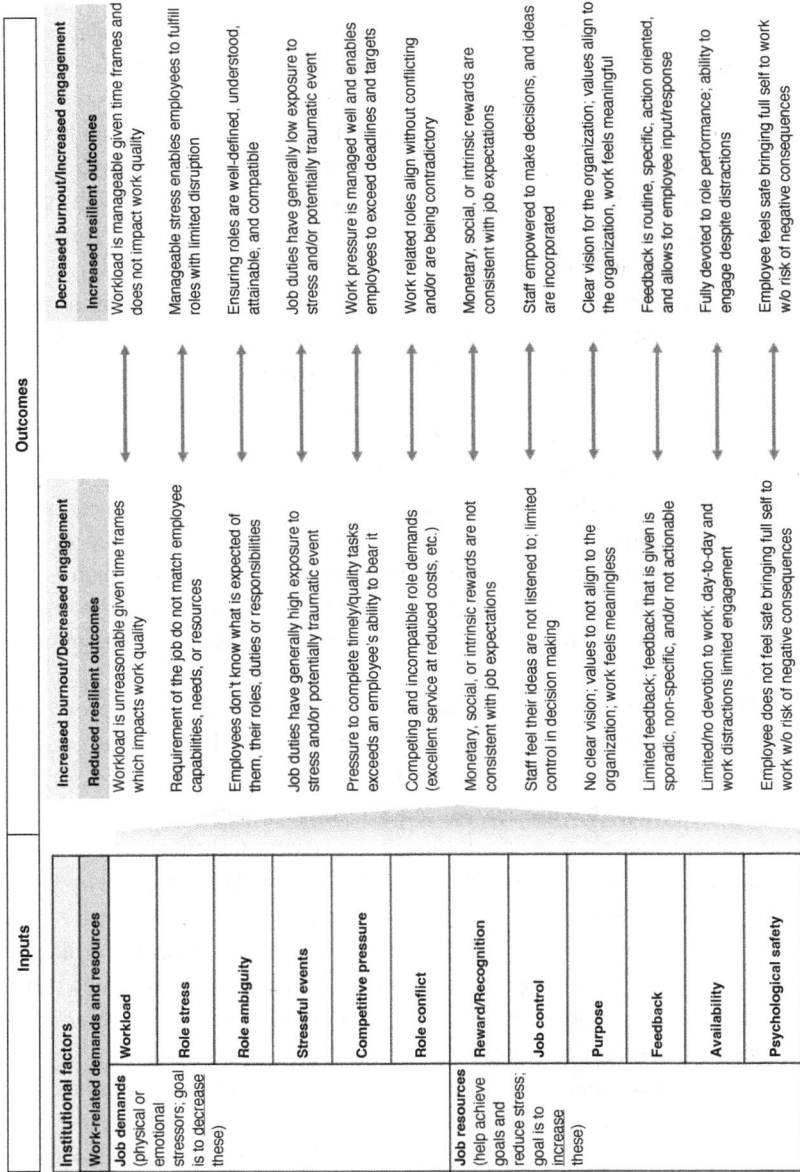

Inputs		Outcomes	
Institutional factors		Increased burnout/Decreased engagement — **Reduced resilient outcomes**	Decreased burnout/Increased engagement — **Increased resilient outcomes**
Work-related demands and resources			
Job demands (physical or emotional stressors; goal is to decrease these)	**Workload**	Workload is unreasonable given time frames which impacts work quality	Workload is manageable given time frames and does not impact work quality
	Role stress	Requirement of the job do not match employee capabilities, needs, or resources	Manageable stress enables employees to fulfill roles with limited disruption
	Role ambiguity	Employees don't know what is expected of them, their roles, duties or responsibilities	Ensuring roles are well-defined, understood, attainable, and compatible
	Stressful events	Job duties have generally high exposure to stress and/or potentially traumatic event	Job duties have generally low exposure to stress and/or potentially traumatic event
	Competitive pressure	Pressure to complete timely/quality tasks exceeds an employee's ability to bear it	Work pressure is managed well and enables employees to exceed deadlines and targets
	Role conflict	Competing and incompatible role demands (excellent service at reduced costs, etc.)	Work related roles align without conflicting and/or are being contradictory
Job resources (help achieve goals and reduce stress; goal is to increase these)	**Reward/Recognition**	Monetary, social, or intrinsic rewards are not consistent with job expectations	Monetary, social, or intrinsic rewards are consistent with job expectations
	Job control	Staff feel their ideas are not listened to; limited control in decision making	Staff empowered to make decisions, and ideas are incorporated
	Purpose	No clear vision; values to not align to the organization; work feels meaningless	Clear vision for the organization; values align to the organization, work feels meaningful
	Feedback	Limited feedback; feedback that is given is sporadic, non-specific, and/or not actionable	Feedback is routine, specific, action oriented, and allows for employee input/response
	Availability	Limited/no devotion to work; day-to-day and work distractions limited engagement	Fully devoted to role performance; ability to engage despite distractions
	Psychological safety	Employee does not feel safe bringing full self to work w/o risk of negative consequences	Employee feels safe bringing full self to work w/o risk of negative consequences

FIGURE 5.3. Balanced Scale Model of Job Demands and Job Resources

Job demands

- Workload
- Role stress
- Role ambiguity
- Stressful events
- Competitive pressure
- Role conflict

Job resources

- Reward/Recognition
- Job control
- Purpose/Meaningfulness
- Feedback
- Availability
- Psychological safety

Note. Strong empirical evidence supports the concept that job demands and resources can contribute to diminished wellness, burnout, and/or disengagement (see Alarcon, 2011; Bakker et al., 2007, 2014; Cavanaugh et al., 2000; Kahn, 1990; Lee & Ashforth, 1996; Mauno et al., 2007; Moeller et al., 2018; Schaufeli & Bakker, 2004).

FIGURE 5.4. Job Demands Outweigh Job Resources

The natural inclination is for **demands** to take precedence over **resources**

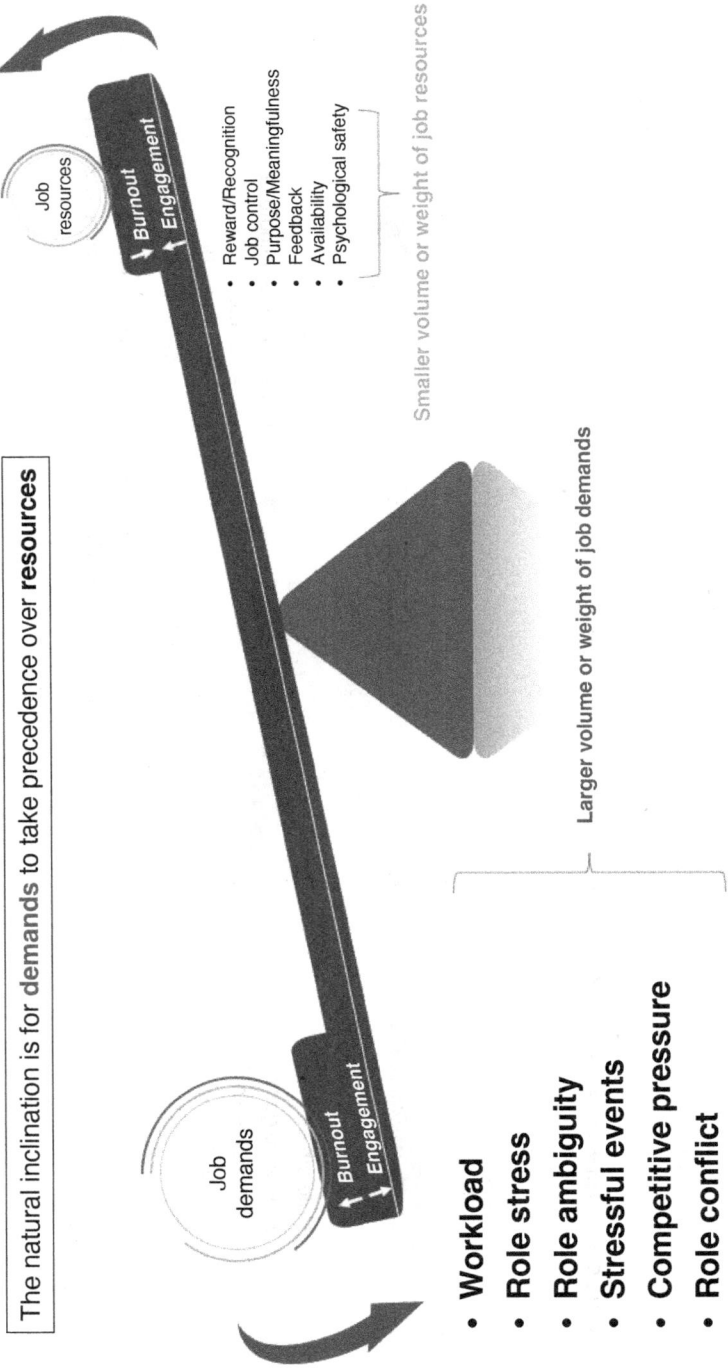

Smaller volume or weight of job resources

- Reward/Recognition
- Job control
- Purpose/Meaningfulness
- Feedback
- Availability
- Psychological safety

Larger volume or weight of job demands

- **Workload**
- **Role stress**
- **Role ambiguity**
- **Stressful events**
- **Competitive pressure**
- **Role conflict**

a high volume of demands but also their substantial weight. For instance, consider an air traffic controller who has a low volume of job demands with a manageable workload, clear job expectations, and minimal role conflict. She also has favorable job resources such as good pay, a positive work environment, and a sense of team connection. Despite favorable job conditions, her role stress entails precise aircraft management, quick decision making, and multitasking and thus carries significant weight, potentially leading to burnout. Without a workforce resilience strategy, she is at a heightened risk of experiencing engaged–exhausted conditions, as highlighted by Moeller et al. (2018; see also Chapter 4 of this volume). Experiencing these conditions substantially raises the likelihood that she will consider leaving her job, as turnover intention is highest among engaged–exhausted employees. The absence of a resilience strategy poses a risk for organizations, as it may result in the departure of actively engaged and high-performing individuals from critical roles.

Let's reconsider the analogy involving Tommy "Mad Dog" Harrison. Envision a scenario in which the 150-pound Tommy is on one end of the teeter-totter, absolutely outweighing 50-pound dynamo Irving McCalister, on the other. Instead of opting for a conventional solution, such as adding more weight to Irving or suggesting Tommy shed some pounds, we can explore the question of how to establish balance. By analyzing the mechanics of the teeter-totter, we can seek another, perhaps unconventional, method to solve this problem: Tommy ungracefully dismounts from the device and lumbers off to the axis point. Using his superhuman arm strength, he hoists the axis bend with one hand and gives the pivot point—the fulcrum—a swift kick, relocating it closer to his seat. Consequently, the fulcrum is no longer at the center but much closer to Mad Dog. Now, both Tommy and Irving, legs dangling, are eye to eye, despite their disparate weights.

How does this concept connect to the business realm? It involves not just haphazardly mixing job demands and resources but strategically revolutionizing the power balance within an organization. This strategy includes shifting organizational fulcrums (or addressing the workplace systems), envisioning them as powerful levers steering the course of the resilience strategy at the organization (see Figure 5.5). These fulcrum shifts have the power to address multiple demands and resources at once, laying the foundation for a culture of workforce resilience. In this scenario, the approach doesn't entail simply adding or eliminating a hint of demands or a dash of resources; rather, it uses organizational levers to coordinate the synchronized movement of multiple demands and resources. The natural follow-up question, then, is what, exactly, do these levers represent, at the cultural level?

FIGURE 5.5. Moving the Organizational Fulcrum to Balance Job Demands and Resources

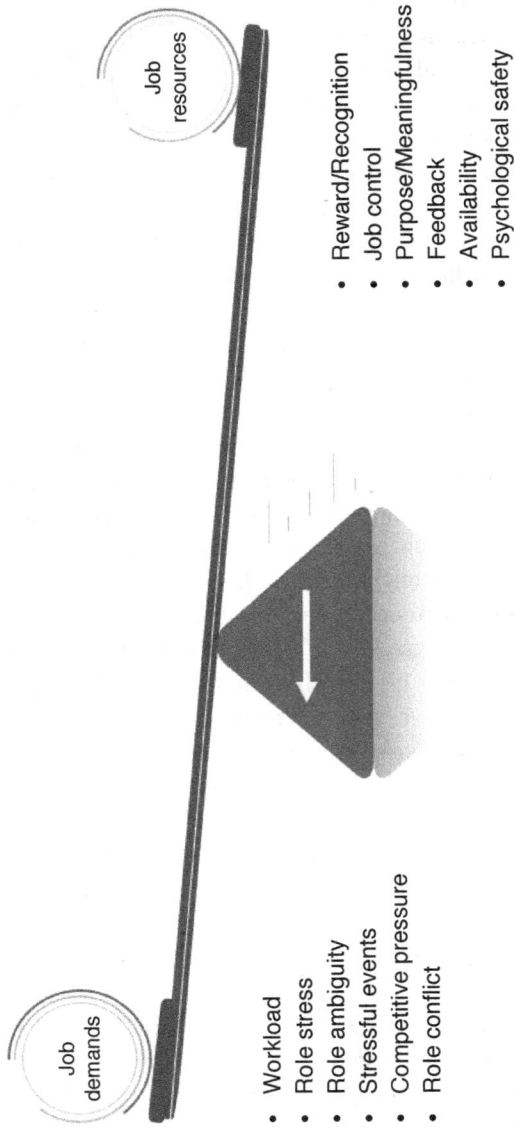

Job demands
- Workload
- Role stress
- Role ambiguity
- Stressful events
- Competitive pressure
- Role conflict

Job resources
- Reward/Recognition
- Job control
- Purpose/Meaningfulness
- Feedback
- Availability
- Psychological safety

CULTURAL LEVERS TO MOVE ORGANIZATIONAL CULTURE

When I think about how to shift organizational culture, the most apt analogy is one of those colossally gaudy cruise ships (yes, that one) you see in a port city from time to time. Many of these ships, despite their immense size, rely on a modest, unassuming, and inconspicuous component—the (relatively) small rudder—that serves as the key instrument for steering. When the captain aims to execute a subtle course adjustment, they must skillfully direct the rudder and other steering instruments. Though passengers may not readily perceive these gradual turns, they are integral to the journey. The captain must make decisions well ahead of time, as steering large ships requires careful planning for effective navigation and course changes.

The 1912 Titanic tragedy poignantly underscores the dire consequences of misjudged decisions and lack of foresight, serving as a reminder of the importance of careful planning and execution in navigation. In the 37 seconds after spotting the iceberg, the crew, hampered by limited time, faced a challenging situation. Historical analyses suggest that altering the Titanic's course was likely beyond the captain's control (History.com Editors, 2019). The lookout, stationed high in the crow's nest, revealed during Senate testimony that although he had binoculars, his request to use them was denied. Had he seen the iceberg several hundred feet earlier, he could have directed the captain to change course, profoundly impacting the Titanic's historical significance.

In an organization, leaders must function like both the captain steering the rudder and the lookout holding the binoculars. They need the foresight to detect potential hazards and the capability to direct the organization using cultural instruments. This dual role allows them to guide the organization toward greater engagement and protect employees from burnout. But in an organization, what serves as the rudder? This section of the chapter explores the dynamics of four cultural levers that have the power to shape and direct an organizational culture. I present evidence supporting each lever, examining how it can effectively steer organizational culture toward better performance, vis-à-vis engagement, and away from burnout.

Before going further, it's important to emphasize a key point. The levers within an organization are intricately tied to its values and its practices, which have a reciprocal relationship. Values serve as the bedrock of organizational culture, shaping the mindset and actions of the workforce, and practices are the tangible expressions of these values that influence day-to-day behaviors. For example, many organizations list "the welfare of the workforce" or some variant as a core business value on their fancy brochure but struggle to put it into practice. Conversely, some companies provide employee assistance programs or similar services and practices to address employee needs. However, the use of these services might be minimal (fewer than 1% of the employees in many companies), as wellness is not clearly defined as an explicit company value.

Each lever I share acts either as a conduit for company values or as a means to shape company culture. In essence, the lever is a reflection of values and practices needed to actualize these principles within a company. If a company lacks interest in well-being or claims to prioritize it but fails to invest, these levers may not be useful. On the other hand, for companies deeply invested in the workforce, particularly those intertwining well-being with their company's mission and vision, these levers prove invaluable, not just for employee well-being but also for the bottom line. They play a pivotal role in transforming organizational culture, which, in turn, contributes to over half of the performance variance observed among companies (Tosti & Jackson, 1994). Additionally, three out of every four employees acknowledge that workplace culture affects their productivity, efficiency, and ability to do their best work (Eagle Hill Consulting, 2018). So, improving workplace culture is not just a commendable ethical practice; it's a strategic move with tangible financial implications for the company.

Cultural Lever 1: Performance Management

The *happy-productive worker hypothesis* is the name of a theory that, as it sounds, states that employees perform better when they are happy, and several studies support its validity (Brief, 1998; Spector, 1997). However, the concept of "happy" varies, with some studies linking it to job satisfaction and others to overall well-being. In a seminal study, Wright and Cropanzano (2000) found that psychological well-being, and not job satisfaction (or age, gender, tenure), consistently predicted how well someone performed on the job. This finding echoes those of other studies (e.g., Wright & Bonett, 1993, 1997), further validating the idea that enhanced employee well-being contributes significantly to improved performance.

Beyond well-being, the discussion expands to explore workforce resilience—a delicate balance between job demands and resources—and the role of PM in shaping this equilibrium (see Figure 5.6). As discussed in Chapter 4, workload emerges as a critical factor, with studies warning against the potential harm of heavy, unmanaged workloads on employee well-being and performance (Fan & Smith, 2017; Jomuad et al., 2021). Research such as Bruggen's (2015) emphasizes the "inverted U-shaped connection"

FIGURE 5.6. Moving the Performance Management Fulcrum

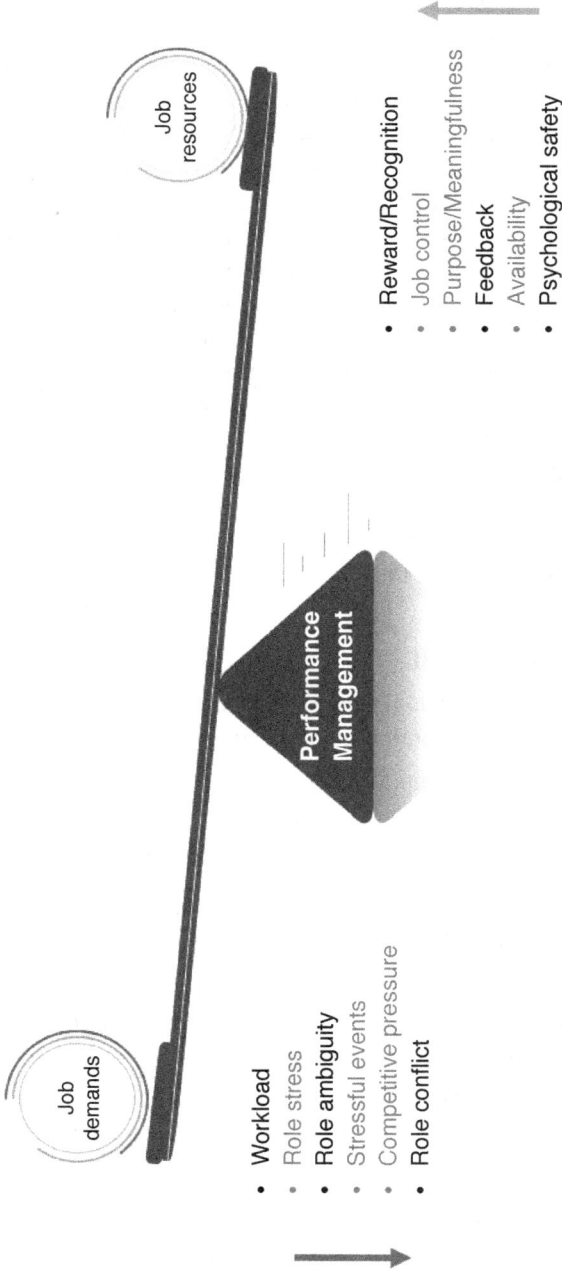

Job demands
- Workload
- Role stress
- Role ambiguity
- Stressful events
- Competitive pressure
- Role conflict

Performance Management

Job resources
- Reward/Recognition
- Job control
- Purpose/Meaningfulness
- Feedback
- Availability
- Psychological safety

(p. 2377), revealing that employee performance reaches its peak under moderate workloads, emphasizing the positive impact of well-managed or moderate work conditions.

PM, at its core, enables organizations to understand and improve employee job performance. This system can range from paper-and-pencil record keeping to complex tools and software with advanced performance analytics. Within the framework of workforce resilience, organizations can craft a PM system to moderate job demands and optimize resources. A well-designed PM system achieves these goals by balancing workloads, reducing role ambiguity and conflict through clear role definition, providing integrated feedback, and recognizing and rewarding employees based on their performance (see Figure 5.6). Adopting this counterbalancing approach via PM contributes to cultivating a culture of psychological safety, a key component of Kahn's (1990) conceptualization of work engagement. A workplace that fosters psychological safety has substantial benefits, reducing turnover and stress, and enhancing employee engagement, productivity, and collaboration (Minnick, 2023).

Some key considerations organizations should bear in mind when designing a PM system with a focus on enhancing workforce resilience include the following:

- **Balanced workload**
  - Highlight individual workloads through the PM system, ensuring equitable task distribution among team members.
  - Conduct regular performance assessments to identify instances of excessive workload, prompting necessary adjustments through feedback mechanisms and facilitating timely management interventions.

- **Job conflict**
  - Detect signs of job conflict by illuminating team interactions and performance dynamics through the system, enabling early intervention.
  - Identify areas of disagreement or tension in performance assessments, facilitating targeted resolutions to mitigate conflicts.
  - Incorporate conflict resolution strategies and resources into the system, offering guidance to managers for effective management and resolution of disputes within the team.

- **Role ambiguity**
  - Define, document, and reward employees based on clear job roles and responsibilities within the PM system.

- Ensure fair task distribution among team members to avoid confusion about responsibilities.
- Conduct regular performance assessments to identify unclear or overlapping roles, prompting necessary adjustments for clear direction.
- Foster open communication channels, enabling employees to seek clarification actively, reducing ambiguity, and fostering a shared understanding of expectations.

- **Rewarding performance**
  - Integrate performance metrics into the system to evaluate individuals objectively based on achievements in key job duties.
  - Tie recognitions, bonuses, or promotions to performance metrics as incentives, motivating excellence.
  - Provide a transparent framework within the system for linking rewards to specific accomplishments, promoting fairness and accountability.

- **Recognition and feedback**
  - Feature regular feedback exchange between managers and employees within the PM system, fostering continuous improvement.
  - Implement recognition programs in the system to highlight teamwork, reinforce positive behaviors, and minimize potential sources of conflict.
  - Cultivate accountability through upward feedback, allowing employees to share insights on managerial performance within performance reviews.
  - Ensure timely feedback within the system so employees are aware of strengths and areas for improvement, contributing to professional development.

- **Psychological safety**
  - Support a culture of psychological safety through the PM system by encouraging open communication and idea sharing.
  - Implement anonymous feedback mechanisms within the system, allowing employees to express concerns or ideas without fear of reprisal.
  - Frame performance discussions within the system constructively, emphasizing growth and development and promoting a positive and psychologically safe work environment.
  - Conduct regular check-ins and performance discussions within the system, creating opportunities for open dialogue, enabling constructive conflict resolution, and promoting a harmonious work environment.

Cultural Lever 2: Job Crafting

I recall the tale of Lisa, a veteran New York City bus driver weary of the monotony in her daily routine. Battling a growing sense of apathy that seeped into her mood and family life, Lisa found her motivation waning. Clocking out had become the sole incentive at the start of her shift. One day, a loyal passenger sparked a revelation by remarking, "I bet you've heard some wild stories over your time on the road!" Inspired, Lisa began chronicling memorable and humorous tales from her passengers. To combat routine, she transformed her bus rides into lively journeys, sharing intriguing snippets about the city and recounting wild stories. At first, it seemed as if her audience were stuck in their own worlds, but Lisa persisted, undeterred. Soon, passengers migrated closer, suppressing laughs behind newspapers or exchanging knowing glances. They started using her first name, engaging in lively greetings and farewells, and even sneaking in personal questions about her family. Lisa's self-initiated transformation turned her bus into a lively stage, injecting humanity into her routine and transforming it into a more engaging and fulfilling experience.

What stands out in Lisa's story is her self-initiated transformation to combat boredom, turning what seemed like a fun activity into a redefinition of her job. Unknowingly, she engaged in *job crafting*, reshaping her approach to bus driving to align with her need for personal interactions (Wrzesniewski & Dutton, 2001).

You may have noticed a potential contradiction, notably suggesting Lisa shouldn't bear the burden of fixing burnout but should craft her job. Yet this dualistic viewpoint may warrant a closer look. When examined through the lens of well-being and ultimate behavior change, Lisa's self-initiated tasks, which are grounded in autonomy, intrinsic motivation, and psychological ownership, help to foster enduring behavioral change and heightened satisfaction, surpassing the outcomes achieved when behavioral change is imposed on employees.

Employees craft their jobs in three general ways. *Task crafting* involves modifying job responsibilities, *relational crafting* shapes interactions with colleagues, and *cognitive crafting* changes one's mindset about task significance (Wrzesniewski & Dutton, 2001). Lisa, for instance, continued driving the bus and maintained the same stops but she reshaped her relationship with her job by infusing spontaneous tour elements (task), building connections through storytelling (relational), and adopting the mindset of a full-time storyteller, part-time bus driver (cognitive).

Job crafting demonstrates a multitude of positive outcomes at both individual and organizational levels, as indicated by studies of heightened work meaningfulness (Tims et al., 2016) and reinforced organizational attachment (Wang et al., 2018), both crucial elements mirrored in Lisa's story.

The extent of these outcomes depends significantly on how we operationalize job crafting. Tims and Bakker (2010) aligned this practice with the job demands–resources (JD-R) model. Their framework includes the specific behaviors that individual employees use in reshaping their roles and highlights positive outcomes such as heightened work engagement, satisfaction, person–job fit, work meaning, and identity. On an organizational scale, these outcomes ripple into improved job performance, enhanced job design, and reinforced organizational commitment. Notably, job crafting emerges as a strategic approach for employees navigating change while prioritizing their well-being.

Illustrating the profound connection between job crafting and well-being, Tims and colleagues (2013) centered on a substantial sample of chemical plant workers actively shaping their personal well-being by adjusting job demands and resources. Initially sharing insights into their work engagement, job satisfaction, and burnout levels, participants received computer-generated feedback. This feedback, including scores for job demands and resources, featured brief examples suggesting improvements such as socializing after work or having lunch with colleagues. The purpose of these suggestions was to maintain job crafting as a personal initiative driven by the employees themselves. As anticipated, employees who engaged in job crafting during the first month witnessed an increase in structural and social resources across the duration of the study. The increase in job resources not only elevated engagement and job satisfaction but also led to a notable reduction in burnout among the employees.

Figure 5.7 illustrates specific job demands and resources that can be addressed through job crafting. For example, shifting the job crafting fulcrum to the left can help reduce the volume of workload, role stress, ambiguity, and conflict. In part, this is moderated through job control.

Let's revisit Lisa, the bus driver seeking more meaning and connection in her work. She evaluated her role and aligned her behaviors with her personal values of purpose, connection, and availability ("embodying her full self" as per Kahn's [1990] conceptualization). Lisa's experience is an ongoing, evolving process that requires time and concerted effort, similar to job crafting. She takes notes, shares quips, and modifies her stories based on what connects with her passengers.

However, job crafting has a few potential dark sides. For instance, a chef who prioritizes interaction with customers over cooking does not meet the restaurant's objectives. While the chef might be happier doing this, her limited time in the kitchen and providing mentorship will be detrimental to the restaurant. Additionally, if an organization doesn't value well-being, embedding job crafting into the culture will be challenging and unlikely to thrive.

FIGURE 5.7. Moving the Job Crafting Fulcrum

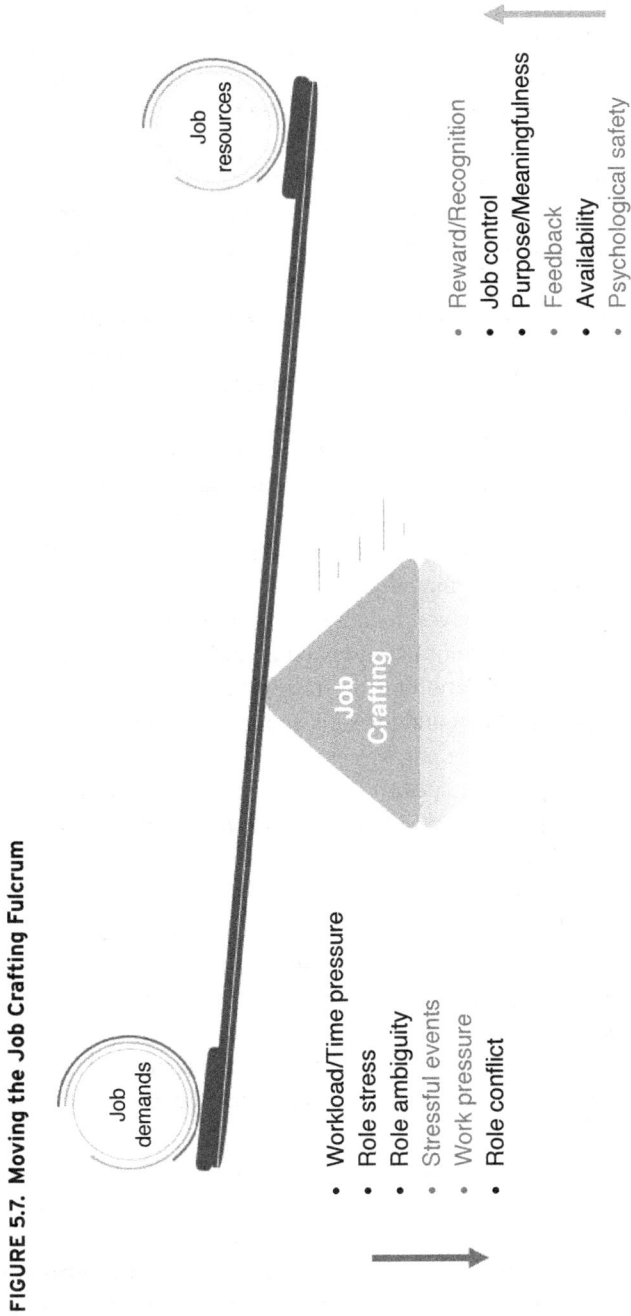

Job resources

Job demands

Job Crafting

- Workload/Time pressure
- Role stress
- Role ambiguity
- Stressful events
- Work pressure
- Role conflict

- Reward/Recognition
- Job control
- Purpose/Meaningfulness
- Feedback
- Availability
- Psychological safety

Consider the following examples of how task, relational, and cognitive crafting can influence both job demands and resources which, in turn, help enable a culture of workforce resilience (see Chapter 7 for specific industry examples illustrating these practices).

- **Reducing workload and time pressure**
  - Task crafting: Faced with a demanding schedule of back-to-back appointments and overwhelmed by the workload, a hairdresser might choose to delegate certain administrative duties to a new team member with the capacity to handle them effectively.
  - Cognitive crafting: By reframing the perception of time pressure, a business executive may prioritize tasks by employing strategies such as using urgency-importance matrices, time blocking, and delegating effectively to ensure she is focusing on high-impact responsibilities aligned with organizational goals.

- **Reducing role stress**
  - Task crafting: A mechanic experiencing role stress due to the monotony of his tasks may redesign his responsibilities by taking on more complex repair challenges or attending classes that can diversify his skill set.
  - Relational crafting: By establishing positive relationships with colleagues and setting a goal of meeting one new teacher each week, a teacher experiences reduced role stress. He cultivates a robust social network that improves connectivity and assists in addressing job challenges (such as motivating unmotivated students!).

- **Reducing role ambiguity**
  - Task crafting: An IT specialist can reduce role ambiguity by clearly defining and restructuring tasks. She may create detailed task lists, establish clear workflows, and proactively communicate her role expectations with her manager within her first week on the job.
  - Cognitive crafting: Participating in workshops, industry conferences, and collaborative projects allows a marketing professional to reframe ambiguity as an opportunity, cultivating a positive and proactive mindset in approaching marketing challenges.

- **Reducing role conflict**
  - Relational crafting: To address role conflict, a project manager may enhance her role clarity by proactively updating her understanding of responsibilities and initiating routine meetings with her boss to establish clear communication and alignment on her role expectations.

- Cognitive crafting: To alleviate stress from conflicting roles, a sales representative acknowledges the synergy between building client relationships and meeting sales targets. By reframing conflicting demands as mutually beneficial, he leverages his top strength in relationships to contribute effectively to his sales goals, fostering a more harmonious approach to his work.

- **Improving job control**
  - Task crafting: A graphic designer can take ownership of specific design projects and tailor them to align with her personal strengths of creativity and technical proficiency to enhance her job control.
  - Relational crafting: By proactively fostering strong relationships with her team and superiors through innovative team-building exercises, a software developer can establish a supportive network. This network provides her valuable resources and more control over her work environment.

- **Improving purpose and meaningfulness**
  - Cognitive crafting: By aligning daily tasks with the goals of the organization, a nonprofit coordinator enhances the perceived importance of her role. Recognizing the direct contribution of effective volunteer management to the mission of the nonprofit fosters a sense of purpose and meaningfulness in her work.
  - Task crafting: Actively selecting tasks that align with personal values and contribute to the overall mission of the organization, an environmental scientist gains a sense of purpose and fulfillment.

- **Improving availability and engagement**
  - Cognitive crafting: By managing distractions and staying fully engaged, a writer can adopt a mindfulness approach. Mindfulness practices involve focusing on the present moment, enhancing concentration, and improving overall availability for role performance.
  - Relational crafting: A customer service representative can become more resilient to distractions and interruptions by intentionally building positive relationships with colleagues to create a supportive work environment that fosters engagement.

Cultural Lever 3: Analytics

If the core of a company's culture lies in its values, practices, and connections, the usual way to strengthen these links is often through—you guessed it—

technology. You're probably well acquainted with (and might even be wearing) a digital wearable, or perhaps there's a wellness app (think breathing exercises, relaxation, medication) within arm's reach. At work, video conferencing platforms like Zoom or Microsoft Teams connect you with your team, streamlining your collaboration. In the workplace, digital technologies become the contemporary threads weaving individuals together, simplifying the embodiment and expression of the company's values. And this isn't just a passing trend. According to the U.S. Bureau of Labor Statistics (2023), data science is projected to grow 35% from 2022 to 2032, much faster than the average for all occupations.

While advanced tech platforms and wearable devices can enhance data collection and analysis, they are not strictly necessary for small businesses to benefit from data science. Even with limited budgets, small businesses can leverage basic data analysis techniques and simpler tools to improve their operations and contribute to employee well-being. Technology often serves as the front door to expressing analytics, but there is also a backdoor: traditional methods. Let's quickly break down the origins of analytics and provide an example of how a pencil and paper can be all you need.

Analytics traces its roots to the Greek word "analytika," denoting "loosening" or "set free" (Online Etymology Dictionary, n.d.). Essentially, it involves breaking down intricate problems into smaller, more manageable components for thorough examination and understanding. Imagine those holiday lights hibernating on the top garage shelf—the meticulous and, perhaps, pains taking process of unfurling those knots into a coherent strand of colored lights mirrors the linguistic roots of analytics. In essence, analytics encapsulates the idea of methodically unraveling complexities, with or without technology.

Let's see this concept in action with Joe, the owner of a quaint bookstore in a small town. Despite the absence of advanced technology in his business, Joe is determined to understand workforce trends and enhance employee engagement among his small team. To foster a thriving work environment, Joe initiates regular team meetings, encouraging open communication so that employees share thoughts, ideas, and concerns. Actively listening to his team during these sessions, Joe writes down valuable insights into their experiences, preferences, and challenges. Joe then introduces an anonymous suggestion box, the Idea Vault, which provides his employees a private platform to submit thoughts and suggestions. Recognizing the importance of face-to-face interactions, he organizes monthly team-building activities to boost morale and observes team dynamics in a relaxed setting. Joe makes notes on attendance, successful aspects, and areas for improvement. In addition, Joe implements a recognition program and publicly acknowledges employees by name for their contributions to customers, colleagues, and the business. He transforms these recognition moments into tangible rewards, such as gift cards or time off, further enhancing the impact of acknowledgment. Joe has used analytics, in its rudimentary form, to meet the needs of his employee base, ultimately improving the culture of his bookstore.

The cynic or self-proclaimed "realist" may argue that any form of data tracking—paper and pencil or otherwise—is intrusive, and the intrusion outweighs the benefits. In an article cleverly titled "The Creepy Rise of Bossware," Carnegie (2023) explored this tension. She shed light on companies such as Amazon, which not only uses such tools to manage warehouse staff but allegedly predicts unionization thoughts among workers, extending its reach to traditional office jobs. Citing Diego Naranjo, head of policy at the international advocacy group European Digital Rights, Carnegie emphasized the escalating paranoia and lack of trust from upper management, which now permeates remote work environments.

While the prevalence of employee monitoring, colloquially known as "bossware" in employee circles, is on the rise, it is imperative to strike the right balance. I advocate that effectively managing the equilibrium between employee autonomy and well-being represents an initial step toward cultivating a resilient organizational culture. However, when this balance is mishandled or leaders overextend their analytical reach, employee monitoring becomes counterproductive to the drivers of resilience and significantly affects psychological safety, trust, and autonomy. Organizations must skillfully navigate this delicate balance to avoid adverse effects on employee well-being and overall organizational resilience.

In essence, analytics can manifest through cutting-edge technologies to illuminate employee wellness trends, influencing behavior instantly. Alternatively, it can be an approach akin to Joe's—meticulously tracking successful strategies and areas for improvement and, when feasible, offering social or financial rewards to reinforce behaviors contributing to a culture of well-being. In his comprehensive exploration of how technology shapes culture, Clark (2022) emphasized, "The melding of data-driven analytics with a human touch plays a significant role in strengthening company culture. Just as companies leverage technology to comprehend their customers, they should similarly tap into employees' needs and desires to enhance internal culture."

Whether embodied by Joe, the budding ethnographer, or a sophisticated platform, analytics plays a pivotal role in shaping organizational culture. Ultimately, analytics—whether paper and pencil or digital—connects people, creates shared meaning, and builds value. In the contemporary digital landscape, the significance of perceived proximity—how close or distant someone feels—in some cases sometimes surpasses the importance of physical closeness (for more details, see Wilson et al., 2008). Perceived proximity has large implications for how managers explore strategies for managing a remote workforce. Moreover, even in a fully on-site or hybrid workforce, adding employee-led initiatives, mentorship programs, and in-person events is a humane approach to organizational culture and a strategic imperative for building a thriving, innovative, and resilient workplace.

In the complex organizational teeter-totter shown in Figure 5.8, analytics serves as a powerful force driving the delicate balance between job demands and resources. Of particular importance is feedback, which offers myriad ways to help balance this equation, especially when part of dynamic feedback loops. Feedback loops involve the ongoing exchange of information and responses among different levels, teams, or individuals within an organization. These loops are integral for sustaining communication, fostering continuous improvement, and ensuring alignment.

Organizations often use three types of feedback loops:

- **Performance feedback loop**
  - Description: Regular feedback on individual and team performance
  - Purpose: Enhance employee development, improve efficiency, and align performance with organizational goals
  - Role of analytics: Measure and analyze key performance indicators, providing quantitative insights for performance assessment
  - Analytics in action: Tracking sales representatives' monthly targets, identifying areas for improvement, and recognizing top performers

- **Employee engagement feedback loop**
  - Description: Collection of feedback on employee satisfaction, well-being, and engagement
  - Purpose: Understand employee sentiments, address concerns, and create a positive workplace culture
  - Role of analytics: Analyze employee survey data and engagement metrics to identify trends, areas for improvement, and the overall health of the organizational culture
  - Analytics in action: Assessing employee survey results to identify exhausted–engaged cohorts and implement targeted initiatives to improve workforce resilience

- **360-degree feedback loop**
  - Description: Feedback collected from various sources, including peers, subordinates, and supervisors

FIGURE 5.8. Moving the Technology/Analytics Fulcrum

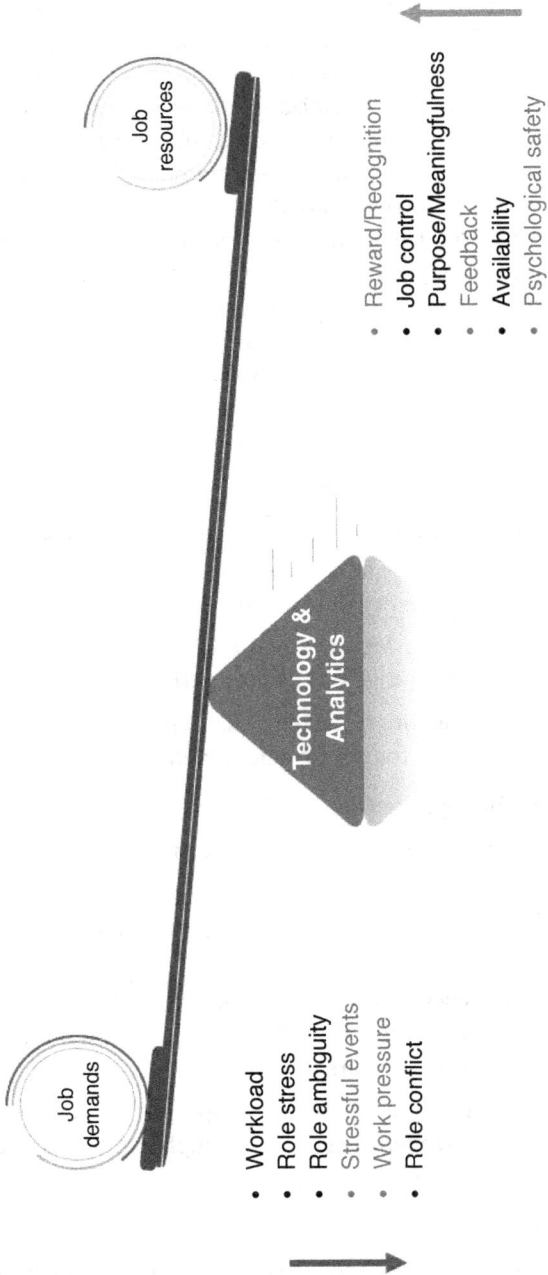

Job demands
- Workload
- Role stress
- Role ambiguity
- Stressful events
- Work pressure
- Role conflict

Technology & Analytics

Job resources
- Reward/Recognition
- Job control
- Purpose/Meaningfulness
- Feedback
- Availability
- Psychological safety

- Purpose: Provide a comprehensive view of an individual's performance, fostering personal and professional growth
- Role of analytics: Aggregate and analyze 360-degree feedback data to identify patterns, strengths, and areas for improvement to aid in targeted development strategies
- Analytics in action: Assessing feedback from peers, supervisors, and subordinates to create a holistic view of an employee's leadership skills and areas for improvement

The transformative impact of analytics extends beyond merely increasing the weight or volume of feedback. The feedback process, when data-driven, also has the effect of alleviating the burden of job demands.

Consider Mary, a clinical psychologist who has worked for several years in a military hospital. Mary's productivity is evaluated using relative value units (RVUs), a metric used by hospitals to gauge payments to health care providers. Her clinic's analytics-driven performance feedback loop reveals that, in the past month, she has fallen short of her RVU goal by 25%, as she has been spending more time providing informal consultation groups and trainings to new psychology residents. Mary and her clinic director both spot this trend through the clinic's interactive dashboard that offers real-time insights into work patterns across the clinic.

During discussions with her clinic director, Mary expresses her growing enthusiasm for providing formal supervision to the residents. They agree to amend her current role to align closer to her strengths though still meeting the clinic's revenue target and settle on a revised role, transitioning from 100% client work to 75% client work and 25% formal supervision, including signing off on residents' notes to help capture the remaining portions of her revenue target. To formalize this change, Mary and the clinic director collaboratively draft expectations, responsibilities, and RVU targets for her new role. They agree to revisit the job dashboard monthly and her job duties quarterly and to amend as needed.

This compromise not only empowers Mary, much like Lisa the bus driver, to shape her role according to her interests but also enhances her job control. Through the insights provided by analytics, Mary's role stress, ambiguity, and work pressure all decrease. Furthermore, Mary optimizes her workload to align better with her skills and interests. As a result, Mary experiences less exhaustion, heightened engagement, and a deeper commitment to her work at the hospital. In essence, the job crafting process, fueled by analytics, aligns her personal interests with job duties, restoring equilibrium to her job demands and resources.

The fusion of technology and analytics plays a role in shaping organizational culture. As a strategic tool, analytics can take on various forms, from the simplicity of Joe's grassroots paper-and-pencil initiative to the complexity of Mary's insightful role adjustments. Both instances exemplify individual leadership, with one led by a formal leader and the other by a dedicated staff member. However, the question arises: How can an individual like Joe or Mary drive cultural change when analytics, whether digital or otherwise, is typically considered a tool or approach owned by leadership? This conundrum will be thoroughly explored in the remaining chapters of this book. For now, the primary point is that analytics remains a fundamental catalyst for organizational transformation. Particularly noteworthy is its role in cultivating a culture that fosters engagement and safeguards against burnout.

Cultural Lever 4: Strategic Communications

George Bernard Shaw is often credited with the bold declaration, "The single biggest problem in communication is the illusion that it has taken place," which reverberates powerfully, particularly when considering the real world consequences of communication breakdowns. Look no further than contemporary examples, such as communications surrounding COVID-19 in the United States. Despite earnest efforts to circulate information, the rapid influx of new details created challenges in maintaining consistency, clarity, and coordination. The resulting chaos, stemming from what some would argue were contradictory instructions and muddled messages, vividly illustrates the imperative of clear and accurate communication in preventing disastrous outcomes.

This truth became evident in April 2010 when the Deepwater Horizon oil rig, managed by BP, undertook an exploratory drilling operation in the Gulf of Mexico. The resulting explosion led to a catastrophic blowout, claiming the lives of 11 people and leaving 17 others injured. The rig burned and sank in just 2 days, triggering the most extensive offshore oil spill in the history of the United States (Sellnow, 2010). The operation, which was a collaborative effort involving multiple companies including Transocean and Halliburton, faced critical communication breakdowns as it progressed.

These breakdowns unfolded as a series of missteps, revealing the potential for significant environmental disasters when communication fails. The first breakdown emerged in information flow, notably the communication of risks. Despite the complex nature of deep-sea drilling and the potential for catastrophic events, the three companies involved (BP, Transocean, and Halliburton) failed to adequately communicate the high-risk nature of the operation (Goldenberg, 2010). As a result, key personnel on the rig were not fully aware of the potential dangers associated with the drilling. Another breakdown in information flow occurred in the coordination of safety measures. The three companies involved were not aligned with the Deepwater Operations Plan, which aimed to minimize risk as much as possible. Misunderstandings and lack of clarity in the communication of safety tests led to missteps and incorrect decisions, ultimately contributing to the disaster (S. Smith, 2011). Moreover, information inadequacy was evident in the evaluation of the cement seal on the well. It became apparent that the well fell short of industry standards and failed three out of four laboratory tests conducted prior to the Deepwater Horizon explosion on April 20. Incomplete information sharing about the integrity of the seal resulted in a lack of awareness regarding potential vulnerabilities. This information gap prevented the identification and addressing of safety issues (Goldenberg & Kollewe, 2010).

In the aftermath of the blowout, targeted communications to the public and regulatory authorities were deficient. BP faced criticism for its handling of crisis communication, in particular conveying the severity of the spill and the steps being taken to address it (Sellnow, 2010). Criticism was directed at CEO Tony Hayward in particular for his handling of the crisis communication. Hayward's admission that he did not fully comprehend the gravity of the situation and subsequent PR missteps, including insensitive comments such as "I want my life back," portrayed a lack of empathy and added to the public's perception of callousness (Sellnow, 2010, para. 4). These missteps further burdened the company's reputation.

The narrative reflects on communication breakdowns evident in the Deepwater Horizon incident, emphasizing the failure to communicate risks effectively, coordinate safety measures, share adequate information, and target communications. These breakdowns highlight the need for robust communication to prevent disasters. Specifically, information flow, information adequacy, and targeted communications are identified as elements for sustaining a healthy organizational culture and averting potential disasters. In the context of employee well-being, prioritizing open and effective communication ensures that employees are well informed, engaged, and supported. This approach fosters a safe, healthy, and predictable work environment and promotes a content and thriving workforce.

Shaw's insight serves as a poignant lens to view the events. The illusion of effective communication in the drilling operation masked deficiencies that led to a severe environmental catastrophe. The Deepwater Horizon incident serves as a reminder that communication breakdowns have far-reaching consequences and emphasizes the importance of transparent and accurate communication in complex operations. Ultimately, these narratives underscore the need for robust communication practices for organizational success and the well-being and safety of individuals within and beyond the workplace.

Decoding Strategic Communication

Strategic communication, in its conventional sense, means deliberately sending messages that match the goals of the organization. Such communication may involve a CEO illustrating how individual roles contribute to the company's needs or an airline communicating with families during an emergency landing. But strategic communication should (but does not always) transcend beyond targeted messaging. A refined definition of strategic communication recognizes the interconnectedness of targeted messaging, information flow, and information adequacy (see Table 5.3).

Strategic Communication Dynamics: Well-Being, Performance, and Organizational Outcomes

Limeade, a software company and well-being stalwart, emphasizes the importance of information flow and adequacy, linking them to key aspects of the employee experience and the business bottom line, including well-being, burnout, and engagement (Limeade, 2020). Focusing on a workforce employee cohort based in the United States, Limeade reported that employees who perceived free information flow within their organization were (a) 3 times more likely to feel included, (b) 4 times more likely to trust their organization, (c) 3 times more likely to feel connected, (d) over 3 times more likely to feel valued, and (e) nearly 3 times more likely to perceive a positive

TABLE 5.3. Focus, Purpose, and Elements of Targeted Communication, Information Flow, and Information Adequacy

Aspect	Focus	Purpose	Elements
Targeted communication	Tailoring messages for specific audiences	Achieving understanding, engagement, and desired responses from audiences	Audience segmentation, personalized messaging, and context relevance
Information flow	Seamless and timely exchange of information	Efficient and effective communication within the organization	Clear channels, real-time updates, and structured dissemination
Information adequacy	Sufficiency, accuracy, and relevance of data	Providing comprehensive and reliable information for decision making	Data completeness, accuracy verification, and relevance assessment

employee experience. The report also revealed that employees who felt they had received adequate information were (a) nearly 3 times less likely to feel burned out, (b) 5 times more likely to feel their organization cares, (c) almost twice as likely to feel they have well-being in their life, and (d) almost twice as likely to feel engaged in their work.

The outcomes are impressive yet unsurprising. When information flows freely and accurately, individuals develop a sense of connection and trust in their organization, which fosters enhanced performance and bolsters the corporate bottom line. Despite the apparent simplicity of timely and accurate communication, these fundamental practices are often downplayed or disregarded, occasionally leading to catastrophic consequences, as evidenced by impactful events like the Deepwater Horizon disaster, the Fukushima Daiichi Nuclear Disaster in Japan, and the global financial crisis of 2008.

If information flow represents the smooth transmission of data within an organization, information burden emerges as its adversary, characterized by inconsistencies, duplications, irrelevance, and the need for extensive effort. In a survey by Gartner (as cited in Klein et al., 2023), nearly 38% of employees reported feeling overwhelmed by an "excessive" volume of communications that results in their spending approximately 3 hours and 27 minutes weekly navigating information burden. These barriers impede information flow, giving rise to a "high-burden" culture that can affect job stress, time pressure, role stress, and potentially compromise psychological safety within the workplace.

The complexity of modern workspaces is amplified by technological advancements that bombard professionals with extensive and often conflicting information. This information overload can result in cognitive strain and affect employee performance (Biondi et al., 2021). To test this, Gamble et al. (2018) analyzed human decision making at the Army Research Laboratory at Aberdeen Proving Ground under varying cognitive loads and information accuracy. Participants assessed the reliability of two information sources, unaware that one provided highly accurate and the other less accurate information. The researchers found that people trusted the more accurate information. When faced with cognitive challenges, they were even better at using accurate information to enhance performance. This finding emphasizes the role of information accuracy in boosting cognitive performance under challenging conditions, such as when cognitive load is high. Consider the contrary example in the case of Deepwater Horizon, discussed earlier, in which high cognitive load and less accurate information undermined effective decision making.

Haumer and team (2021) studied the impact of personalized and targeted messaging on communication processes within organizations. They discovered that crafting messages to fit individual personality types amplifies employee engagement during periods of organizational change. However, when messages fail to align with individual personalities, employee engagement decreases noticeably. While it's unlikely for an organization to know each person's personality type, the core message emphasizes the value of a systematic approach to communicating with stakeholders, targeting the right people, and timing messages appropriately.

In summary, strategic communication significantly influences employee well-being, burnout prevention, and engagement and has a direct impact on the corporate bottom line. Especially during crises, accurate information and precisely tailored messages take precedence over information burden. Recognizing the interconnected nature of communication, well-being, and organizational outcomes underscores the importance of addressing challenges like information overload. This recognition aligns with the JD-R model (see Figure 5.9) and illustrates how job demands such as information overload contribute to time constraints, work pressures, and stress, effectively straining employees and creating a burden of job demands. Conversely, job resources, including free and accurate information flow, can help align people with their roles, make them feel recognized, provide purposeful work, and ensure psychological safety, thus supporting well-being and performance. The core message is clear: Prioritizing thoughtful, targeted, and accurate communication is vital for the success of both individuals and organizations. Table 5.4 provides a brief summary of how strategic communication influences the top four key job demands and resources through information flow, information accuracy, and targeted communication.

CHAPTER SUMMARY

- The term "resilience" has been critiqued as overused and vague, often absolving organizations of responsibility by placing undue emphasis on individual capacity to cope with challenges, thus obscuring deeper systemic issues and potentially misguiding corporate wellness initiatives.

- Workforce resilience is an organizational process (job demands and job resources) that shapes workforce culture (engagement and strain pathway) to optimize employee well-being (increase engagement, decrease burnout).

- Twelve job demands and resources are crucial to workforce resilience and ultimately organizational performance, including workload, role stress, role ambiguity, stressful events, competitive pressure, role conflict, rewards/recognition, job control, purpose, feedback, availability, and psychological safety.

FIGURE 5.9. Moving the Strategic Communications Fulcrum

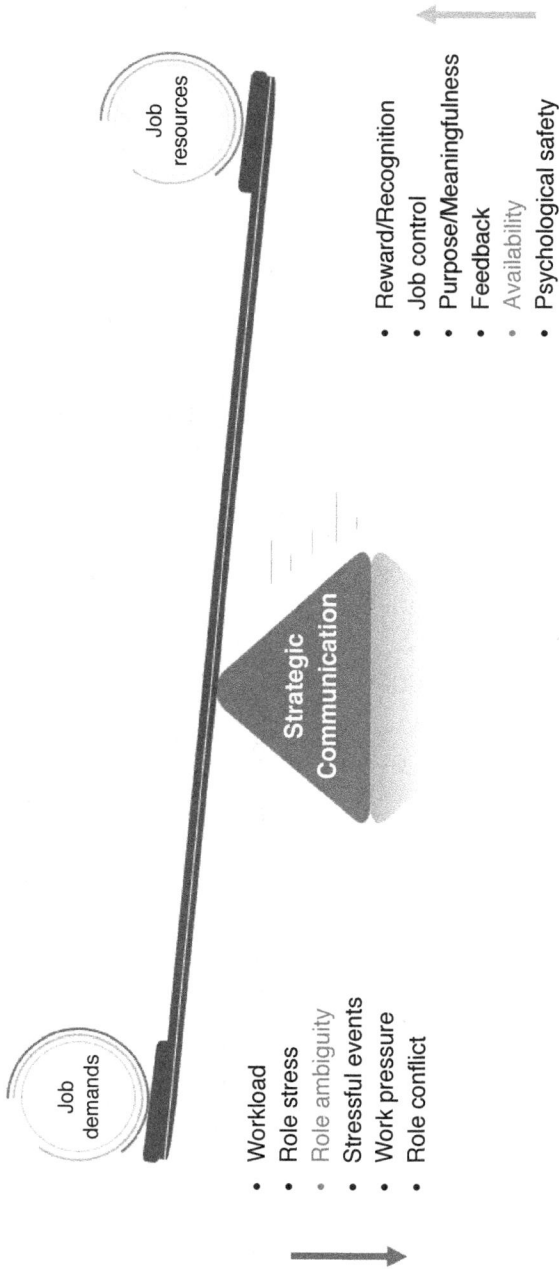

Job demands

- Workload
- Role stress
- Role ambiguity
- Stressful events
- Work pressure
- Role conflict

Strategic Communication

Job resources

- Reward/Recognition
- Job control
- Purpose/Meaningfulness
- Feedback
- Availability
- Psychological safety

TABLE 5.4. Impact of Strategic Communication on Key Job Demands and Resources

Job demands/ resources	Information flow	Information accuracy	Targeted communication	Example of integration
Workload	A project management tool that provides real-time updates on task progress and dependencies	Accurate information on task progress (e.g., Task A is 80%, Task B is complete) to prevent confusion and rework	Software developer receives detailed progress updates related to coding tasks, while a project manager receives broad updates on overall project status and potential bottlenecks	An intuitive task management system automatically updates team members on project progress, minimizes confusion, and ensures each team member receives relevant information, thus optimizing workload
Role stress	An employee handbook that systematically communicates clear job responsibilities and procedures	Accurate information detailing job duties, expectations, and procedures	Targeted training sessions addressing specific stressors and role-related challenges	Performance management evaluates employee performance against handbook-outlined role duties; subsequently, targeted training promotes transparency and effectively mitigates role-related stressors, thanks to clear performance outcome guidelines

Recognition	Establish a system in which team members can nominate their colleagues for outstanding contributions or achievements	Use data analytics tools to collect and analyze performance data, enabling the identification of specific contributions and achievements in an objective and data-driven manner	Regularly and publicly communicate the number, types, and frequency of rewards, including both employees' choice nominations and those driven by performance analytics, to ensure transparency and recognition across the organization	Establish a platform for peer nominations and data-driven recognition, regularly and publicly communicating reward details covering both employee choices and performance analytics-driven recognitions to ensure transparency and organizational acknowledgment
Psychological safety	Include a feature allowing employees to provide upward feedback anonymously, encouraging honest and open communication	Include mechanisms for users to provide feedback on the accuracy of shared information to create a continuous feedback loop, allowing for corrections and improvements	Host town halls to recognize and address the unique experiences and perspectives of different individuals or teams within the organization to foster a sense of inclusivity	Establishment of an integrated platform fostering a comprehensive feedback ecosystem by enabling anonymous employee expression, validating information accuracy, and using virtual town halls for inclusive recognition, ultimately promoting psychological safety, honesty, and continuous improvement

- Four cultural levers have the power to shape and steer an organizational culture: (a) Performance management, as suggested by the happy-productive worker hypothesis, is vital for enhancing job performance by promoting employee well-being and effectively managing workloads; (b) job crafting improves job satisfaction and organizational performance by allowing employees to modify tasks, manage relationships, and shift mindsets; (c) analytics significantly enhance organizational culture and employee performance by simplifying complex problems and showcasing the versatility from high-tech solutions to basic methods; and (d) strategic communications shape organizational outcomes by managing information flow and accuracy, boosting employee well-being, preventing burnout, and enhancing engagement, thus affecting the bottom line.

CHAPTER QUESTIONS

- How can I, as a leader, transform corporate wellness initiatives to tackle systemic challenges rather than just enhancing individual capacities to manage stress?

- Which of the 12 identified job demands and resources am I managing effectively, and which ones need more of my focus?

- In what specific ways can I help recalibrate the balance of job control, rewards/recognition, and workload to boost both workforce resilience and performance?

- How have I encouraged or implemented job crafting on my team or for me, personally? What tangible impacts has it had on my and/or my team's job satisfaction and performance?

- How is my organization currently using analytics to monitor and enhance employee wellness within the organization? Can I see potential to expand its use in specific areas?

- What specific actions can I suggest to refine strategic communications, boost employee well-being, and drive better organizational results under my leadership?

6 THE RESILIENT LEADER IMPERATIVE

Enthusiasm is common. Endurance is rare.

—Angela Duckworth, *Grit*

In Chapter 1, I explored various challenges and shortcomings of well-intentioned programs that failed to achieve their goals. In Chapters 2 through 4, I explored common beliefs about burnout, and in Chapter 5 I examined cultural strategies to balance job demands and resources, thus fostering engagement and preventing burnout. Now, I turn to those who wield these levers: leaders at every level of the organization.

This chapter focuses on the mutable traits of leaders that are pertinent to everyone within the organization. These resilient traits provide leaders with the insight and fortitude to catalyze many of the changes discussed in Chapter 5. Indeed, effecting a cultural shift presents significant challenges if leaders lack the resilient qualities necessary to instigate change. This chapter also presents an exploration of the intricate dynamics between leaders

https://doi.org/10.1037/0000454-007
Rethinking Employee Resilience: Why Our Current Approach to Worker Burnout Is Failing, and How to Fix It, by D. Pelton

and employee resilience, examining how leaders can both cultivate their own resilient qualities and impart them to the workforce. Core to the analysis is an essential question: Amidst adversity, how can leaders enhance their own resilience while fostering a corporate culture that encourages the development of these traits?

IGNITING CULTURAL TRANSFORMATION: THE LEADERSHIP SPARK PLUG

Imagine the organizational culture as a car engine, with each team serving as a combustion chamber. In an organization, as in an engine, an explosion within the chambers propels the entire system forward. However, a spark is required for this explosion to happen. In an engine, the seemingly modest spark plug is the vital catalyst. In an organization, leaders, much like spark plugs, are indispensable. They provide the energy to the team, enabling it to function effectively and achieve its goals. While the potency of this spark may vary based on positional rank and authority, every member of an organization holds the potential to drive cultural change.

What about spark plug duds? You know, the uninspiring leaders that not only fail to ignite the team but also inject poison into the system, sometimes intentionally, sometimes inadvertently. Like all people, they have psychological blind spots, but these classically toxic leaders often draw from idiosyncratic personality traits that are inherently damaging to people and culture.

Reflect on the most toxic leaders you've encountered. From my discussions with thousands of leaders (and personal experience), I believe that their deficiencies often stem from emotional and relational shortcomings rather than technical skills. How often have you found yourself thinking something like "I'm not particularly inspired by Sam because he's not great at his job . . . but he is a nice person"? It's more common to hear things like "Sam's a narcissist," "Sam has zero integrity," or the classic "Sam only cares about himself." How many times have you uttered any of these phrases about a leader in your life?

UNVEILING THE FOUR CORE QUALITIES OF RESILIENT LEADERS: COPES

Certain emotional and relational qualities emerge as indispensable for effective leadership, but these qualities aren't immutable, hardwired personality constructs. Rather, they can be cultivated and honed through learning and practice. Drawing on insights from empirical research and my clinical experience—

interacting with thousands of patients, coaching hundreds of executive leaders, and developing countless leadership development and resilience programs— I argue that four traits in particular are essential for igniting change and nurturing resilient leaders. Those core qualities are conscientiousness, optimism, emotional endurance, and social relationships, or COPES (see Figure 6.1). I think COPES is also a very fitting label, given that resilience is about how we respond to, and cope with, adversity. At its core, the COPES factors encapsulate the essence of our humanity across four key domains: behavioral (conscientiousness), cognitive (optimism), emotional (emotional endurance), and relational (social relationships). Substantial empirical evidence supports the role of each component and subcomponent role in resilience, suggesting that harnessing these traits can enhance one's resilience.

Beyond theoretical understanding, it's crucial to consider the tangible impacts of cultivating traits like conscientiousness, optimism, emotional endurance, and social relationships. There are many, so I will be brief. Conscientious individuals tend to exhibit organizational skills, dependability, and diligence, which are associated job performance (Barrick & Mount, 1991), stable interpersonal relationships (Donnellan et al., 2005), and life expectancy (Bogg & Roberts, 2004). Emotional endurance enables individuals to cope effectively with stress, setbacks, and adversity, and effective coping is associated with physical benefits such as reduced blood pressure (Gordon & Mendes, 2021), improved sleep (Beck et al., 2022), and improved executive functioning (Liu et al., 2020). Optimistic individuals often experience positive mental and physical health (Conversano et al., 2010), effective coping

FIGURE 6.1. COPES Model of Resilience

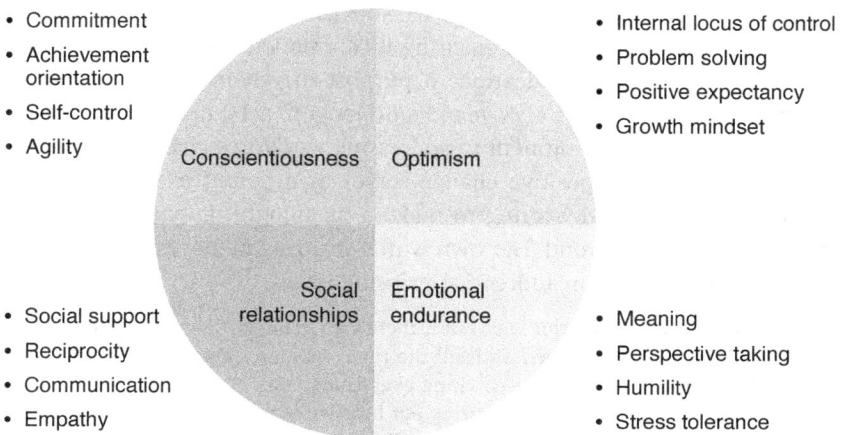

- Commitment
- Achievement orientation
- Self-control
- Agility

- Internal locus of control
- Problem solving
- Positive expectancy
- Growth mindset

Conscientiousness | Optimism

Social relationships | Emotional endurance

- Social support
- Reciprocity
- Communication
- Empathy

- Meaning
- Perspective taking
- Humility
- Stress tolerance

Note. COPES = conscientiousness, optimism, emotional endurance, and social relationships.

abilities (Hanssen et al., 2015), strong relationships (Stambor, 2006), and success in achieving their goals (Lench et al., 2021), as they approach challenges with a positive mindset and persistence. Highly relational individuals score high in measures of well-being (Pezirkianidis et al., 2023), are protected against mental health issues such as depression and anxiety, and have lower mortality rates overall (Holt-Lunstad et al., 2010). In summary, these traits significantly enhance outcomes related to productivity, mental health, and overall quality of life, all of which are closely associated with resilience.

Imagine having a leader who embodies these traits. How would it influence you, or your team? Equally important, where do your strengths lie, and where do you need to cultivate growth? Consider the following four case studies of individuals who exemplify the COPES qualities. My hope is that you will recognize some of these traits in yourself.

Conscientiousness: The Organizational Architect

In the realm of leadership, the trait of conscientiousness stands out for its core qualities of organization, dependability, and diligence. One exemplary figure that brings this trait to life is Indra Nooyi, the former CEO of PepsiCo. Throughout her tenure, Nooyi demonstrated remarkable agility, especially in response to the shifting landscape of consumer preferences toward healthier snacks. Despite encountering initial pushback, her unwavering commitment to her vision enabled PepsiCo to adeptly transform its product offerings, embracing the ethos of "performance with purpose" (Nooyi & Govindarajan, 2020). What truly distinguished her leadership approach was not just her resoluteness but also her capacity to heed her team's input, fostering inclusivity amidst transformative change.

This adaptability proved pivotal as Nooyi navigated PepsiCo through a period of strategic evolution, ensuring its continued relevance in a swiftly evolving market. Her dedication to purpose-driven leadership is further underscored in her book, *My Life in Full* (Nooyi, 2021), in which she delves into her profound commitment to addressing workforce challenges. Nooyi's relentless pursuit of positive change serves as a potent example for conscientious leaders endeavoring to make a meaningful impact within their organizations and beyond. Her own words encapsulate her ethos, reflecting an unwavering focus on addressing pressing issues:

> I don't know why I am this way, but if there's an issue, until it's resolved I just can't sleep. I'm just focused on it all the time. I mean, right now I'm focused on the care issue, and I'm researching everything I can about care. I'm totally consumed by this care issue, figuring out how we're going to support care for the caregivers, for the essential worker. (Ignatius, 2021, 10:06)

Nooyi's ability to lead with conscientiousness yet maintain a focus on achieving positive results underscores her effectiveness as a leader in driving PepsiCo's transformation. Her leadership style embodied several key attributes, including self-control, agility, commitment, and achievement orientation—all of which can fall under the broad banner of conscientiousness. These attributes, including the definition, relationship to conscientiousness and resilience, and an example from Indra Nooyi's life, are detailed in Table 6.1.

Optimism: The Visionary Mindset

Optimism is key to resilience as it influences how individuals perceive setbacks. Those with an optimistic mindset see obstacles as temporary and manageable, and this mindset fosters perseverance and motivation to overcome adversity effectively. Oprah Winfrey exemplifies this trait; in an early career interview, she emphasized the power of thoughts in shaping one's life and responding to challenges. In the early stages of Winfrey's career, she participated in an interview in which she emphasized the fundamental components of optimism, highlighting how thoughts shape a person's life and in particular their ability to respond to challenges. She poignantly concluded with what she described as an "aha" moment, recognizing, "If you want your life to be more rewarding, you have to change the way you think" (Winfrey, n.d.-a). This isn't just idle talk. Winfrey's journey from poverty and adversity in rural Mississippi to becoming an influential media mogul underscores her resilience and determination. Despite facing significant hardships, including poverty, abuse, and family instability, she found solace in education and storytelling (Saner, 2018).

A core aspect of optimism is perception of control—whether we believe we control our lives internally or attribute outcomes to external forces. Embracing an internal locus of control, Winfrey attributed success or failure to her own actions and decisions, signaling a shift in mindset. She notably remarked, "When I figured out that my thoughts control my whole life—that no matter what hand life deals me, I can always choose my response to it" (Winfrey, n.d.-a). Research confirms that an internal locus of control is an essential prerequisite for resilience because it empowers individuals to confront challenges with a positive mindset (optimism), confidence, and determination (Felicia et al., 2022).

Winfrey's journey also exemplifies problem solving, a vital component of both optimism and resilience. Optimistic individuals confront challenges with confidence, actively seeking solutions rather than yielding to setbacks (Scheier et al., 1986). They employ effective problem-solving skills to navigate and

TABLE 6.1. Key Attributes of Conscientious Leaders

	Self-control
Definition	The ability to modify or alter cognitive, emotional, and behavioral reactions (Baumeister et al., 2007)
Relation to conscientiousness and resilience	Individuals with self-control exhibit resilience in adversity by employing cognitive reappraisal strategies to reinterpret threatening situations (Mischel et al., 2011). Conscientiousness enhances this process, as it fosters disciplined efforts in managing stress and maintaining a positive outlook.
Example	Nooyi's ability to maintain objectivity and composure in the face of challenges showcases her remarkable self-control. This trait enables her to navigate complex situations effectively and make well-considered decisions.
	Agility
Definition	"Resilient agility" (Prieto & Talukder, 2023) for an individual entails withstanding adversity while staying adaptable
Relation to conscientiousness and resilience	The interconnected relationship between resilience and agility refers to the combined capability to perform effectively in rapidly changing contexts (Prieto & Talukder, 2023). Conscientiousness plays a pivotal role in this dynamic, as individuals who exhibit discipline and goal-oriented behavior are equipped to navigate challenges successfully.
Example	Nooyi demonstrates agility in her leadership by swiftly adapting to changing circumstances and market dynamics. Her proactive approach to recognizing and responding to shifts in consumer preferences exemplifies her agility as a leader.
	Commitment
Definition	Actively engaging in life activities and showing genuine interest and curiosity about the world (Maddi, 2006)
Relation to conscientiousness and resilience	Conscientious individuals, known for their disciplined and goal-oriented nature, tend to demonstrate commitment across different life domains. This commitment, in turn, cultivates a proactive mindset and fosters resilience, enabling individuals to persevere through challenges and adapt effectively to adversity.
Example	Nooyi's unwavering dedication to her vision and goals underscores her commitment to driving organizational success. Her perseverance in the face of resistance and skepticism highlights her strong sense of commitment to achieving positive outcomes.

TABLE 6.1. Key Attributes of Conscientious Leaders (*Continued*)

	Achievement orientation
Definition	An individual's drive to succeed, set challenging goals, and pursue excellence in their pursuits
Relation to conscientiousness and resilience	Conscientious individuals who have high achievement motivation outperform their peers (Richardson & Abraham, 2009). This tendency to excel is closely linked to resilience, as their perseverance and determination in pursuing goals contribute to their ability to overcome setbacks and adapt to challenges effectively.
Example	Nooyi's relentless pursuit of excellence and results-driven approach reflects her strong achievement orientation. She sets ambitious goals and works tirelessly to accomplish them, driving both personal and organizational success.

surmount obstacles, forging ahead with innovative approaches. By leveraging positive expectancy, a core component of optimism, they maintain a positive mindset, believing in and envisioning favorable outcomes. Despite facing dismissal from her initial TV role as a news anchor in Baltimore and being labeled "unfit for TV," Winfrey refused to let this setback define her. Instead, she leveraged it to create "The Oprah Winfrey Show," one of the most acclaimed daytime television shows of all time (FasterCapital, 2024).

Finally, Winfrey's optimism is evident in her growth mindset, which emphasizes improvement through dedication and effort. She viewed setbacks as opportunities for learning and growth rather than as permanent limitations and emphasized, "Every experience and encounter, particularly your mistakes, are there to teach you and force you into being more of who you are" (as cited in Clarida, 2013). Her optimism, marked by an internal locus of control, problem-solving skill, positive expectancy, and a growth mindset, defines her approach. This optimism was evident in her television show; she fearlessly tackled taboo topics, amplified marginalized voices, and encouraged viewers to face challenges with courage and resilience. Ultimately, Winfrey's journey demonstrates how optimism can transform adversity into personal and professional fulfillment.

Emotional Endurance: The Unquenchable Resolve

While not commonly discussed in research or popular media, emotional endurance is a concept I have considered over the years as I have heard stories of people facing and overcoming challenges. Emotional endurance is often associated with emotional stamina or stability and is referred to as the ability to bounce back, recover, and flourish from emotional hardships, maintain stability, and cope effectively with stress and setbacks. Endurance connotes hardship; just as runners build endurance through practice and by pushing themselves out of their comfort zone, individuals develop emotional endurance by facing difficulties.

Jose Salvador Alvarenga's survival story is a prime example of emotional endurance. He gained international attention after surviving 438 days adrift in the Pacific Ocean (Franklin, 2015). In November 2012, Alvarenga set out on a fishing trip from Mexico. However, he was caught in a storm that blew his small boat off course, leaving him adrift. During his ordeal, Alvarenga exhibited a remarkable capacity to find meaning even in the direst circumstances. His unwavering focus on survival, despite starvation, dehydration, and exposure to the elements, echoes Frankl's (1959) teachings about finding purpose in adversity. Alvarenga noted, "If one depressed person avoids committing suicide then the book is a success. . . . Your mind has to be relaxed as you think about survival. Don't think about death. If you think you are going to die, you will die . . . there are challenges and punishment in life but you have to fight!" (as quoted in Franklin, 2015, p. 262).

Alvarenga also demonstrated perspective taking, drawing from past trials and emotional experiences to navigate and endure his harrowing journey. A friend of his noted that Alvarenga's survival wasn't surprising, attributing it to his reputation as the "toughest" man due to his past experience in a guerrilla army in El Salvador, where he underwent rigorous training (Crowley, 2014). Facing and surviving difficult challenges in the past provided Alvarenga with the perspective and resilience to persevere through his ordeal at sea, unlike his companion who gave up prematurely. Alvarenga likely experienced similar emotions before—fear, anxiety, depression, hopelessness—but successfully overcame them, which bolstered his emotional endurance for the challenges he faced.

Throughout his ordeal, Alvarenga demonstrated humility by acknowledging his own limitations and relying on his expertise as a fisherman (Franklin, 2015). He respected the forces of nature and understood that survival demanded acceptance of his circumstances. Over time, he adapted by recognizing patterns in sea life and employing various survival techniques, such as catching and consuming small sharks for their nutrient-rich livers, harvesting sea turtles for their blood to sustain him, and immobilizing sea birds for food by breaking their legs.

In addition to meaning, empathy, and a modest demeanor, Alvarenga used various healthy coping strategies to maintain stress tolerance while enduring the physical and psychological hardships of life at sea. He used meditation, prayer, and a focused mindset to find inner peace and maintain hope for rescue. When asked what he wanted people to take away from his 438-day ordeal, Alvarenga summed up emotional endurance aptly by noting, "Maybe if people read this story they will realize that if I can make it, they can make it. . . . Be strong. Think positive. If you start to think to the contrary, you are headed to failure. . . . You have to survive and think about the future and your life" (as quoted in Franklin, 2015, p. 262).

Social Relationships: The Interpersonally Proficient

In the realm of resilient leadership, the ability to form interpersonal relationships easily stands out as the vital final quality. Numerous studies emphasize the role of strong social connections in navigating challenges and emerging triumphant in adversity. It's crucial to recognize that while social–relational skills are fundamental, they often complement other leadership qualities. Let's take a closer look at the previously discussed individuals and how they exemplified these social–relational traits.

Oprah Winfrey's journey is a compelling example of relational resilience, underscored by the influence of key figures in her life. Her grandmother, Hattie Mae, emerged as her earliest role model, most notably instilling the priceless gift of literacy from a young age (Cook, 2022). Similarly, her fourth-grade teacher in Nashville, Mrs. Duncan, played a role in nurturing Winfrey's intellect and fostering confidence in her academic abilities (Winfrey, n.d.-b). Despite facing significant childhood hardships, Winfrey attributed much of her foundational support to these influential social supports.

For relational reciprocity, the Oprah Winfrey Leadership Academy for Girls in South Africa serves as a beacon. Winfrey herself hailed it as her greatest legacy, offering a lifeline to students who have braved childhood poverty and trauma, showcasing resilience, courage, and spirit (Oprah Winfrey Charitable Foundation, n.d.). While you and I likely cannot match Oprah's scale of contribution, even small acts of support and assistance can bolster our resilience. In fact, research indicates that helping and supporting others is linked to positive health outcomes, including reduced mortality (Poulin et al., 2013).

Indra Nooyi's remarkable ability to connect with people from diverse backgrounds underscores the importance of effective communication in fostering relational resilience. Despite initial setbacks, she diligently worked to refine her communication skills, emphasizing clarity, simplicity, and understanding (Gallo, 2022). This dedication not only propelled her career within PepsiCo but also exemplified how strategic communication can strengthen relationships and drive success in professional endeavors.

In Jose Salvador Alvarenga's harrowing survival saga, empathy emerged as a trait that sustained him throughout his ordeal. Despite facing unimaginable challenges, Alvarenga demonstrated compassion and care toward his younger and less experienced companion, even after his tragic death several weeks into the journey. Despite facing his own struggles, Alvarenga remained compassionate and supportive, demonstrating a deep understanding of the human condition and the importance of helping others in times of need. He noted, "I helped him as much as I could. I would hug him. I told him, 'We'll be rescued soon. We'll hit an island soon'" (Lah, 2016). Despite the companion's occasional outbursts of despair and violence, Alvarenga remained steadfast, providing comfort and reassurance up until his friend's death several weeks into the journey.

In summary, resilient leaders possess many of the characteristics that constitute a resilient conceptualization of leadership. Most leaders excel in one domain, but they may not be as strong in others, and some may even have relative weaknesses. The goal is not perfection in each aspect but rather recognition of the multifaceted nature of resilience.

It's important to acknowledge that resilience may manifest differently for all leaders, yet remains anchored to the following general framework:

- **Conscientiousness** embodies traits such as organization, dependability, and diligence, exemplified by leaders like Indra Nooyi, who demonstrate adaptability and resilience in navigating challenges. As a predominantly behavioral construct, conscientious individuals exhibit self-control, agility, commitment, and achievement orientation, enhancing their resilience by effectively managing stress, adapting to challenges, and pursuing goals with determination.

- **Optimism** influences how individuals perceive setbacks, fostering perseverance and motivation to overcome adversity effectively, exemplified by Oprah Winfrey's journey from adversity to success. As a predominantly cognitive construct, optimism empowers individuals to leverage problem-solving skills, positive expectancy, an internal locus of control, and a growth mindset. By confronting challenges with confidence, resilience, and a focus on personal and professional growth, optimistic individuals navigate adversities effectively.

- **Emotional endurance** is characterized by the ability to bounce back from emotional hardships, maintain stability, and cope effectively with stress; it is exemplified by Jose Salvador Alvarenga's survival saga at sea. As a predominantly emotional construct, emotional endurance empowers individuals to find meaning in their situations and exhibit perspective taking, humility, and healthy coping strategies. These qualities enable them to navigate and endure physical and psychological hardships with resilience and determination.

- **Social relationships**, especially strong social connections, foster resilience by providing emotional support and practical aid and by fostering inclusivity amidst transformative change. As a predominantly relational construct, individuals with strong social relationships derive benefits from emotional support and reciprocal dynamics, empathy, and clear communication with others. These qualities enhance their resilience by fostering a sense of belonging, connectedness, and mutual assistance, enabling them to navigate challenges effectively.

Let's briefly explore how certain character traits can impede resilience. Earlier, I mentioned toxic leaders and their personality styles. While resilience traits like empathy offer valuable benefits such as fostering compassion and humility, traits like self-pity, self-righteousness, self-absorption, and self-sufficiency act as obstacles to resilience. These traits often stem from core personality characteristics like narcissism and borderline tendencies, shaping individuals' self-perception and interactions. I've encountered numerous patients burdened by entrenched and unyielding self-pity, which has made it challenging to assist them. Hence, it's crucial to recognize factors that nurture resilience and distinguish them from corrosive self-referential traits that hinder it.

LEADERSHIP STRATEGIES FOR EMPOWERING TEAMS

Acknowledging the profound impact of leadership within teams, NBA superstar Chris Bosh emphasized the role of leadership setting the culture within teams. He noted, "Leaders set the tone for their peers. Peers look up to them and say, 'They're doing it, so I'm doing it'" (as quoted in Agbelusi, 2020).

Considering the essential traits of resilient leadership, the inevitable question emerges: How does a leader effectively influence these traits within their team? Forsyth (2014) emphasized the impact leaders have on others, acknowledging that "leadership is one of the great mysteries of social life" (p. 12). He highlighted that effective leadership is not simply about giving orders or expecting passive compliance but rather is a nuanced blend of art and science that needs to account for the complexities in motivating and guiding others. Forsyth noted that while some followers may struggle to resist direct commands, savvy leaders employ various persuasive tactics—personalized thank-you notes, public acknowledgments, small rewards—to encourage follower loyalty and cooperation. He concluded that the most successful leaders seamlessly combine direct and indirect methods, crafting their influence "so subtle that it is scarcely noticed by their followers" (Forsyth, 2014, p. 12).

Let's examine COPES and integrate Forsyth's (2014) notion of subtle influence, exploring how resilient leaders can mold these qualities to foster resilience within their teams. This subtle influence is the essence of transmitting characteristics such as conscientiousness, optimism, emotional endurance, and social responsibility. But how is this influence expressed in daily practices? I present a case study for using the COPES model to illustrate its practical application.

CONSCIENTIOUSNESS IN COMMUNICATION

In the legacy of Indra Nooyi, the hallmarks of conscientious leadership—meticulous organization, steadfast dependability, and unwavering diligence—are unmistakable. Yet Nooyi's unwavering commitment to refining her communication style, particularly in service of the workforce, truly sets her apart. This dedication not only allowed her to steer the company and its workforce in the right direction but also fostered an atmosphere of trust, confidence, and transparency.

What does this look like in the day-to-day workforce? Consider Sarah, a vibrant team leader in a burgeoning tech startup, embodying conscientious leadership at its core. Sarah doesn't just share project updates; she infuses them with context, rationale, and invaluable insights, creating a culture of psychological safety and trust within her team. Under Sarah's guidance, team members feel empowered to express opinions, voice concerns, and contribute ideas freely. This open and transparent communication environment becomes the bedrock for teamwork, innovation, and the ultimate success of the startup.

Let's zoom in on a moment in the startup's journey: a period of organizational restructuring. As uncertainties loom large, Sarah steps up, proactively engaging in regular communication. She tackles challenges head-on, acknowledging the uncertainties while providing a clear roadmap for the future. Here's where Sarah's leadership truly shines. By openly discussing the restructuring process, potential outcomes, and anticipated benefits, she demystifies the situation for her team. Through her transparent approach, team members feel not only involved but also empowered in decision making, instilling a deep sense of confidence and security within the team.

As a leader, consider incorporating some of Sarah's strategies to strengthen your connections with your team and amplify their impact:

- **Infuse context and rationale.** Like Sarah, go beyond simply sharing project updates. Provide context and rationale behind decisions and tasks to help your team understand the big picture. This approach fosters transparency and trust, laying the foundation for open communication.

- **Empower team members.** Encourage your team to express their opinions, voice concerns, and contribute ideas freely. Create an environment in which everyone feels valued and heard, just as Sarah does. This empowerment enables individuals to take ownership of their work and contribute to the team's success.

- **Use proactive communication.** In times of uncertainty or change, take a page from Sarah's book and engage in regular communication. Address challenges head-on and provide a clear roadmap for the future. Transparency about the situation and the way forward builds trust and alleviates anxiety among team members.

- **Demystify processes.** Follow Sarah's lead in demystifying complex processes or changes within the organization. Openly discuss the reasons behind decisions, potential outcomes, and anticipated benefits. This transparency helps team members understand the situation fully and feel more confident in their roles.

- **Empower decision making.** Involve your team in decision-making processes whenever possible. Solicit their input, consider their perspectives, and make them feel like valued contributors to the team's success. Empowering them in this way fosters a sense of ownership and commitment.

OPTIMISM THROUGH GROWTH MINDSET

In the realm of leadership, optimism is a cornerstone trait, fueled by qualities such as problem-solving abilities and a positive outlook. But what truly drives optimism is the growth mindset—a belief in the potential for skill development through dedication. This mindset not only bolsters resilience during challenging times but also fosters a proactive approach to overcoming obstacles and personal growth, ultimately shaping the trajectory of optimistic leaders.

Consider Robert, a prominent leader within the university's business department. Robert embodies the ethos of a growth mindset in every aspect of his leadership role. Rather than viewing challenges as insurmountable hurdles, he sees them as opportunities for growth and development. When confronted with setbacks, Robert tackles them head-on, approaching them with curiosity and a solution-oriented mindset.

A defining characteristic of Robert's leadership is his embrace of failure as a steppingstone to success. He recognizes that setbacks are an inevitable part of the growth process and leverages them as valuable learning experiences. Instead of dwelling on past mistakes, Robert encourages his team members to analyze them objectively, extract lessons, and apply them to future endeavors. This approach not only fosters continuous improvement but also nurtures a culture of resilience and innovation within the department.

Furthermore, Robert's dedication to personal development sets him apart as a leader. He actively seeks out opportunities to expand his skills and knowledge, whether through professional development courses, mentorship programs, or self-directed learning. By modeling a growth mindset, Robert inspires his team members to invest in their own growth and development, fostering a culture of continuous learning and improvement.

Robert's influence extends far beyond his immediate team, permeating the departmental culture with optimism and a relentless pursuit of growth. His leadership serves as a testament to the transformative power of a growth mindset for driving individual and organizational success.

What might this look like in your day-to-day? Try one or more of the following strategies:

- **Lead by example.** Take on challenges with a forward-thinking attitude, showing team members how obstacles can lead to growth. Face difficulties with openness and creativity, signaling that setbacks are not roadblocks but opportunities for progress.

- **Encourage learning.** Motivate team members to pursue new skills and knowledge. Provide access to development opportunities such as courses, mentorships, and personal projects. Actively support their efforts to improve and grow professionally.

- **Promote resilience.** Normalize the idea that failure is a learning tool. Encourage team members to review mistakes without fear and extract insights for future success. Create an atmosphere in which learning from setbacks is not only accepted but expected.

- **Foster collaboration.** Foster a culture of collaboration and continuous improvement within your team. Encourage open communication, idea sharing, and constructive feedback to promote innovation and resilience.

- **Recognize efforts.** Acknowledge and celebrate the efforts and achievements of your team members. Recognize their dedication to personal and professional growth, and express gratitude for their contributions to the team's success.

EMOTIONAL ENDURANCE IN CRISIS

Emotional endurance emerges as a cornerstone quality that is deeply intertwined with personal growth and resilience and is essential for leaders navigating the unpredictable terrain of their roles. Consider the gripping tale of Alvarenga's survival at sea—qualities such as perspective taking, humility, and the ability to find meaning in adversity proved invaluable. Such experiences, analogous to real-world crises, refine leaders' thinking and decision-making skills under duress and enhance their emotional resilience.

Cecilia, a sales manager at a bustling department store, exemplifies emotional endurance in her leadership journey. Cecilia faces a daily barrage of challenges, from meeting lofty sales targets to defusing tense customer interactions and managing team conflicts. Yet she meets these obstacles head-on, armed with unwavering composure and resilience. This resilience isn't innate; it's a learned response, forged through life challenges that have given her empathy and perspective.

Standout characteristics of Cecilia's emotional endurance are her unyielding positivity and resilience in adversity. Instead of succumbing to setbacks, she perceives them as opportunities for growth and learning and draws on past experiences as enduring reminders of her perseverance. Cecilia's steadfast demeanor inspires her team and fosters a culture of resilience and optimism within the department. Under Cecilia's guidance, the team learns to confront challenges directly and by incorporating perspective taking, which enables them to understand and empathize with diverse viewpoints and thus fosters a resilient and cohesive work culture. The culture she fosters prioritizes safety, facilitated through open communication and a constructive feedback mechanism. This environment equips employees with confidence, driving both individual and collective success.

Consider the following strategies for leading your team with emotional endurance:

- **Encourage continuous improvement.** Stress the value of turning setbacks into opportunities for learning, similar to how Cecilia approaches challenges. Inspire team members to tap into their past successes as evidence of their strength and determination.

- **Promote open communication.** Create a safe space for open expression and constructive feedback within your team. Encourage transparent communication and dialogue, allowing team members to share their thoughts and feelings without fear of judgment.

- **Cultivate a supportive network.** Facilitate connections among team members to create a supportive network in which they can lean on each other during challenging times. Encourage collaboration and peer support, fostering a sense of camaraderie and shared resilience within the team.

- **Celebrate resilience.** Recognize and celebrate instances of emotional resilience and perseverance within your team. Acknowledge their efforts to confront challenges head-on and commend their ability to bounce back from setbacks.

- **Foster mentorship.** Establish mentorship opportunities within your team, mirroring Cecilia's guidance. Pair senior members with junior members to promote skill development and cultivate a supportive community.

SOCIAL RELATIONSHIPS WITHIN TEAMS

An interpersonally proficient leader is characterized by relational traits that are fundamental to building resilience. Qualities like social support, reciprocity, communication, and empathy are essential. While leaders may have many other strengths, the expression of these traits through relationships activates resilience.

Charles, for example, leads a customer service call center. He epitomizes the essence of social responsibility in his leadership approach. Beyond his technical prowess, Charles is renowned for his unwavering commitment to community and environmental sustainability initiatives. His office isn't merely a workspace; it's a vibrant hub of collaboration and support, where team members freely exchange ideas and extend a helping hand when needed.

Charles's leadership ethos centers on reciprocity, fostering an environment in which team members thrive on mutual support and recognition. Under his stewardship, every contribution, whether sharing expertise or offering encouragement, is valued and acknowledged. This dedication to reciprocity is evident in his communication approach, characterized by transparency and candor. He actively encourages the exchange of information and invites feedback by posing queries such as "What challenges are you encountering?" and "How can I better support you?" Through attentive listening and proactive troubleshooting, Charles meticulously nurtures a culture of trust and unity within his team.

Perhaps his most enduring traits is his empathy. He actively listens to his team's concerns, offering unwavering support and creating a safe space for open expression. Drawing from challenges he has faced in her own life, Charles is cognizant of how to explicitly relate to the team's challenges, fostering a palpable sense of psychological safety so that members feel comfortable sharing their thoughts and feelings.

Charles's leadership story highlights several key takeaways and recommendations based on the value of social relationships:

- **Emphasize social responsibility.** Prioritize social responsibility by actively engaging in community and environmental initiatives, fostering a sense of purpose and connection beyond the workplace.

- **Cultivate a culture of reciprocity.** Encourage a culture in which team members support and recognize each other's contributions, fostering an environment of mutual respect and collaboration.

- **Promote transparent communication.** Foster open and transparent communication channels so that team members feel comfortable sharing their thoughts, concerns, and feedback without fear of judgment.

- **Practice active listening and empathy.** Actively listen to team members' concerns and demonstrate empathy by providing unwavering support and understanding, fostering an environment in which open expression is encouraged.

- **Promote peer support.** Establish networks for team members to provide advice, guidance, and emotional support. Encourage mentorship and buddy systems to foster mutual assistance and camaraderie.

CHAPTER SUMMARY

- Leaders ignite energy within teams and drive the entire organizational culture forward.

- Leadership failures are often attributed to a person's emotional and relational shortcomings rather than to a lack of technical skills. This attribution emphasizes the importance of these softer skills.

- Critical leadership qualities such as emotional intelligence and relational skills are not innate and can be developed through targeted learning and practice.

- The COPES model—conscientiousness, optimism, emotional endurance, and social relationships—outlines the core qualities needed for resilient leadership, all of which can be developed.

- Conscientiousness involves high levels of organization, dependability, and diligence, which are directly correlated with improved job performance and relationship stability.

- Optimism is characterized by a positive outlook on life, enabling leaders to perceive challenges as temporary and manageable. This outlook enhances resilience and overall success.

- Emotional endurance refers to the ability to sustain emotional stability and resilience through adversity, allowing leaders to maintain focus and performance under stress.

- Strong social relationships are crucial for providing support, fostering a collaborative environment, and enhancing the overall well-being and resilience of leaders and their teams.

CHAPTER QUESTIONS

- What specific actions am I taking to energize my team and propel forward momentum?

- What would my team say are my emotional or relational gaps, and how can I address them?

- Which strategies can I employ immediately to enhance my emotional intelligence and relational skills?

- How does my level of organization and dependability affect my team's performance and stability?

- What would my team say about my leadership performance during stressful situations?

- What actions can I take to strengthen the social bonds within my team?

PART **III** CHANGE STRATEGIES

7 CASE STUDIES IN HARMONIZING RESILIENCE AND WORKFORCE CULTURE

The only thing of real importance that leaders do is to create and manage culture. If you don't manage culture, it manages you.

—Edgar Schein

You may be familiar with the resonant quote, "Culture eats strategy for breakfast," often found laminated and tucked away in a company breakroom, serving as a rallying cry for human resources (HR) departments. This unconventional perspective challenges traditional wisdom that asserts strategy shapes culture. Instead, the statement proposes an intriguing reversal and suggests that, regardless of the meticulous crafting of a business strategy on paper, the prevailing organizational culture wields a substantial influence over its practical success or failure. In other words, culture matters, and it's time to take notice.

In practice, a brilliant strategic plan may face challenges if the internal culture does not support or align with it. Organizational culture, with its

https://doi.org/10.1037/0000454-008
Rethinking Employee Resilience: Why Our Current Approach to Worker Burnout Is Failing, and How to Fix It, by D. Pelton

TABLE 7.1. Companies Addressing Workforce Resilience Across the Four Cultural Levers

Performance management	Job crafting	Analytics	Strategic communication
Continental	Google	Genpact	Buffer
Bayer	Atlassian	Purolator	Button
Handu Group	LinkedIn	Kuehne+Nagel	Typeform
Adobe	3M	Microsoft	Full Contact
Genpact	Patagonia		
GE	Siemens		
Google	Unplugged		
Cisco			
Netflix			

unwritten norms, values, and employee behaviors, plays a crucial role in shaping actual outcomes within a business.

Focused on practical implementation, this chapter kicks off with an in-depth exploration of real-world industry examples showcasing each of the four cultural levers introduced in Chapter 5. I shine a spotlight on companies that have not just embraced these concepts in theory but have translated them into impactful practices (see Table 7.1). At the end of each narrative, I pose a series of first-person questions and leave room for you to jot down responses in the space provided.

CULTURAL LEVER 1: PERFORMANCE MANAGEMENT

As explored in Chapter 5, a performance management (PM) system fundamentally empowers organizations to oversee and enhance employee job performance. Within the construct of workforce resilience, organizations can shape a PM system to mitigate job demands and optimize resources in a variety of ways, such as harmonizing workloads, clarifying role definitions to minimize ambiguity and conflict, offering comprehensive feedback, and acknowledging and rewarding employees based on their performance. This chapter provides a look at how a variety of companies are implementing these strategies.

Continental Airlines: Rewarding Team Over Individual

In HR discussions, a recurring debate revolves around whether it's more effective to incentivize individual performance than team performance. Although teamwork occupies a sizable portion of an employee's workday—some estimate up to 80% (Cross et al., 2016)—the emphasis on individual achievement persists in compensation, promotions, rewards, and recognition. Leaders often prefer individual incentives because they are easy to measure and administer, yet these rewards may contribute minimally to team dynamics and performance or may detract from them (Libby & Thorne, 2009; Schweyer, 2021). However, research suggests that in many cases, particularly in highly interdependent work, team-based rewards yield better performance than individual rewards (Ladley et al., 2015; Schweyer, 2021). You read that right. While the reasoning is complex, the simple explanation is that as teams become more interdependent, they feel more psychologically safe, communicate better, and collaborate to create an impact that can surpass the sum of individual contributions. Yet team incentives are underutilized: A 2014 survey indicated that only 28% of publicly traded U.S. companies had incorporated them, while 66% weren't considering team incentive programs (Greeven et al., 2023).

Let's shift to a real-world example. In February 1995, Continental Airlines was facing financial distress and initiated a novel team-based incentive program, offering every hourly employee a $65 bonus for each month that Continental ranked in the top five for on-time performance. Simester and Knez (2000) analyzed the impact of the program, noting that approximately 35,000 eligible employees received checks, totaling around $2.3 million. This program played a pivotal role in Continental's financial recovery, preventing bankruptcy and generating net profits of $224 million in 1995, up from a net loss of $613 million in 1994. This upward financial trend continued year over year and was related to improved on-time performance, a reduction in baggage delays, and fewer customer complaint statistics post-implementation.

Simester and Knez (2000) noted that the establishment of autonomous work groups played a central role in driving improvements within Continental Airlines. These groups, similar to specialized teams such as baggage handlers or ticket agents at airports, helped address the problem of "free riding"—a situation in which individuals benefit from group efforts without contributing (e.g., think of that one person in high school who never pitched in on your group project but still got the grade). This program addressed the issue by operating within autonomous groups in which employees collectively agreed to exert high effort, monitor, and sanction their colleagues to enforce the group decision. Ultimately, this approach led to increased incentives for effort and performance. The senior management at Continental observed positive shifts in employee behavior, including increased effort, mutual monitoring, and notable reductions in turnover, on-the-job injuries, and sick days. Employee interviews at various Continental airports further affirmed the widespread acknowledgment of the effectiveness of the bonus program.

Continental's bold shift to team-based incentives wasn't just a financial turnaround; it became a model for others, including its competitor TWA, illustrating the impact of collective motivation on performance. Beyond rescuing the airline, the initiative highlighted the concrete advantages of prioritizing team incentives and bringing employees together in a shared pursuit of common goals.

Table 7.2 is the first of a series of application tables that contain self-reflection questions, example responses to the questions from disidentified employees from a variety of organizations, and a place to record observations and actions. Think about how you would respond to each prompting question and record your answers in the "My observations/My actions" sections.

Bayer: Radical Gratitude

In a popular article, Buckingham and Goodall (2019) highlighted the National Football League as a high-stakes industry that understands the true value of feedback. Referencing legendary coach Tom Landry's approach with the Dallas Cowboys, the authors emphasized Landry's focus on creating individual highlight reels for players, focusing on their successful moments rather than dwelling on mistakes. According to Buckingham and Goodall, Landry reasoned that

> while the number of wrong ways to do something was infinite, the number of right ways, for any particular player, was not. It was knowable, and the best way to discover it was to look at plays where that person had done it excellently. From now on, he told each team member, 'we only replay your winning plays.' (p. 12)

Taking inspiration from this philosophy, Bayer implemented a similar strategy in their recognition platform for their business in China. In personal communication with me (Voelker, personal communication, 2024), a spokesperson of Bayer China highlighted the impactful nature of the Discover Better employee recognition program. Powered by a dynamic digital platform designed to mirror popular social media interfaces like Facebook and accessible via the company intranet or WeChat portal, the Discover Better program allows employees to effortlessly express gratitude and encouragement to their peers with personalized thank-you cards, cultivating a shared collection of "Better Moments" that resonate throughout Bayer. It features various feedback cards such as "Applause" and "High Five," allowing managers to recognize efforts with or without monetary rewards. This initiative isn't just about acknowledging good work; it's about fostering a vibrant culture of appreciation throughout the organization while it enhances employee interaction and engagement.

TABLE 7.2. Continental Application

1. Are our company mission, vision, and values publicly available and understood by the workforce? Is well-being part of our value structure?

Sales director example: Yes, all of this is publicly available. "Collaboration" is a core pillar of our people strategy from what I read on our website, but nothing explicit about employee welfare or well-being. Frankly, I don't even know why collaboration is a value–this isn't something our leaders talk about in their town halls.

My observations:

2. What factors is our company emphasizing when deciding which behaviors deserve rewards and which ones don't?

Supply chain analyst example: Our company says they value well-being, but we certainly don't reward people for well-being. We reward widgets–the volume and impact of what someone produces. That's fine; just don't tell me you value well-being.

My observations:

3. Does our organization currently recognize and reward team behaviors? If not, which specific team behaviors do you believe deserve recognition and reward?

Risk manager example: This job is competitive, so we reward individuals. I wish we rewarded teams. I think we should look at the quality and quantity of output by individual versus teams. That should be part of our incentive structure.

My observations:

4. Does our PM system allow for a component that rewards teamwork?

Educational consultant example: I'm hesitant to say what we have is a "PM system." We just write a whole lot of prose, submit it, and then if we're lucky we get a small pay raise and bonus. So we need to crawl before we walk.

My observations:

5. Is there opportunity to explore the impact of team recognition on employee motivation, satisfaction, and retention? What about innovation and problem solving?

Human resources (HR) leader example: [As an HR leader], we haven't put much time thinking through individual versus team recognition, but we have a compelling case and gobs of data.

My observations:

6. What is one thing I can do this week to recognize the collective efforts of my team(s)?

Product manager example: On our leadership call on Wednesday, I am going to publicly recognize three people on my team. I'll share their names, what they did, and the impact it had on the team and the end result.

My actions:

Since its launch, the platform boasts a 65% login rate and more than 30,000 thank-you cards sent in its first year, predominantly nonmonetary. This success shows a genuine culture of gratitude at Bayer and not only has boosted internal morale but also has established Bayer as a leader in employee recognition practices in the local market.

There isn't enough space in this chapter to fully examine the values and impact of gratitude. Nonetheless, numerous studies assert the value of gratitude for fostering positive relationships, providing social support, and enhancing workers' well-being. It has been shown to reduce negative emotions in the workplace and contribute to organizational health and success (for a comprehensive review, see Di Fabio et al., 2017). Picture the transformative effect on your organization if each person exhibited a single act of gratitude every day, and consider the potential impact on the overall culture and the positive shift it could bring.

In her book *SuperBetter* (McGonigal, 2015), author and game designer Jane McGonigal explored the transformative power of cultivating a gameful mindset to overcome challenges and enhance well-being. She addressed various aspects of resilience and underscored the importance of social resilience in building relationships that become valuable resources during times of need. Specifically, McGonigal's discussion of social resilience highlighted the role of connections in finding support and resources. She brought attention to the practice of gratitude, noting that expressing thanks not only fosters positive emotions but also has lasting effects on one's perception of the world. Citing studies on gratitude, McGonigal underlined its transformative power. She echoed the sentiments of Chowdhury (2019), who emphasized the release of neurotransmitters such as dopamine and serotonin, contributing to an immediate sense of happiness. Fletcher's (2015) comparison of gratitude to a "natural antidepressant" further underscores its positive effects, akin to medications.

McGonigal (2012) drew attention to the physical expression of gratitude, such as a prolonged handshake (just 6 seconds!), which can elevate oxytocin levels in the bloodstream. She also advocated for incorporating gratitude into daily life, such as by sending a daily thank-you note once a day by email, chat, or text message.

To deepen the understanding of gratitude, McGonigal (2015) incorporated insights from Dr. Kelly McGonigal, a Stanford psychology professor. Gratitude, she noted, extends beyond a simple thanks. She emphasized that an ideal and more radically transformative approach to gratitude would include the following:

"1) Find the benefit. What good came to you because of this person (and be specific)?

2) Acknowledge the effort. What might have been hard for them?
3) Spot the strength. What good do you see in the person you're thanking?"
   (p. 355)

For instance, you might express to your colleague, "I want to extend my gratitude for voicing your support during today's meeting. Your specific acknowledgment of the deliverables I've accomplished, which others might not have been aware of, truly made a difference (finding the benefit). I recognize the courage it took to speak up in such a way and put yourself out there, and I greatly appreciate your effort (acknowledging the effort).

Your diplomatic approach and authenticity have earned you immense respect from others on the call. It's evident that lifting others up is a quality you consistently embody, and I genuinely value this strength of yours (spotting the strength). Thank you for your meaningful contributions!"

Imagine expressing gratitude like this at least once a day. Consider the influence a mere 5 minutes could wield on organizational culture, fostering psychological safety among team members. How would you feel if you got this kind of thank you? According to Sugawara et al. (2012), you would have a rush of dopamine (such as while eating lots of chocolate) and feel good. Emotions can be contagious, too (see Chapter 3). Simple expressions of gratitude have the potential to transform the meaning and purpose we attribute to our day-to-day work.

Please review the questions and examples in Table 7.3. Then, apply insights you have learned about the concept of radical gratitude from Bayer and others, specifically focusing on practical observations or actions.

Handu Group: We Pay You to Team Well

Handu Group, a prominent e-commerce player, has instituted an innovative internal entrepreneurship model, especially through its flagship brand HStyle. Departing from traditional hierarchies, the company has transformed its structure and organized into specialized product teams handling end-to-end processes, such as design, production, and sales. Each team, comprising at least three members with distinct roles, operates autonomously. This organization fosters agility and responsiveness to real-time consumer feedback. Initially centered on a single product, HStyle's exponential growth is credited to cross-functional teams guided by clear annual task indicators such as sales, gross profit, and inventory turnover (Greeven et al., 2023). Similar to fine-tuning a piano, each team of 3+ consistently refines products to enhance the consumer experience.

TABLE 7.3. Bayer Application

1. Reflecting on the coaching philosophy of Tom Landry with the Dallas Cowboys, how might I focus on "individual highlight reels" of my team, emphasizing successful in real time over mistakes?

Graphic designer example: This week, as I collaborate with Sarah, I will proactively highlight and celebrate her successful designs in real time during our team meetings, providing specific details about the strengths I observed and emphasizing their positive impact on both her colleagues and the quality of her work.

My observations/actions:

2. As a team leader, what could "we only replay your winning plays" look like day to day?

Data scientist example: In upcoming meetings, I'll spotlight daily celebrations of team successes, commencing with Markus and his groundbreaking implementation of an innovative algorithm in a complex data modeling project, which resulted in a substantial enhancement of prediction accuracy. I'll emphasize this recognized strength and share the profound impact of his work.

My observations/actions:

3. Is there an opportunity to implement of a recognition platform (digital or paper-and-pencil) with nonfinancial rewards and/or gamified interactions?

Marketing coordinator example: Teresa will establish a paper-and-pencil recognition board in a central office space, encouraging handwritten notes or sketches that celebrate individual and team achievements.

My observations/actions:

4. Considering the studies that emphasize the significant value of gratitude in fostering positive relationships and enhancing well-being, how might incorporating a daily practice of expressing gratitude transform the overall culture and dynamics within my organization?

General example: Monique allocates 5 minutes at the end of each team meeting for team members to share appreciations and express gratitude, fostering a positive and appreciative atmosphere during daily huddles.

My observations/actions:

5. What one person and in what forum (public or private) could I spend 1 or 2 minutes thanking this week?

General example: At least once this week, I will express gratitude to someone who made an impact on me, acknowledging their effort, finding the benefit, and spotting their strength.

My observations/actions:

Daily real-time rankings create a competitive environment, driving effective performance. Role clarity is prioritized, as employees need to know exactly what is required to improve (the very visible) real-time rankings. In this system, recognition and rewards motivate teams positively. And in cases of team splits at HStyle, the innovative incentive structure comes into play.

Greeven et al. (2023, para. 8) recently highlighted reinvention of performance management, noting, in regard to HStyle's unique approach to teaming, that

> If a team splits up and some members form a new team, the leader of the new team must pay a fee to the original team for its previous training of the acquired staff. Moreover, the company's financial system automatically transfers 10% of an acquired staffer's bonus to the original team leader every month for one year. This system encourages each team to reorganize and generate new autonomous teams.

As a hypothetical example, imagine that Team Innovator, led by John, decides to split up, and some of his team members form a new team, Team Pioneer. Sarah, as the new leader of Team Pioneer, is required to pay a fee to John for the training of the staff she acquired. Imagine also that the company's financial system automatically transfers 10% of the bonus earned by each acquired staff member to John, the original team leader, every month for a year. Although Sarah and her team have a financial investment, they also have potentially significant gains, including the chance to lead a new team and explore fresh projects or ideas and possibly extra bonuses if the new team excel and/or branches off to create new teams. This comprehensive approach, fostering continuous learning and collaboration, not only recognizes the investment made in developing team members but also incentivizes deliberate team restructuring. It cultivates an environment of innovation and adaptability within the organizational structure and contributes to workforce resilience. This strategy encourages leaders to mentor effectively and empowers teams to thrive in a dynamic setting.

Please review the questions and examples in Table 7.4. Then, apply insights you have learned about incentive structures from Handu Group, specifically focusing on practical observations or actions.

Adobe's Evolution: Transitioning From Annual Performance Reviews to Check-Ins for the Future of Employee Development

Adobe's strategic departure from traditional annual performance reviews was prompted by significant pitfalls in their existing approach (Burkus, 2017).

TABLE 7.4. Handu Group Application

1. Does incentivizing teamwork align with the values and culture of my organization?

Accounting group example: While I haven't witnessed incentivizing teamwork directly, I believe it would align well with our organization's values and culture. Our emphasis on collaboration and cooperation suggests that rewarding teamwork could reinforce these principles and cultivate a culture of mutual support and collective effort.

My observations/actions:

2. Have we clearly defined and measured what team success looks like?

High school principal example: Yes—I have defined clear, measurable metrics for team success, facilitating discussions to establish transparent criteria and benchmarks. I monitor team performance against these metrics, providing guidance for continuous improvement.

My observations/actions:

3. Does our inventive structure have a teaming component, specifically in the context of team restructuring?

City planning example: Nope. We need to make changes to incentivize teamwork during restructuring, for example proposing rewards for team performance, peer recognition programs, and aligning individual goals with team objectives.

My observations/actions:

4. If we have team rewards, are they tied to specific, achievable goals?

Federal health worker example: I'd like to introduce team rewards linked to clear goals to boost motivation and success. I'd suggest creating a plan, defining achievable objectives, setting performance criteria, and offering tangible rewards. Tracking progress, encouraging communication, and adjusting as needed would be key to my approach.

My observations/actions:

5. Is our reward system clear, transparent, and equitable?

General example: Our current reward system lacks clarity, transparency, and equity and has inconsistencies in recognition and bonuses. For instance, some employees are rewarded without meeting performance standards, causing confusion and resentment. The opaque decision-making process further diminishes trust and morale.

My observations/actions:

The forced distribution model, which involves "forcing" employees into one of four performance tiers, consumed 80,000 hours of managers' time and was perceived as cumbersome and bureaucratic by employees (Adobe, n.d.). Adobe witnessed a significant increase in voluntary attrition in the months following performance reviews, indicating dissatisfaction and highlighting potential drawbacks of the traditional system (Burkus, 2017). In light of these challenges, Adobe decided to sunset annual performance reviews in 2012, recognizing the need for a more people-focused approach to PM. This marked the beginning of Adobe's journey toward a transformative system known as "check-in."

Check-in centers on continuous, two-way communication between employees and managers. The system focuses on real-time feedback, performance discussions, and career growth dialogues, and it is a departure from the rigid and time-consuming forced distribution model. To support the successful execution of check-in, Adobe created a public-facing 17-page toolkit that outlines the check-in process and aligns it with three key phases: expectations, feedback, and development (Adobe, n.d.). This toolkit caters to different roles within the organization, such as employees and people managers, and offers worksheets that enhance transparency and eliminate role ambiguity.

By encouraging ongoing, regular check-in conversations, Adobe streamlined workload management, eliminated formal ratings, and empowered managers to make nuanced and informed decisions, including compensation decisions, based on individual performance. Adobe (n.d.; see also Psico-Smart Editorial Team, 2024) noted significant positive outcomes since implementing check-in, including enhanced communication, increased employee satisfaction, and a notable reduction in employee turnover. Their departure from the traditional performance review system has not only created a more collaborative work environment marked with psychological safety but has also positioned check-in as a factor in driving employee development and engagement.

Please review the questions and examples in Table 7.5. Then, apply insights you have learned about performance management from Adobe, specifically focusing on practical observations or actions.

ADDITIONAL ORGANIZATIONS

In addition to the previously discussed models, numerous organizations are reshaping their PM structures to "move the fulcrum," fostering a more balanced view of demands and resources and ultimately cultivating a more

TABLE 7.5. Adobe Application

1. In assessing our current performance management system, can I pinpoint specific challenges or drawbacks? How do these align with the issues encountered by Adobe in their transition?

   General example: Our annual performance feels compliance driven and just a check-the-box exercise. Frankly, I didn't know there was any other way. I am going to talk with my team about their impressions of our PM process to see if I am an outlier or if other people feel this way.

   My observations/actions:

2. Is feedback a recognized value within my organization? If so, how it is instituted and standardized across different levels and teams?

   General example: Top-down feedback is valued, but bottom-up feedback isn't. We need a way to rate our bosses, and it should be part of our PM process. I am glad to hear this is an emerging trend, but my company has not yet embraced it.

   My observations/actions:

3. Does my organization have a formalized process for regularly checking in with employees? If so, to what extent is it used and effectively implemented?

   General example: We are encouraged to check in with our team leaders, but the burden is put on staff to schedule these meetings. Therefore, it feels like the more proactive people—for example the ones scheduling weekly meetings with the boss—are more favored in our company.

   My observations/actions:

4. Do I possess a clear understanding of the elements that should be included in a check-in, akin to Adobe's detailed 17-page toolkit?

   General example: We are told to check in, but there is no standardized process, which I don't mind. But often it's us just talking, which might be the point. So, a handbook would be helpful.

   My observations/actions:

5. Is there someone, be it a leader or subordinate, with whom I can check in this week?

   General example: Yes, there is. I am going to find 30 minutes with my supervisor. I'll create an agenda beforehand as I want to cover my year-end goals, how she perceives I am performing relative to my goals, and any developmental feedback she might have.

   My observations/actions:

6. Do I see potential value in adopting Adobe's model, encompassing expectations, feedback, and development?

   General example: Yes, lots of value. Right now, we are told to check in when it makes sense, but many times we are not clear on who is leading the meeting!

   My observations/actions:

resilient workforce. Table 7.6. offers a summary of a select number of publicly available organizations. This overview is not exhaustive, as it omits certain PM components in favor of others. Additionally, because it relies solely on publicly available data, the information provided may have evolved.

Against the backdrop of archaic performance assessment methods, a cadre of forward-thinking organizations are challenging the norm, sparking a renaissance in workplace culture and efficiency. From Continental Airlines to Bayer, these pioneers are revolutionizing the workplace by prioritizing teamwork, gratitude, and continuous feedback. Gone are the days of ruthless individual competition—instead, companies are rewarding collective efforts, fostering collaboration, boosting morale, and driving unprecedented financial turnarounds. Meanwhile, Handu Group is dismantling rigid hierarchies in favor of agile, autonomous teams that fuel innovation and adaptability, and Adobe, the tech giant, is leading the charge in reimagining performance reviews, replacing annual appraisals with regular, two-way check-ins that empower employees and foster trust. With industry giants like Genpact, GE, Google, Cisco, and Netflix (see Table 7.6) fearlessly leading the charge, it's abundantly clear: The future of work belongs to the risk takers—the innovators who challenge norms, disrupt outdated practices, and champion employee well-being as the cornerstone of success.

Best Practices

As the case examples suggest, these companies adhere to a set of best practices:

- **Clarify mission, vision, and values.** Clearly define and disseminate the organization's mission, vision, and values in a place that is easily accessible for all employees. Embed well-being into corporate strategy, typically in the talent or people pillar.

- **Recognize teams.** Foster collaboration and psychological safety through team incentives, such as team performance bonuses and recognition programs. Align rewards with team success. For instance, all members of a sales team that exceeds quarterly targets could receive bonuses or profit sharing.

- **Express gratitude and recognition.** Like Bayer, enhance workplace culture by implementing gratitude practices. Provide daily, public acknowledgment of individual and team efforts in team meetings and calls, emails, and texts.

- **Promote autonomy and team structure.** Like Handu Group, create a structure that enables autonomy and specialization within product teams.

TABLE 7.6. Impact of Performance Management on the Workforce Resilience of Five Organizations

Organization	Description	Performance management approach	Impact on job demands and job resources
Genpact (Burton, 2023)	Employee sentiment-linked bonuses	Employee perception takes precedence as, since 2020, the company linked 10% of the bonuses for its CEO and top 150 leaders to employee sentiment. This sentiment is regularly captured through artificial intelligence that helps determine an employee mood score based their experience at Genpact.	Genpact's approach is notably progressive, as it ties leaders' salaries to the organizational culture. This innovative strategy has the potential to influence most, and perhaps all, job demands (JDs) and job resources (JRs).
GE (Silverman, 2016)	Flexible compensation approach	GE has moved away from strictly scheduled annual raises by piloting distribution of pay raises and incentives at different times throughout the year. Managers are equipped with various tools, including time off, to reward and motivate employees.	This intermittent reinforcement approach can induce behavioral changes, including increased persistence, motivation, habit creation, and risk-taking behavior. While its impact may extend to multiple JDs and JRs, it is particularly notable in the realm of rewards.
Google (PerformYard, n.d.-a)	Upward feedback	Google incorporates upward feedback in its PM process. Targeted questions, which could include workload or role-related questions, enable employees to rate their managers' performance.	This approach has the potential to influence feedback and psychological safety positively while reducing role ambiguity, role conflict, and workload.
Cisco (Zavvy, n.d.)	Elevating teams through managerial investments	Cisco adopts a holistic view of performance, emphasizing managers' investments in team development and staff skill enhancement. Specific questions focus on team impact to evaluate how managers use their strengths to uplift the team's performance.	Cisco's approach prioritizes employee growth an, success, and it fosters a culture of psychological safety. It significantly contributes to shaping positive JDs and JRs by emphasizing collaborative team efforts and skill enhancement.
Netflix (PerformYard, n.d.-b)	"Do as we do, not as we say"	Netflix employs a unique HR strategy that involves rewarding and promoting employees who align with the company's core values, as well as their well-established culture document. This approach aims to cultivate a high-performance culture within the organization.	Netflix's commitment to aligning promotions and rewards with company values minimizes role conflict. This strategy ensures that individuals not adhering to the company's values are respectfully let go, contributing to a workplace with minimal role conflict.

Consider routine incentivization of team restructuring to promote innovation and learning.

- **Facilitate continuous check-ins and feedback.** Shift from annual reviews to regular check-ins for real-time feedback. Use platforms that enable continuous, two-way communication.

- **Offer flexible compensation and recognition.** Explore flexible compensation approaches for timely and personalized recognition. Consider intermittent, unexpected incentives, financial and otherwise, over annual incentives.

- **Align with core values.** Align promotions and rewards for employees with organizational core values. Cultivate a high-performance culture by reinforcing clear expectations, providing regular feedback, and promoting behaviors that align with core values.

- **Integrate upward feedback.** Implement mechanisms for upward feedback to improve communication and to keep leaders accountable. Regularly incorporate inquiries about role-related conflict into check-ins and address these issues whenever feasible.

CULTURAL LEVER 2: JOB CRAFTING

Recall Lisa, the bus driver discussed in Chapter 5. She was growing weary of the tedium and monotony in her job and embraced a transformative approach, reshaping her relationship with her role. While her approach didn't alter her core work duties, it allowed her to redefine specific tasks, forge new connections, and adopt a different mindset. As a result, she experienced increased happiness, felt more connected to her passengers, and rediscovered the joy in her job. Through proactive reshaping of her role, Lisa not only alleviated boredom and apathy but also enjoyed enhanced well-being and job satisfaction.

Job crafters such as Lisa frequently find ways to infuse meaning and purpose into their roles by redefining their job relationships, effectively imbuing their personality into their work. The essence of job crafting lies in its potential for positive transformations. What sets Lisa's narrative apart is her proactive effort to implement these changes, highlighting the empowering nature of job crafting.

Importantly, job crafting isn't just a personal remedy; it holds broad implications for both individuals and organizations. Studies consistently indicate its positive outcomes (e.g., Tims & Bakker, 2010; Wrzesniewski & Dutton, 2001), including heightened work meaningfulness and engagement—both elements mirrored in Lisa's journey. The key to unlocking these benefits lies in how we operationalize job crafting, notably in the context of organizational resilience, given its potential for a substantial impact on personal and organizational well-being.

Side Project Time

Let's start by exploring side project time. *Side project time* stands as a powerful manifestation of job crafting within the professional realm. It refers to an allocated period during the workday or workweek during which employees are encouraged to invest their time and skills into personal projects that align with their interests or passions. This intentional provision of time for personal endeavors allows employees to redefine and enhance their job roles and to foster creativity, innovation, and a sense of autonomy.

Google, a pioneer in this practice, popularized the concept with its renowned 20-percent time rule (Murphy, 2020). Since 2004, Google engineers have enjoyed the freedom to dedicate 20% of their paid work time to personal projects. The parameters are flexible and allow work on projects that may not yield immediate returns but could unveil significant opportunities in the future. Notably, more than 50% of Google's major revenue-generating products, including AdSense, Gmail, Google Maps, Google News, Google Earth, and Gmail Labs, have emerged from this initiative (Kotler, 2021). As of the most recent update from a Google spokesperson in 2020, the program continues to be in place (Murphy, 2020).

Atlassian, an Australian enterprise company, adopted the 20% project model in 2008 (J. Rotenstein, 2009). This dedicated time sparked innovations, including significant software updates for the Jira project management tool, culminating in the successful completion of 48 projects within a year.

Evolving their approach, Atlassian now conducts Innovation Week every 5 weeks (20% of work time), during which the entire organization pauses regular work, forms ad-hoc teams, and addresses diverse challenges (Fagan, 2021). One notable project involved the Atlassian security team creating a Slack bot, named Security Scorecard, to visualize security requirements and display team-specific information in Slack channels. Following the changes introduced during Innovation Week, a consistent 80% of the team reported that they had enhanced the quality time available for their 20%-time work. This improvement underscores the positive impact of the shift and highlights improved collaboration and satisfaction when employees are empowered to undertake projects of their own choosing.

LinkedIn has experimented with a more structured approach, introducing the [in]cubator program: Any employee or team, once a quarter, can propose and pitch projects to the executive staff. Approved teams get up to 3 months of dedicated time for their projects, which can cover a variety of topics, including internal tools, new product lines, infrastructure improvements, and HR programs. Acting as small investments, the [in]cubator projects may yield significant returns. Notably, the project go/book, an internal tool revolutionizing how meetings are scheduled at LinkedIn, emerged as a major success, prompting approval for a second round of development (Scott, 2012).

3M's historic 15% Time initiative, introduced post-World War II, played a pivotal role in creating the iconic Post-It Note, which now generates over $1 billion in annual revenue (Kotler, 2021). This early success not only highlights the enduring impact of providing employees dedicated time for self-directed projects but also aligns with 3M's ethos, "innovate or die." In keeping with this legacy, the 15% Time initiative allows all employees to allocate 15% of their work hours for exploring and developing innovative projects. Previous initiatives under this program, such as clear bandages, reflective optical films, and improved painter's tape, are market successes that have helped to encourage a culture of creativity and ingenuity at the company.

Initiatives involving side project time play a vital role in job crafting, allowing employees to redefine their roles and contribute creatively. However, they are not without critics. For example, Schrage (2013) highlighted the internal struggle within Google to strike a balance between fostering innovation and considering the performance data of its employees. Schrage emphasized the ongoing debate within the company on whether the most talented employees generate the most valuable innovation by rigorously focusing on ongoing projects or through curiosity-driven and passion-driven initiatives. He advocated for a nuanced approach, mindful of the diverse skills and people who benefit from discretionary time to innovate. Additionally, many companies encounter challenges in embracing a similar side-project philosophy because of organizational conservatism regarding new ideas (Goetz, 2011).

Patagonia: "Let My People Go Surfing"

In a job crafting approach similar to side project time, Patagonia's "let my people go surfing" philosophy empowers employees to shape their schedules, integrating breaks for activities like surfing. Unlike a rigid 20% time allocation, this policy offers flexibility, allowing employees to pursue personal activities whenever they choose. While maintaining full-time commitments, employees are free to determine their working hours. A distinctive feature of this flexibility is that if an employee spots favorable waves during a meeting in Patagonia's scenic corporate office overlooking the Pacific Ocean, they have the freedom to pause work and head to the beach (Kotler, 2021). Yes, you read that correctly. This isn't just a corporate brochure promise; in 2023, a Patagonia spokesperson said that employees indeed retain the "permission to go surfing when the conditions are good with the expectation that work gets done" (Mann & Varanasi, 2023). This policy is intrinsic to Patagonia founder Yvon Chouinard's "let my people go surfing" ethos and underscores the belief that scheduling autonomy not only prioritizes rest but also aligns with circadian rhythms, promotes exercise, and fosters a state of flow—a philosophy he expounded in his book of the same name (Chouinard, 2006). Far from mere rhetoric, Patagonia remains committed to providing employees the freedom to surf, arguing that it's an essential component for enhancing motivation and overall workplace performance.

Siemens' Strengths-Driven Job Roles

A specific job resource closely tied to employee engagement is illustrated in Kahn's (1990) framework for engagement, which encompasses meaningfulness, safety, and availability. The concept of availability stands out as a linchpin, intricately tied to job crafting—the strategic shaping of one's role to align with personal strengths in a way that enhances their capacity to fully engage at any given moment. Illustrating this principle in action is Siemens AG, a venerable Germany-based engineering and technology powerhouse with a global footprint spanning over 300,000 employees.

Siemens collaborated with the consultancy Strengthscope to integrate a unique framework into their recruitment process (Strengthscope, n.d.). Prospective job candidates have the option to take an assessment that will enrich the interview and explore how their strengths align with opportunities at Siemens. Interestingly, within this assessment lies a nuanced examination of "overdrive risk"—a facet highlighting instances in which maximizing a particular strength might lead to diminishing returns (Brewerton, 2022). For instance, a detail-oriented person may risk overextending themselves on a project, triggering a counterproductive spiral. This awareness allows for the candidate and HR to position this candidate strategically into a role that plays to their strengths. The resounding endorsement from candidates

(98%) and hiring managers (90%) emphasizes the efficacy of this assessment and skill matching process (Strengthscope, n.d.).

The success of the program prompted Strengthscope's global rollout across 27 countries, marking a transformative shift in Siemens' talent acquisition approach (Strengthscope, n.d.). In a broad context, the widespread adoption of Strengthscope significantly contributes to job crafting and availability. By aligning candidates with roles that play to their strengths, candidates and employers all win. Candidates may find enhanced satisfaction, performance, and personal growth by knowing (and leveraging) their strengths, while employers may benefit from a more productive and engaged workforce.

Unplugged

An intriguing innovation of a company aptly named Unplugged is a transformative digital detox retreat that spans 3 or 4 days. Founded by Hector Hughes and Ben Elliott, Unplugged emerged from their own struggles with burnout and excessive screen time; the experience highlights the pressing need for individuals to disconnect and recharge. Hughes (personal communication, February 21, 2024) shared that the idea for Unplugged came after he attended a 10-day silent retreat in the Himalayas after a period of intense work in a technology startup. Seven days later, he quit his job, marking the genesis of Unplugged. The essence of Unplugged lies in its digital detox concept, which Hughes says is unique among cabin getaway businesses. Guests are prompted to lock away their phones in a secure box upon arrival; a key provided in a sealed envelope creates deliberate friction in accessibility that facilitates disconnection and relaxation.

Hughes (personal communication, February 21, 2024) highlighted the significance of the program's duration, citing what he termed the "72-hour effect" and suggesting that this timeframe is necessary for participants to truly disconnect and experience the benefits of the retreat. He commented that the first day can be a challenge, akin to withdrawal, and noted, "The first day people are a little bit more active, they feel like they've lost the limb, getting off their phone and then they just access this kind of deep sense of calm."

Alas, there are lifelines. Unplugged offers alternative tools that serve purposes similar to smartphones, such as a physical map (yes, they still exist), a retro Nokia phone for emergency calls, and a Polaroid camera. According to Hughes (personal communication, February 21, 2024), these provisions "eliminate all the excuses people might have to use their phone." Unplugged also offers organized activities like reading, listening to the radio, and outdoor exploration to foster mindfulness and relaxation. Hughes observed that after the first day, participants often find that time passes quickly while they are engaged in simple activities like walking, cooking, and reading. Hughes (personal communication, 2024) shared that employers are actively promoting Unplugged retreats to boost employee well-being and productivity, with an 80% uptake rate significantly surpassing the industry standard of 17% for benefit utilization. This commitment aims to combat burnout and improve work–life balance, acknowledging the negative impacts of excessive screen time. The company's emphasis on digital detoxification aligns with the growing awareness of the detrimental effects of excessive screen time on mental health and overall productivity; digital detox is a valuable addition to corporate wellness initiatives.

Unplugged retreats have proven successful, achieving a 96% occupancy rate and planning an expansion from 20 to 50 or 60 cabins across Europe by the end of 2024 (Hughes, personal communication, 2024). Participants leave rejuvenated, with heightened focus and a critical perspective on normalized societal stress. Hughes noted they experience significant relief from constant stress and anxiety and advocated for simple post-retreat strategies such as using a "phone jail" to maintain digital discipline. Unplugged differentiates itself by underscoring the adverse effects of technology and promoting daily application of disconnecting practices, emphasizing a return to a naturally calmer state.

Please review the questions and examples in Table 7.7. Then, apply insights you have learned about job crafting, specifically focusing on practical observations or actions.

Section Recap

Imagine if, like the employees at Google and other forward-thinking companies, you had one day a week dedicated to side project time, in which you could pursue tasks aligned with your passions. How would that make you feel? Empowered, relaxed, and more committed? Or perhaps overwhelmed or stressed out by the ambiguity? Take a moment to reflect on your emotions and write them down. If the idea resonates positively, consider taking the first step this week. It could be as simple as bringing more of your authentic self into meetings, provided you feel psychologically safe to do so.

In today's dynamic work environment, job crafting is reshaping traditional roles and organizational cultures. These initiatives not only enhance individual satisfaction and well-being but also drive organizational resilience

TABLE 7.7. Job Crafting Application

1. In what ways can I individually initiate changes in my job role to harness the empowering nature of job crafting, as exemplified in Lisa's narrative? Start small by first identifying your strengths, people in your network, and your goals.

Product developer example: I thrive on researching and developing new products, yet currently, it only consumes about 10% of my time; I've scheduled a meeting with my boss this Monday to present my plan for elevating this to 20% in the next month, while concurrently crafting a coverage strategy for my other responsibilities.

My observations/actions:

2. How can I empower and encourage my team to play to their strength and align job duties closer to their passions?

Hotel staff example: This Wednesday, I plan to guide my team in identifying their top five strengths and initiating a discussion on how well their current tasks align with those strengths.

My observations/actions:

3. Where can I incorporate a similar approach to "Side Project Time?" What are the initial conversations I can have?

Marketing team example: In our team meeting this Friday, I aim to introduce the concept of "Side Project Time" and suggest implementing dedicated "Innovation Hours" each week for our marketing team to explore projects aligning with our individual interests.

My observations/actions:

4. What principles from Patagonia's "Let My People Go Surfing" edict can I apply in my work either for me or for my team?

Nursing team example: This week, I am going to collaborate with my team on a flexible scheduling approach inspired by Patagonia's philosophy in our nursing team, allowing staff to take short breaks or engage in activities like mindfulness exercises during quieter periods, promoting well-being without compromising patient care commitments.

My observations/actions:

5. Where am I in danger of "overdrive risk" where I am vulnerable to potential counter-productive spirals by strategically positioning individuals based on their strengths? Who can keep me accountable?

Accountant example: Given my natural inclination towards Attention to Detail Overdrive, I will identify times in the past when I got burned out by working too much on something that didn't require that much effort. This week, I will schedule periodic breaks and delegate at least one task.

My observations/actions:

(continues)

TABLE 7.7. Job Crafting Application (*Continued*)

6. What's getting in my way of being more available–physical, emotional, or psychological resources–to personally engage in my work?

Business example: Acknowledging my tendency to blur the lines between work and personal life, I've observed that I often extend my work hours unnecessarily and struggle to decline work-related requests. Recognizing the impact on my life, I'm committed to aligning my actions with my values, prioritizing home and family.

My observations/actions:

---

and innovation. As companies navigate the complexities of the modern workplace, integrating job crafting strategically is a powerful tool to unlock untapped potential and create a future in which work transcends mere utility to become a source of fulfillment.

Best Practices

The companies discussed in this chapter follow a series of best practices, as summarized in the following points:

- **Embrace job crafting and transformational approaches.** Encourage individuals to proactively reshape their roles to align with their interests and strengths, fostering a sense of purpose and fulfillment in their work.

- **Implement side project time.** Provide dedicated periods for employees to work on personal projects. This strategy promotes creativity, innovation, and autonomy and enhances job satisfaction and motivation.

- **Adopt Patagonia's "let my people go surfing" philosophy.** Prioritize flexibility and autonomy in the workplace to support employee well-being and work–life balance, contributing to a positive organizational culture.

- **Integrate strengths-driven job roles.** Align candidates' strengths with their roles to enhance employee engagement, satisfaction, and performance. This strategy also optimizes organizational effectiveness.

- **Promote being "unplugged."** Encourage employees to disconnect from work-related tasks and environments. This strategy supports well-being, fosters a healthy work–life balance, and improves overall productivity.

- **Establish peer mentorship and support groups.** Establish peer mentorship programs or support groups to facilitate knowledge sharing, learning, and mutual support among employees undergoing the job crafting process.

- **Host task redesign workshop**s. Host workshops to revamp tasks and roles to better suit employee strengths and interests. This strategy enhances job satisfaction and performance, which drives organizational success.

- **Facilitate cross-functional collaboration projects**. Cross-functional collaboration projects foster creativity, learning, and skill diversification among teams, promoting a culture of innovation and teamwork.

- **Recognize employees for job crafting efforts**. Recognize and celebrate employees who have successfully crafted their roles to inspire others and reinforce a culture of appreciation and empowerment within the organization.

- **Initiate continuous improvement initiatives**. Establish mechanisms for ongoing evaluation and refinement of job crafting initiatives to align with organizational needs and employee preferences, driving continuous improvement and adaptation.

CULTURAL LEVER 3: ANALYTICS

Tristan Harris, a former Google design ethicist and cofounder of the Center for Humane Technology, has been a vocal advocate for ethical technology design and responsible usage. Departing from Google in 2016, he dedicated himself to advancing ethical technology practices and addressing the societal impact of digital technologies. Harris's views reflect the delicate balance between employee autonomy and well-being: "There's a difference between technology that's 'on your team' versus technology that's 'against you'" (see Bookey, n.d.). His emphasis is on distinguishing technology that empowers individuals from that which exploits them. As part of his work for the Center, the Center for Human Technology, he advocates for technology that enhances well-being, supports democracy, and aligns with humanity's best interests.

Indeed, certain industries have adeptly navigated the delicate balance between technology and employee well-being. Throughout this book, I avoid endorsing the idea of monitoring a workforce through analytics, acknowledging that such monitoring has the potential to rightfully trigger defensive reactions among employees. Concerns often arise within the employee base because of the way information is shared, particularly when there's a lack of clarity about the collected data and its purpose. In alignment with Harris's insightful skepticism, in this section I explore specific instances in which technology, ostensibly designed for benevolent purposes, actively elevates the employee experience and fosters workforce resilience.

Genpact AI Impact: Amber, Genome, and Watercooler

When discussing PM earlier in this chapter, I highlighted Genpact, a global professional services firm, which ties employee engagement to 10% of the bonuses for its CEO and top 150 leaders. You want radical culture change? Start there. Burton (2023) went further, extensively detailing how Genpact focused on three platforms for their transformation: Amber, the employee engagement bot; Genome, an AI-enhanced internal learning portal; and Watercooler, an AI integration that connects employees across the company.

Amber has effectively replaced traditional employee engagement surveys; it engages with employees regularly and generates mood scores based on sentiments. It interacts with new hires eight to 10 times a year in their initial 6 months and with all other employees at least four times a year. As it accumulates data, it becomes more intelligent, ultimately contributing to upper management bonuses and more. In an interview with CNBC, Genpact's CEO Tiger Tyagarajan (2020, 2:09) discussed how the company used Amber during the COVID-19 pandemic. He noted as an example "a pocket of people in Bucharest in Romania where we have 4,000 people, but this group of 100 seems to have a score that doesn't sound right in terms of, 'I don't feel good about what I'm doing. I feel depressed.' (We provide) interventions, launched 1-800 numbers, launched counselors, and much more than before."

Burton (2023) noted that at Genpact, learning and development is done through Genome, an AI-enhanced platform launched in 2019. Informed by Amber's insights, Genpact identified 75 skills crucial for the future workforce. AI was then used to identify internal experts, or "gurus," who contributed knowledge to more than 600 skills. Courses, called "waves," are voluntary, and Amber flags employees with low mood scores to encourage their participation. The courses, with some taking as little as 15 minutes, have had a three times impact on engagement and retention. Genpact also employs AI to facilitate virtual watercooler moments, recognizing the importance of fostering connections in a remote work environment. Using AI, Genpact assesses weak ties within the organization and connects employees who would benefit from interacting outside their immediate networks.

Think about the impact these initiatives can have on a workforce. As highlighted, Genpact has experienced notable increases in engagement and retention, important elements for workforce resilience. Specifically, on-the-job demands and resources are positively affected. For example, Amber not only enhances feedback but, as a critical resource, contributes to an equitable rewards structure that fosters engagement. Genome aligns individuals with their strengths, effectively enhancing purpose and meaningfulness. Employees can acquire skills closely aligned with their roles and thus reduce ambiguity and increase job control. The virtual watercooler facilitates connections, fosters a sense of belonging, and enhances psychological safety. In essence, Genpact's approach demonstrates how AI can be a transformative force in employee engagement, learning, and fostering connections, laying the groundwork for a radical culture change in the workplace.

Please review the questions and examples in Table 7.8. Then, apply insights you have learned about Genpact's approach to using analytics, specifically focusing on practical observations or actions.

Purolator Health's Mood Insights: Fueling Well-Being and Safety

In a groundbreaking collaboration, Cleveland Clinic Advisory Services teamed up with Purolator, a leading Canadian courier giant, to pioneer Purolator Health—a comprehensive program addressing social, physical, mental, and financial well-being. Originating from the heightened stress of the pandemic, Purolator's initiative responded to a 30% surge in delivery volume with only a 7% increase in the workforce, showcasing an industry under strain (Varley & Glaser, 2023).

Breaking away from the courier industry's conventional focus on physical well-being, Purolator placed a unique emphasis on mental health, evident in initiatives such as doubling the annual mental health benefit maximum, introducing virtual therapy, and unveiling the Mood Insights app (Varley & Glaser, 2023). Fueled by AI-based predictive mood tracking, this app empowers drivers to monitor their well-being throughout the day. Enhanced mood can reduce stress and ultimately improve driver safety, given the observed link between driver stress and workplace accidents (CB Staff, 2023). The anonymized data is then shared with team leaders to address emerging issues proactively. Purolator's CEO, John Ferguson, stressed the impact of the app, highlighting its ability to detect mood issues in terminals or groups (Evans, 2022). The app allows for local interventions and the provision of necessary resources to address challenges effectively. The voluntary app uses various inputs to categorize regions in which individuals may be facing difficulties, enabling Purolator to offer targeted support in the transportation sector.

TABLE 7.8. Genpact Application

1. How does my organization leverage technology to capture and measure employee sentiment effectively?

Business example: I am confident my company collects employee data to make decisions, but I don't know what they do with it. For example, I log daily hours, they track my days off, know when I travel. But who knows if they do anything with it, or is just collects dust on some spreadsheet.

My observations/actions:

2. In the absence of advanced technology, is there a "paper-and-pencil" approach to track and improve employee engagement?

Small diner example: We have routine meetings where we share what's working well and not. We occasionally have a survey we fill out, but its not clear what improvements are made based on our feedback.

My observations/actions:

3. What strategies can your organizations adopt to tie employee engagement to performance incentives, similar to Genpact's approach?

Magazine publisher example: I know our company collects data on our well-being. I know because we fill out surveys and we see (some of?) the data in all-hands meetings. I imagine they don't want to tis this data to upper management rewards because (1) they don't think the data is reliable or (2) they know the results will negatively affect their bonus. Either stop asking for our sentiment or put your money where your mouth is.

My observations/actions:

4. How can your company identify and prioritize key skills crucial for the future workforce, and what role can AI play in this process?

Technology startup example: We identify key future workforce skills through regular skills gap analyses, collaboration with industry leaders, and employee input. AI plays a pivotal role by analyzing data, offering predictive insights, and enhancing personalized learning plans for our employee base.

My observations/actions:

5. Considering the remote work environment, how can your company foster meaningful connections and a sense of belonging among employees, even without advanced AI tools?

Human resources company: As a fully remote company, we cultivate a strong sense of belonging with regular virtual team-building activities, open communication channels, and online social events. Our Friday "team share" sessions, featuring themes like favorite dishes, where someone shares a recipe and why its meaningful to them. We've seen increased participation, engagement, and laughter over the past 3 months, transforming from around 30% attendance to near-perfect weekly attendance.

My observations/actions:

The evidence supported their strategy: Purolator's health and safety initiatives resulted in a substantial 25% decrease in total injuries since 2019, with a noteworthy 42% reduction in injuries causing lost work time (Varley & Glaser, 2023). Over 3 years, the company witnessed a 67% increase in the use of the employee and family assistance program, alongside a remarkable 20% decline in mental health-related disability claims from 2021 to 2022. Additionally, in the aftermath of the COVID-19 pandemic, when many companies were losing talent to competitors, Purolator experienced a noteworthy 12% reduction in attrition (CB Staff, 2023). Dr. Shaan Chugh, a key architect of the program, underscored its impact on people's well-being: "When people are healthy and happy, they're more committed and dedicated to their work on a day-to-day basis."

Purolator's program not only highlights the link between employee well-being and organizational performance but positions the company as an exemplary model that addresses workforce challenges and fosters a resilient workplace culture. By enhancing feedback mechanisms and safeguarding privacy while providing actionable guidance, the program has contributed to the creation of a psychologically safe environment. The minimization of role-related stress is evident as drivers can provide real-time feedback with the assurance that it will be promptly addressed. The implementation of a real-time app holds the potential to mitigate overall work and time pressures and to contribute to a resilient and adaptive workforce.

Please review the questions and examples in Table 7.9. Then, apply insights you have learned from Purolator's approach to using analytics, specifically focusing on practical observations or actions.

Kuehne+Nagel: Pioneering Well-Being With Career Explorer

In a strategic move, global logistics powerhouse Kuehne+Nagel has revolutionized its approach to employee experience with the introduction of an innovative internal talent marketplace (Phenom People, 2022). Tackling the challenge of enhancing visibility for internal job opportunities on a global scale, the company unveiled Career Explorer, an AI-powered employee portal. This portal not only elevates the employee experience through personalized recommendations but also equips recruiters with invaluable insights for proactive engagement with internal candidates.

The impact of Career Explorer has been nothing short of transformative. In a mere 2.5 months, Kuehne+Nagel achieved a remarkable 22% increase in the conversion rate for internal candidates and a commendable 20% reduction in the time to fill internal requisitions. The impressive 74%

TABLE 7.9. Purolator Health Application

1. Absent of data analytics, what questions can I ask to understand my teams mental health or well-being, while respecting individual privacy and preferences?

Religious worker example: I work on staff at a local church where we currently have limited resources for quantitative mood or well-being tracking. Despite this, I conduct routine check-ins with my team, and I could ask nonintrusive questions like whether they would be open to participating in voluntary well-being initiatives or mental health support programs. Also, I can ask if they have a preferred method or platform for sharing well-being status.

My observations/actions:

2. In what ways does my organization prioritize mental health within our well-being initiatives.

Mental health worker: Interestingly, despite being in the field, we don't do much for our own mental health. While well-intentioned, our hospital seems to conflate well-being with mental health, with the former being about self-help, and the latter being exclusively tied to psychotherapy. There's a huge gap in the middle that we are missing.

My observations/actions:

3. What can my organization do to tailor well-being programs to address specific challenges faced by our workforce during times of increased stress?

Customer service representative: We need to start by collecting data. Our annual talent surveys do very little, and there's a latency issue. So, we may be addressing a problem that is no longer a problem, or not know of a problem in real time.

My observations/actions:

4. How integral is the connection between employee well-being and reduced attrition in your organizational context?

Sales manager example: I do think its important. While I don't see all the data, I am making the intuitive leap that it is important given the uptick in messaging about well-being, especially during economic downturns. My skeptical side suggests it might be a preparation for layoffs, but my optimistic view leans towards a proactive approach to ensure a positive and supportive workplace environment.

My observations/actions:

---

employee satisfaction rate stands as a testament to the positive influence of the portal on the workforce (Phenom People, 2022). Kuehne+Nagel's unwavering commitment to employee well-being is clearly reflected in these tangible results, setting a gold standard for organizations worldwide. As the company explores additional avenues such as gigs, referrals, and an alumni portal, Kuehne+Nagel emerges as a trailblazer actively investing in initiatives that leave a lasting impact on their employees' professional journeys.

Organizations must adapt to attract and retain talent by addressing issues such as role stress and job control. Tools like Career Explorer offer transformative solutions, helping employees navigate the corporate landscape by aligning opportunities with their strengths and aspirations. This approach not only boosts engagement but also helps prevent burnout, creating a workplace where talent thrives.

Please review the questions and examples in Table 7.10. Then, apply insights you have learned about Kuehne+Nagel's approach to analytics, specifically focusing on practical observations or actions.

Microsoft's Emotion Detection: An AI-Enhanced Approach to Combatting Workforce Stress

In July 2020, a Microsoft team comprising data scientists, management consultants, and engineers conducted an experiment to assess the impacts of the abrupt transition to remote work triggered by the COVID-19 pandemic (Singer-Velush et al., 2020). Employing workplace analytics and anonymous sentiment surveys, the team examined collaboration patterns, work-life balance, and employee well-being. Departing from conventional approaches, Microsoft harnessed deidentified email, calendar, and instant message metadata—considered passive data, or information amassed without direct input—to provide insights and inform workforce recommendations. Given these real-time and seemingly unbiased data, Microsoft developed recommendations including short yet frequent meetings, revision of problematic norms, and facilitation of virtual social meetings.

Less than a year later, a development occurred, reminiscent of the futuristic concept in Philip K. Dick's (1956) short story "Minority Report," but with a more advanced twist. Rather than predicting future crimes, this innovation focused on detecting future anxiety. Microsoft applied for a patent for Emotion Detection, which has the potential to serve as a technological guardian of employee health and well-being (TechCentral.ie, 2021). The Emotion Detection system is a sophisticated mechanism collecting biometric data from fitness trackers, digital assistants, and smartwatches. Using blood pressure and heart rate data, the system can gauge stress levels during work tasks. When anxiety breaches a set threshold, the system triggers wellness insights and recommends actions such as taking a break for enhanced well-being.

Emotion Detection yields an "anxiety score" by considering various inputs, including audio and video meeting data, haptic sensor feedback showing how hard keys are pressed on a keyboard, and time spent drafting email (TechCentral.ie, 2021). When the score hits a high point, the algorithm prompts personalized recommendations: "If the service receives information from an email application indicating a user spent more time reading

TABLE 7.10. Kuehne+Nagel Application

1. Are there specific aspects of Kuehne+Nagel's approach that align with our organization's values and goals, and how can we tailor similar initiatives to our unique context?

Big business example: I really like my company and would love to make a career here. The problem is out company talks a lot about the employee experience, but I rarely "feel it." It feels like empty words. I would LOVE to be contacted proactively by an internal recruited looking to align me somewhere else that matches my interests and strengths.

My observations/actions:

2. How can our organization leverage technology and AI to enhance the employee experience, like Kuehne+Nagel's "Career Explorer" initiative?

HR leader example: AI is the hottest topic in HR and frankly, we are a bit behind the curve here. We are prioritizing where and when to use AI and recruitment is one of our focus areas. We're going to be making a series of investments in AI soon, and it will be good to point to a company that has done this well.

My observations/actions:

---

an email from a manager than a predefined threshold, the user's blood pressure and heart rate for that particular time will be evaluated" (TechCentral.ie, 2021, para. 5). A resultant wellness insight may advise stepping away and returning later. As another example, if email traffic peaks at 9:00 a.m., the user could benefit from having breakfast before diving into responses (Jones, 2021).

What distinguishes this system is its departure from conventional employee monitoring tools fixated on performance metrics. Microsoft's approach places a premium on employee well-being and provides insightful wellness recommendations that go beyond the confines of productivity-centric monitoring. These technological interventions have real-time insights, personalized recommendations, and proactive measures that have the potential to elevate employee wellness, address stressors, reduce burnout, and contribute to an overall improvement in well-being.

Please review the questions and examples in Table 7.11. Then, apply insights you have learned about Microsoft's approach to analytics, specifically focusing on practical observations or actions.

Section Recap

In today's dynamic work landscape, integrating analytics isn't just an option—it's a necessity for organizations looking to fortify resilience and deepen

TABLE 7.11. Microsoft Application

1. Microsoft's Emotion Detection system presents a novel way to address employee stress. How can our company explore similar technologies or innovative solutions to proactively monitor and manage stress levels within our workforce?

Talent leader example: We don't have the budget to bring in smart watches and link it to real-time data. Sounds nice, but not practical. More realistically, we could leverage existing HR data we have—like time off, weekend work, etc. and consider implementing more anonymous sentiment surveys.

My observations/actions:

2. Microsoft's departure from conventional employee monitoring tools focuses on employee well-being rather than just performance metrics. How can we shift our approach to prioritize well-being and provide insightful wellness recommendations that transcend productivity-centric monitoring?

Accounting example: What's interesting is that my company does collect wellness metrics—weekend work, travel, time off—but they are couched as "HR" metrics, so some rebranding of metrics might be needed. But on top of this I just don't know what they do with these wellness metrics. But, I for sure know what they do with performance metrics—they use them to rate us. So would be nice is wellness metrics would be part of our performance equation.

My observations/actions:

3. How can we integrate real-time insights, personalized recommendations, and proactive measures into our organizational culture?

Small business owner example: We don't have much technology or budget, but we can start by establishing regular check-ins or surveys to gather feedback from employees on their well-being. We can then use this data to identify patterns, areas for improvement, and even recommendations through manual processes, such as assigning mentors or wellness ambassadors to provide individualized support based on employees' needs.

My observations/actions:

---

employee engagement. Inspired by thought leaders such as Tristan Harris, companies like Genpact and Purolator are leveraging innovative AI solutions to revolutionize employee well-being initiatives. Genpact's pioneering platforms Amber, Genome, and Watercooler demonstrate how AI fosters connections, facilitates learning, and proactively addresses mental health concerns. Meanwhile, Purolator's Mood Insights app has notably reduced injuries and attrition among its drivers, marking a shift toward prioritizing well-being over traditional performance metrics.

Initiatives like Kuehne+Nagel's Career Explorer and Microsoft's Emotion Detection system further exemplify the transformative power of analytics.

The AI-driven recommendations from Career Explorer have boosted employee satisfaction and streamlined internal processes, while the use of biometric data within Emotion Detection offers a proactive approach to managing workplace stress. These groundbreaking efforts underscore the unmatched potential of analytics to help companies cultivate a thriving workplace focused on employee well-being, whether through talent development or stress management, even in organizations without advanced technology.

Best Practices

The companies in these case examples implement a series of best practices, detailed as follows:

- **Measure what you value**
  - Evaluate employee assessments to align with corporate values, focusing on sentiment analysis to gauge employee satisfaction and well-being.
  - Analyze HR statistics related to well-being indicators such as satisfaction, attrition, retention, recruitment, engagement, and productivity.
  - Explore integrating sentiment analysis with HR metrics to identify workforce resilience indicators.

- **Create assessments where none exist**
  - Develop sentiment surveys using free online survey software, incorporating measures of burnout and engagement.
  - Conduct assessments to inform organizational decisions such as hiring, recruiting, and retention based on data-driven insights.
  - Address issues revealed by assessments, such as high employee turnover due to burnout, by implementing strategies to alleviate workload stress.

- **Promote transparency and accountability**
  - Ensure transparency in data collection, analysis, and utilization processes within the organization.

- **Invest in user-friendly analytics tools**
  - Implement user-friendly analytics platforms accessible to employees with varying technical proficiency levels.
  - Provide training and support to ensure effective use of these tools for data analysis and decision making.

- **Encourage peer learning and mentorship**
  - Facilitate peer-to-peer learning opportunities for employees to exchange knowledge and expertise in analytics, particularly those relevant to workforce resilience.
  - Establish mentorship programs pairing experienced analysts with individuals seeking to enhance their analytical skills.
- **Create a well-being dashboard**
  - Develop a well-being dashboard offering real-time insights into employee mental health metrics such as stress levels, mood, and energy levels.
- **Data visualization competitions**
  - Organize data visualization competitions to foster creativity and effective communication of insights derived from workforce resiliency data analysis.

CULTURAL LEVER 4: STRATEGIC COMMUNICATIONS

Few stories capture the essence of the communication challenges in the modern corporate world quite like the ancient myth of Atlas and Hercules. Imagine, if you will, the iconic sculpture at Rockefeller Center in New York City, which vividly portrays Atlas laboriously carrying the weight of the world on his shoulders. This tale, rooted in Greek mythology, unfolds with Atlas, a Titan, condemned to bear the heavens for eternity. Hercules is tasked with a different mission—stealing the golden apples guarded by a dragon and belonging to Hera. The narrative takes a captivating turn when Hercules strikes a deal with Atlas. He agrees to assume the burden of the world if Atlas fetches the elusive golden apples. After receiving the apples from Atlas, Hercules cleverly convinces him to take back the weight temporarily, claiming that he needs to arrange padding for his shoulders. Hercules then seizes the opportunity, leaving Atlas to endure the infinite task.

This myth serves as a powerful allegory for the intricate dynamics of transparency in organizational communication. In this ancient tale, intentional opacity results in misfortune. While the corporate landscape often navigates the nuanced shades of gray, the importance of transparency cannot be overstated. In the corporate world, where mixed motives and varied intentions abound, transparent communication not only guides organizations through complex challenges but also serves as a fundamental building block for fostering workforce resilience. Let's next examine organizations that have elevated strategic communications to a cornerstone of their organizational culture, enhancing workforce resilience in the process.

Buffer: Pioneering 360-Degree Corporate Transparency

Buffer, a social media management platform born in 2011, has emerged as a trailblazer in corporate transparency, redefining standards by strategically embracing open communication. Their approach underscores their recognition of the role strategic communications play in shaping organizational identity. In defying historical mishaps like the Atlas–Hercules debacle, Buffer not only conveys information but strategically shapes its narrative, influencing internal alignment, organizational culture, and external perception.

At the heart of Buffer's ethos lies the powerful principle, "Default to transparency" (K. Lee, 2018). Their approach isn't just about revealing salaries; it's a philosophy woven into every aspect of Buffer's operations. For Buffer, the instinct is to make everything public and transparent by lifting the veil on salary structures, revenue figures, user statistics, layoffs, and progress reports. In 2014, Buffer took transparency to new heights by making all this information accessible to the public (Dishman, 2015). This audacious step opened the company's doors to the world, inviting everyone to peek into its inner workings.

Buffer's pay transparency is nothing short of revolutionary. The online dashboard lays bare employee salaries, even the CEO's earnings, reported as $298,958 as of January 2024 (Buffer, n.d.). Using a unique salary calculator, visitors can explore potential earnings based on job title and location, providing unprecedented insights into compensation structures. But the transparency debate isn't all sunshine. In a compelling case for the positive impact of transparency, Dishman (2015) highlighted potential downsides such as envy, decreased cohesion, and workplace divisiveness. As in many circumstances, something can have inherently good intentions and still backfire.

Into the realm of corporate transparency, Jenny Terry, the director of business operations at Buffer, brings a refreshing personal perspective to the debate. Living and breathing the company's commitment to openness, Terry's endorsement goes beyond theory, showing the real impact on Buffer's recruitment landscape (Forsdick, 2022). With an immediate surge in job applicants attributed to Buffer's transparent ethos and user-friendly dashboard, candidates can now navigate pay expectations before applying. And the benefits extend far beyond the hiring process. Terry emphasized the tangible outcomes of transparency at Buffer, including a sense of trust among teams, smooth pay negotiations, and a commendable reduction in pay gaps within diverse groups. This firsthand account adds a compelling layer to the ongoing discourse about the practical implications of radical transparency.

Buffer's dedication to openness transcends financial disclosures. It's a game changer for workforce resilience, significantly improving role clarity and fostering a deep sense of purpose. In a culture in which people are encouraged to express thoughts without fear of judgment, Buffer's commitment to radical transparency becomes a lived experience, shaping the daily lives of its team members and creating a workplace that goes beyond the norm.

Please review the questions and examples in Table 7.12. Then, apply insights you have learned about Buffer's approach to corporate transparency, specifically focusing on practical observations or actions.

Button: Communicating Crystal-Clear Career Progression in Mobile Commerce

In the dynamic realm of mobile commerce technology, Button not only leads in innovation but also sets a remarkable standard for transparency and career development. At the core of their commitment is The Growth Ladder, a meticulously crafted framework that serves as a beacon for individuals navigating their career progression (Mardell, n.d.). This comprehensive career framework explicitly defines performance expectations at each level. Categorizing roles into makers and managers, emphasizing both vertical and horizontal opportunities, and outlining professional attributes, The Growth Ladder is a universal language within the organization—a clear roadmap for employees' career growth.

In many organizations, a transparent pathway for career growth is often absent, leaving individuals uncertain about how to navigate horizontal and vertical progression and the requirements for reaching the next milestone. The linchpin of The Growth Ladder's success lies in effective communication. Acting as a catalyst for open and honest conversations about growth, it aligns aspiring employees with key attributes. This transparency is pivotal in addressing issues that affect workforce resilience, notably reducing job demands such as role ambiguity, role conflict, and role stress while enhancing commensurate job demands such as job control, feedback, and purpose.

As a strategic communication catalyst, The Growth Ladder propels the organization toward high engagement and effectively mitigates burnout. By clarifying expectations and providing a roadmap for career progression, it creates an environment in which employees feel a sense of control, receive meaningful feedback, and understand their purpose within the organization. This approach not only fosters professional growth but also actively

TABLE 7.12. Buffer Application

1. Considering Buffer's audacious move to make all information accessible to the public in 2014, how open is your organization to inviting external stakeholders to peek into its inner workings, and what benefits or challenges do you foresee in doing so?

Coffee barista example: I've worked at a local coffee shop for years, and discussions about salaries are often relegated to hushed conversations in the break room confirm. This week, I'll initiate a conversation with my manager to discuss my compensation openly, backed by outside research and evidence of my contributions. I will also explore potential growth paths within the company and consider other opportunities to ensure a comprehensive approach to addressing my salary concerns.

My observations/actions:

2. How does your organization currently approach transparency, and to what extent is it integrated into various operational functions, similar to Buffer's comprehensive approach?

Local hardware store: We maintain transparency by openly communicating with both employees and customers about product information, pricing, and service details. While our approach may not be as comprehensive as Buffer's, we prioritize clear and honest communication in various operational aspects, as forging trust is one of our core values.

My observations/actions:

3. To what degree does your organization default to transparency in its operations, beyond just revealing financial information, and how might adopting such a philosophy impact your company's practices and culture?

Large social media company:

Unfortunately, our communication on privacy policy changes is opaque, lacking clear notifications about significant data collection practices, potentially breaching trust. This really bothers me. So, this week, I will proactively seek feedback from my colleagues to enhance collaboration and identify areas for improvement in our team projects.

My observations/actions:

---

contributes to building a resilient workforce capable of navigating challenges in a dynamic work landscape.

Please review the questions and examples in Table 7.13. Then, apply insights you have learned about Button's approach to career transparency, specifically focusing on practical observations or actions.

Typeform: Hashtags and Rewards in Workplace Culture

Typeform has unveiled a distinctive approach to employee motivation, a novel concept involving the use of Typecoins (T. Smith, 2020). These merit-based

TABLE 7.13. Button Application

1. How transparent is your organization about career growth pathways, and do employees clearly understand the expectations at each level?

Public relations specialist example: Although Joe cannot confirm with absolute certainty, he believes his company lacks transparency in career growth to prevent public relations competitors from gaining an advantage in talent acquisition. Despite this, he is determined to provide clarity to his subordinates about promotion pathways. To achieve this, Joe plans to initiate regular meetings or workshops focused on discussing career growth opportunities, setting clear expectations at each level, and addressing any queries or concerns employees may have.

My observations/actions:

2. Reflecting on effective communication catalysts, what strategies or tools does your organization currently use to facilitate open and honest conversations about career growth?

Operations manager example: In her role as operations manager, Mia consistently organizes impactful team meetings, performance reviews, and career development workshops, serving as effective communication catalysts. These workshops are thoughtfully designed to encourage open conversations, allowing employees to share aspirations, seek feedback, and gain insights into available pathways within the organization. Mia goes the extra mile by utilizing polls to gather feedback at the end, ensuring she understands and addresses the needs of her team effectively.

My observations/actions:

3. In what ways could elements of "The Growth Ladder" be adapted or integrated into your organization's existing career development framework?

Hospital director: We don't have anything as explicit as "The Growth Ladder," but we do have clear expectations aligned to career level. We need to do a better job of not only making the expectations even more apparent (e.g., providing detailed guidelines and examples), but also to be very candid on the promotion process. As an organization, we do value transparency, but can go the extra mile by implementing comprehensive communication strategies and workshops.

My observations/actions:

---

currencies, distributed monthly, are tokens of appreciation that employees can award to colleagues who've made a positive impact. These Typecoins aren't just symbolic; they wield tangible benefits that can be both financial and social. For example, recipients can exchange them for Amazon vouchers, Starbucks coffees, and Uber rides. A live leaderboard tracks the accumulation of Typecoins by each team member, introducing a friendly competitive spirit. Typeform uses their Bonusly platform for peer-to-peer recognition and awarding Typecoins. They also employ it as a systematic method for the team to communicate gratitude for daily acts of kindness. This practice purposefully reflects the company's core values.

Adding a fascinating layer to their communication strategy, Typeform integrates 12 hashtags associated with its values into the Bonusly platform, including #teamwork, #leadership, and #problem-solving. This isn't your run-of-the-mill tagging exercise; it's a deliberate use of communication to reinforce behaviors reflective of the culture (Heljala, 2016). Within the context of workforce resilience, this strategic use of communication emerges as a powerful tool for rebalancing job demands and resources, actively fostering a resilient workforce. Embracing hashtags like #workload, #psychologicalsafety, #purpose, and #jobcontrol—integral to this delicate equilibrium—empowers employees to tangibly recognize and appreciate those shaping a culture of resilience.

Consider Monique, a (hypothetical) astute team leader at Typeform. Attuned to the intricacies of motivation and potential burnout factors within her team, she integrates workforce resilience discussions into her morning stand-up meetings. Questions such as "How comfortable do you feel with your current workload?" and "Is there anything you find particularly challenging or lacking in terms of resources?" serve as a compass for her team. Monique adeptly recalibrates the team dynamics based on workload insights, ensuring effective workload management and instilling a sense of control in their daily tasks. The trust they place in Monique is unmistakable. Consequently, many team members express their appreciation publicly, reflecting the workforce resilience values she diligently fosters.

In the vast landscape of workplace culture, Typeform's use of recognition tools and merit-based currencies underscores a dedicated commitment to a human-centric approach in which effective communication strategies play a pivotal role. This commitment is crucial in the evolving dynamics of the modern work environment, envisioning a workplace in which expressing gratitude through a simple thank you contributes to building a resilient workforce and fostering a positive organizational culture, all anchored in efficient communication strategies.

Please review the questions and examples in Table 7.14. Then, apply insights you have learned about Typeform's approach to workplace rewards, specifically focusing on practical observations or actions.

Full Contact: We Pay You to Go on Vacation

To conclude the exploration of groundbreaking workplace initiatives, Full-Contact takes center stage. Whenever I present FullContact's employee benefits

TABLE 7.14. Typeform Application

1. Similar to Bonusly, what are things you can do to encourages human-to-human recognition without focusing on tracking individual performance?

Nurse practitioner example: I can foster human-to-human recognition by initiating regular peer appreciation rounds, establishing a gratitude board, organizing team-building activities, implementing monthly team recognitions, and encouraging cross-functional collaboration. More specific to our day-to-day duties, I can also integrate hospital-specific initiatives, recognizing outstanding patient care, teamwork during critical situations, and promoting a positive health care environment.

My observations/actions:

2. Considering the 12 hashtags integrated by Typeform—e.g., #teamwork, #leadership, and #problem-solving—which hashtags would you include to reinforce behaviors reflective of your unique culture, which would include a focus on well-being? These hashtags could also be aspirational, representing values we aim to embrace, even if they are not fully present in our current organizational culture.

Legal assistant example: #integrity, #legalExcellence, #clientAdvocacy, #EthicalPractice, #worklifebalance, #burnoutmitigation

My hashtags:

3. What specific communication strategies can your organization employ to actively shape and fortify its cultural fabric, particularly in the context of workforce resilience?

Business executive: This quarter we commit to implement communication strategies such having transparent and open discussions about workload challenges in our monthly townhall meetings, incorporating relevant hashtags that emphasize well-being into our internal communications, and providing platforms for public recognition and appreciation for contributions that align with our values.

My observations/actions:

---

at conferences, it's like witnessing magic. Nearly half the audience reaches for their phones—either to verify the incredulous or to start scouting job opportunities at FullContact. It's that captivating, so let's dive into the enchantment.

Let's first take a look at FullContact's domain. This tech powerhouse specializes in contact management solutions and is known for its dynamic, employee-centric culture that prioritizes workforce well-being. Next, the showstopper—their unparalleled approach to paid time off. FullContact goes above and beyond the mundane vacation policy; they dish out a staggering $7,000 annually per employee to fund employees' "paid, paid" vacations, as they are colloquially known. But here's the twist—to enjoy this perk, employees must completely disconnect during their time off. No emails, no calls, just relaxation.

Chris Harrison (personal communication, March 14, 2024), CEO of Full-Contact, shared with me that the company's vacation policy, initiated as an experiment in 2012, drew inspiration from Brad Feld's philosophy of unplugging from technology for a week every quarter. Feld, a venture capitalist and cofounder of Foundry Group, is now serving on FullContact's board and played a pivotal role in shaping this approach. In the predawn of the second age of social media, Brad shared his insights at TedX 2010, emphasizing how practicing a "quarterly week off the grid" significantly enhanced both his relationships and the overall quality of his life (Feld, 2010).

Harrison (personal communication, March 14, 2024) underscored the symbiotic relationship between policy and culture at FullContact. While the vacation policy mandates time off, the deeply ingrained norms and values of the company have made it a fundamental aspect of their culture. Employees are actively encouraged to share their vacation plans, photos, and experiences, fostering an environment in which taking paid time off is not only accepted but expected. This open dialogue challenges the prevailing stigma of overwork and hesitancy to take breaks. As Harrison succinctly put it, "The policy normalizes the importance of time off, breaking negative mental models of overwork being a badge of honor, the shame culture surrounding vacation, or the fear of being replaced if you take time off."

This innovative approach has yielded remarkable results for FullContact, which boasts an unprecedented 98% retention rate, with 90% of employees staying for 2 years or more, based on trailing 12-month measures (Harrison, personal communication, 2024). Harrison highlighted that despite the associated costs, the benefits are manifold and far-reaching. Notably, it aids in recruitment efforts, generating $3.7 million in earned media alone, providing invaluable exposure to potential recruits. Metrics such as belongingness scores and employee net promoter score (i.e., employee satisfaction) consistently surpass industry benchmarks, underscoring the impact of this progressive vacation policy approach. Looking through the lens of employee well-being, Harrison also emphasized that rested and rejuvenated employees not only experience greater happiness but also demonstrate heightened productivity and creativity. He highlighted that employees have often expressed gratitude, sharing that they wouldn't have prioritized, or even taken, a vacation without this valuable benefit.

Communicating such an innovative benefit required a strategic and impactful approach. FullContact (2012) introduced the Paid, Paid Vacation program through various channels, including company-wide meetings, internal newsletters, and personalized messages to employees. The initial communication aimed to highlight the company's dedication to employee well-being and the belief that everyone deserves a fulfilling break away from work, with financial concerns completely out of the picture.

FullContact's avant-garde talent acquisition approach positions them as elite employers, attracting top industry talent. Beyond policy, it signifies a bold commitment to a thriving and resilient workforce. As Harrison (personal communication, 2024) aptly put it, "Philosophically, we believe our employees perform better when disconnected from the company."

Please review the questions and examples in Table 7.15. Then, apply insights you have learned about Full Contact's approach to incentivizing time off, specifically focusing on practical observations or actions.

TABLE 7.15. FullContact Application

1. Considering FullContact's unique "Paid, Paid Vacation" program, how could a similar concept be adapted to suit the culture and values of your organization?

Small technology business owner example: While I'd love to provide paid vacations, our current budget doesn't allow for it. However, we can shift the perception of PTO. Personally, I struggle to fully disconnect during time off, checking emails and taking calls. Establishing clear boundaries is crucial. Following FullContact's example, I should communicate the importance of being 100% off during PTO. I might even suggest leaving work devices behind for a true break, just like FullContact advises.

My Observations/Actions:

2. Former CEO Bart Lorang emphasizes the importance of working to live rather than the other way around. How does your organization encourage a healthy work-life balance, and what changes, if any, could enhance this aspect?

Web developer example: As a junior web developer in a large corporation, I have impactful ideas such as implementing clearer guidelines for after-hours communication, emphasizing the importance of utilizing vacation time fully, introducing "No Meeting" Days for uninterrupted focused work or personal well-being, and organizing occasional outdoor retreats in natural settings to refresh and foster team bonding.

My observations/actions:

3. What specific communication strategies can your organization employ to actively shape and fortify its cultural fabric, particularly in the context of workforce resilience?

Supply chain manager example: Recently, we introduced "Culture Cafés" where employees engage in themed discussions, fostering a sense of belonging and collective resilience. Additionally, we implement a "Mindful Monday" initiative, integrating mindfulness practices into the workday to enhance well-being and create a positive workplace culture.

My observations/actions:

Section Recap

The case examples of Buffer, Button, Typeform, and FullContact highlight the crucial role of strategic communication for building a resilient workforce culture. Buffer's bold transparency reshapes norms and fosters trust. Button's Growth Ladder clarifies career paths, easing stress. Typeform's innovative use of Typecoins and hashtags reinforces values and fortifies workforce resilience. FullContact's Paid, Paid Vacation initiative, accessible to all, emphasizes the link between well-being and productivity. Organizations must leverage strategic communication to strengthen their fabric and foster resilience. This communications approach involves transparency, clear career paths, recognition, and work–life balance. Effective communication is key to a flourishing workplace culture.

Best Practices

The case examples show how these companies have adopted a series of best practices, which are summarized in the points that follow:

- **Promote organizational transparency**

  - Embrace open communication to shape organizational identity. Communication may include openly sharing company values, mission statements, and strategic goals with everyone involved to foster alignment and a shared sense of purpose throughout the organization.

  - Like Buffer, consider publicly sharing information that is on the mind of current and prospective employees, such as salaries, revenue, and progress reports.

- **Ensure career growth transparency**

  - Establish a comprehensive framework that clearly articulates performance expectations and career progression. Adhere to this framework during performance or promotion reviews.

  - Foster open and honest conversations about growth, for instance how employees can align their personal growth with the goals and values of the organization.

- **Implement communication strategies for cultural fabric**

  - Establish clear boundaries for time off, which may include setting expectations for minimal or no work-related communication, to encourage true disconnect.

- Create spaces for themed conversations, such as weekly lunch discussions on industry trends or book clubs, mindfulness exercises like meditation sessions, and team-building events such as outdoor retreats or game nights, to strengthen the bonds within the company and shape its overall culture.

• **Host town hall meetings**

- Host regular town hall meetings to promote organizational transparency and facilitate two-way communication between leadership and employees.

- Provide updates on company performance, strategic initiatives, and upcoming changes, and encourage employees to ask questions and share feedback openly.

• **Initiate peer recognition programs**

- Implement peer recognition programs to encourage human-to-human recognition and celebrate the contributions of colleagues.

- Allow employees to nominate their peers for recognition based on their positive impact, teamwork, and supportiveness, fostering a culture of appreciation and collaboration.

• **Set aside leadership office hours**

- Offer leadership office hours so that employees can schedule one-on-one meetings with senior leaders to discuss career aspirations, provide feedback, and seek guidance.

- Create opportunities for direct communication and relationship-building between leadership and employees to foster trust, transparency, and engagement.

CHAPTER SUMMARY

• Progressive companies are fostering teamwork, continuous feedback, and gratitude in workplace culture and moving away from individual competition.

• Real-time feedback and two-way communication are facilitated by platforms that are replacing traditional annual review systems.

• Companies are adopting flexible compensation and recognition strategies to deliver personalized and timely rewards, which boosts motivation.

- Upward feedback mechanisms are being used by organizations to enhance leader accountability and effectively address role-related conflicts.

- Firms like Handu Group are dismantling traditional hierarchies to foster agile, autonomous team structures that enhance innovation and adaptability.

- Adobe is redefining performance evaluations by replacing annual reviews with regular, empowering two-way check-ins that build trust.

- Google has implemented side project time, dedicating one day a week for employees to pursue projects aligned with their personal passions, thus enhancing creativity and satisfaction.

- Innovative uses of analytics by companies like Genpact and Purolator are transforming employee well-being initiatives through AI-driven tools and platforms.

- Buffer has adopted radical transparency, openly sharing sensitive information such as salaries and financial status, which fosters trust and supports its culture of openness.

CHAPTER QUESTIONS

- What steps can I take this week to encourage ongoing and actionable feedback across my team?

- What initiatives could I introduce to shift our team's focus from individual achievements to collective success?

- What would be the impact of implementing regular, two-way check-ins across my team, and how can I ensure they foster trust and openness?

- How can I tailor my recognition strategies to better meet the individual needs and motivations of my team members?

- How feasible would it be to implement side project time in our schedule, and what potential benefits might it bring to team engagement and creativity?

- What practices can I adopt to become more transparent and open in my leadership style?

8 NAVIGATING THE PATH TO ORGANIZATIONAL CHANGE

Of course, there is always resistance, always a drag on movement toward better things. The dead hand of the past clutches us by way of living people who are too frightened to accept change.

–Kim Stanley Robinson, *The Ministry for the Future*

In 2002, the dead hand of the past ensnared Enron, plunging the once-obscure Houston energy company from a meteoric rise, with revenues leaping from $13 billion in 1996 to $101 billion in 2000, to bankruptcy. Despite outpacing Microsoft in earnings and in projections to double profits, Enron's swift descent into financial ruin became a stark reality (Forbes, 2013). At the heart of Enron's downfall lay not just rampant systemic fraud but also the disregarded alarms sounded by Vice President Sherron Watkins, who alerted Enron's founder, Ken Lay, to the financial irregularities (UNC Kenan-Flagler Business School, 2015). Watkins' unheeded counsel encapsulated a pivotal crossroads for businesses: clinging to outdated practices that jeopardize ethics, known as *change resistance*, or fostering a culture of critical inquiry for progress, termed *change agility*.

https://doi.org/10.1037/0000454-009
Rethinking Employee Resilience: Why Our Current Approach to Worker Burnout Is Failing, and How to Fix It, by D. Pelton

Why the reluctance to change? This chapter focuses on this question extensively. But before diving deep, I lay the groundwork by outlining two primary strategies for initiating change within organizations. These strategies, employee-led grassroots efforts and visionary top-down initiatives aimed at reshaping organizational culture, are versatile and suitable for environments both open to change and resistant to it. Remember, the goal is to foster a culture that promotes engagement and prevents burnout. As we navigate this journey, we'll encounter resistance, and we aim to explain the psychological process as to why it occurs and consider ways to navigate through it. Let's begin by discussing leader-led change and the disorientation that often precedes it.

CHALLENGE THE STATUS QUO: DOWN THE RABBIT HOLE

Sometimes we must turn the world upside down to see things clearly. In the classic tale, *Alice's Adventures in Wonderland* (Carroll, 1865), Alice is transported down a rabbit hole, from a golden afternoon on the riverbank into a world where everything is nonsense. She is repeatedly frustrated as she encounters riddles without answers, such as "Why is a raven like a writing desk?" After much frustration, she realizes the methods she relied on before no longer serve her in this new place.

Consider the recent surge of artificial intelligence, for instance. This technological revolution has left many, like Alice, feeling upside down, wrestling with concerns of becoming obsolete or even being replaced. Confronted with this challenge, we find ourselves at a crossroads: to adapt and embrace the change or risk being left behind. Navigating this transition can be overwhelming, fraught with stress and uncertainty.

Change is inescapable—and invariably challenging. Many organizations find themselves perpetually stuck, resistant to embracing changes that might disrupt the business yet dissatisfied with the status quo. Even startup organizations, created with bold change at the heart of the mission, can fall prey to this trap. As time passes, work patterns become deeply ingrained, regardless of their effectiveness. Openness and excitement can gradually give way to a stale, change-resistant culture, overshadowing the organization's original zeal. Like Alice, these organizations may find themselves asking, "Who have we become? How did we end up here? And where do we go next?" If not for the convenient diversion of overflowing email inboxes and never-ending to-do lists, this existential crisis would surely be an organization's biggest concern.

Senior leaders, too, are finding it increasingly difficult to have a restful night. A recent survey of 4,700 CEOs across 105 countries revealed that nearly half of them fear their businesses might not survive the next decade because of threats from AI and climate change (Associated Press, 2024). Staying open to change appears riskier than ever—yet it's more crucial than ever for the survival of most companies.

On the other hand, some organizations prioritize innovation excessively, leading to *change saturation*. Continuous change can leave employees feeling disconnected from the values of the organization and overwhelmed, leading to change fatigue. According to a survey conducted by Gartner (Baker, 2020), employee capacity to handle change dropped to 50% of prepandemic levels. Effective and sustainable change requires a clear purpose aligned with the goals and interests of employees or the organization.

Change doesn't have to be a grand spectacle, orchestrated with flashy slide shows and grandiose promises. Quite the opposite. Change can naturally emerge and grow within an environment that encourages it. This is the essence of change agility—the ability to swiftly adjust and adapt a strategy while it's in progress. It's a culture that actively combats stagnation, prioritizing nimbleness and agility.

Who drives this change, you might wonder? Well, that depends on your perspective. Let's start with leaders in the traditional sense, those with positional authority.

CHANGE FROM THE TOP

Visionary leaders play a crucial role in shaping the culture of wellness and resilience within an organization. These leaders are the catalysts who can initiate and nurture a culture ready for change. How do they achieve this? In this section of the chapter, I outline three key points for leaders to consider when instigating top-down change. Although they may not cover every aspect, the psychological principles remain timeless. Leaders must begin with self-awareness and humility, embrace change as a fundamental aspect of everyday business, and possess the insight to identify and address resistance to change.

Check Your Ego at the Door

Change cannot emanate from a leader who lacks awareness and humility. According to the leadership model presented in Chapter 6, consciousness, emotional endurance, optimism, and social relationships are foundational to resilient leadership. While this point may seem obvious, it merits discussion.

Consider the game of Monopoly. A leader's refusal to acknowledge alternative strategies can be likened to drawing the card that commands "Go Directly to Jail," with the stern officer wearing a blue hat and leaving no room for negotiation. Just as you can't build monopolies from jail, you can't foster innovation and cultivate a culture of change if your ego obstructs progress.

When Satya Nadella assumed the role of CEO at Microsoft in 2014, he inherited a company mired in stagnation and internal competition, a legacy of the highly competitive environment fostered by his predecessor, Steve Ballmer (Stolzoff, 2019). This competitive atmosphere had led to teams operating in silos, often working against each other rather than together. Nadella quickly identified that a profound cultural transformation was needed for Microsoft to break free from this stagnation and return to a path of innovation and growth. He set about shifting the company culture from one dominated by "know-it-alls" to one that celebrated "learn-it-alls," emphasizing learning, collaboration, and curiosity over individual achievement and certainty.

One of Nadella's initial actions was to redefine Microsoft's mission. The new mission, to "empower every person and every organization on the planet to achieve more," signals a commitment to collaboration, inclusivity, and growth (Stolzoff, 2019). He championed a culture in which employees were encouraged to learn from failures instead of fearing them and fostered an environment ripe for innovation. Leading by example, Nadella had humility and openness to change that marked a significant shift from the previous leadership ethos. By sidelining his ego and focusing on the collective success of Microsoft, Nadella not only revitalized the company's product line and market value but also repositioned Microsoft as a leader in innovation and growth.

Want to learn how to sideline your ego? Begin by asking yourself these three questions:

1. Why do people follow me? Reflecting on this question will unearth the true reasons behind your influence.

2. How am I serving others today? This introspection will help you understand your contribution to others' lives and work.

3. What are a few words my team would use to describe me? This self-reflection will expose your perception amongst your team members.

These questions will not only help you understand your leadership style better but also reveal the extent to which your ego might be influencing your decisions and relationships.

Adapt Culture to Meet Employee Needs

Let's say you're out of Monopoly Jail and back on the board. It's time to break free from being stuck, but brace yourself—it won't be simple. One of the most formidable tasks for any leader is to embrace challenges to conventional thinking, particularly when that leader has played a part in shaping the current environment. However, cultivating a culture of wellness that bolsters employee resilience necessitates confronting challenges to established methods and perspectives on running the organization. What may be routine in your workplace may not always benefit the organization.

Convictional, a 30-person software company, has embraced this idea by eschewing popular chat apps in favor of an "async" work model. Convictional's approach prioritizes in-depth, written communication and provides employees the flexibility to operate during their peak productivity hours without being interrupted by chat messages. Moreover, they encourage delayed email responses, fostering an environment conducive to deep, uninterrupted work. While this move was met with mixed reactions—chat being a preferred tool for many for its immediacy and easy access to expertise—Convictional values the concentration that comes from uninterrupted work. One employee highlighted the stakes, saying, "The cost of taking an engineer out of flow state is pretty high in a business that's building technology like we are" (Venkatesa, 2022). This philosophy necessitated a cultural shift, especially for new hires accustomed to fast-paced digital interactions, as the company began to steer away from the hustle mentality toward a focus on quality and thoughtfulness in communication. In pursuit of an environment in which quality ideas prevail, the company opted for a challenging initial adjustment for employees but ultimately offered them the flexibility to develop and exchange well-considered thoughts, rather than engaging in rushed and repetitive inquiries.

Leading through change is no easy feat. There will inevitably be dissenters and naysayers, especially when leaders diverge from the status quo, for example by opting for efficiency over traditional collaboration channels (the humanity!). The leader must rely on courage and optimism to navigate this turbulent terrain. In this narrative, it's not about glossing over challenges or denying their existence. It's about confronting them head on and having the audacity to forge ahead.

Overcome Resistance to Change

A close relative to challenging the status quo is aiding the workforce in overcoming resistance to change. Although there are subtle distinctions between the two, they often share a common foundation. Picture them as two sides of the same coin: On one side, there's the fear of standing out as a leader, encapsulated within the refusal-to-challenge-status-quo paradigm. On the flip side, there's skepticism from the employee base toward new initiatives. These dynamics are intertwined, rooted deeply in human nature.

At the core of people's aversion to change lies a complex interplay of psychological factors, perhaps stemming from an instinct for self-preservation. Change triggers a primal response associated with danger, activating the brain's fear center—the amygdala. This fear can manifest as anxiety, resistance, or outright avoidance of change. Additionally, psychological processes such as entrenched habits and fear of the unknown further contribute to resistance. Understanding these underlying psychological mechanisms is crucial for effectively managing and navigating change within organizations. By acknowledging and addressing these innate tendencies, leaders can foster a culture that embraces change and thrives amidst uncertainty.

But how on earth can a leader work through these psychological resistances to change? Consider the following four simple ways.

1. Communicate changes clearly. Honest and clear communication is the hallmark of a top-down approach to change. Creating opportunities for two-way exchanges that employees want to engage with can go a long way when you're planning top-down changes. If employees were not consulted regarding the changes, organizations can offer messaging to help employees anticipate the coming changes, why they are needed, how they would impact employee roles, and any direct benefits or risks.

2. Encourage feedback and iteration. Creating a feedback loop that allows employees to share their thoughts, concerns, and suggestions fosters a sense of ownership and involvement in the change process. Leaders should actively listen to feedback, iterate as needed, and incorporate employee input into decision-making processes.

3. Celebrate small wins. Recognizing and celebrating small victories can help boost morale and maintain momentum during times of change. Acknowledging progress, no matter how incremental, reinforces the notion that change is achievable and worthwhile.

4. Continuously measure changes. Focus on metrics that matter in your analysis, and change your change approach when needed. Embed into your strategy the tools and techniques for prioritizing, understanding, evaluating, and managing the consequences of change.

CHANGE FROM THE BOTTOM

What if top-down change elements aren't in place? Well, there is hope for people in this situation, too, but they can't do it alone.

Influence is a potent force often underestimated in its significance. This power transcends organizational hierarchies, underscoring the truth that every individual, regardless of their role, can wield influence. From the newest recruit to the seasoned CEO, each person holds the potential to make a remarkable impact. Consider a fresh graduate who steps into a large corporation. They may hold a junior position, but they could also have a formidable social media following. This digital influence carries the potential to have a significant impact on the company's brand or reputation. Similarly, an employee with a modest network of just one person can still make waves. Their influence could permeate through various channels and platforms, or it could stem from their sheer enthusiasm and drive. The phrase "everyone has a voice" might sound clichéd, but it carries substantial weight.

For many knowledge workers, the daily grind can be relentless. The constant cycle of checking emails, tackling tasks, attending meetings, and responding to chats can lead to burnout. The day often ends with a sense of disillusionment, as the worker wonders what was accomplished and often continues to work late into the night. This vicious cycle can leave workers feeling out of control and disconnected from their job's purpose. But there's hope for change. Reforms not only are possible but can be initiated by the workers themselves. Take, for example, Lisa, the bus driver introduced in Chapter 5. Her positive experience as a bus-driver-turned-tour-guide, if shared, could inspire her colleagues. If successful, her approach might trigger a ripple effect that leads to a gradual cultural shift within the organization.

Although leaders often prioritize the bottom line, they can also support initiatives like Lisa's that enhance employee experience and customer satisfaction—after all, satisfied customers contribute to business success. Leaders may replicate her success or have her share her positive experience at all-hands meetings. This model could be incorporated into recommended practices for the role, sparking a spiral of change initiated by just one worker whose resilience mindset becomes contagious—in effect, a grassroots movement.

Grassroots Influence: How Employee Movements Reshape the Workplace

Stemming from early 20th-century political activism, grassroots movements embody bottom-up change initiated by ordinary citizens. Much like the intricate root systems of plants, these movements originate from the grassroots level, driven by passion, community mobilization, and a shared ethos. For example, Lisa's influence spreads to colleagues Clarence, Thomas, and Charise, who then have an impact on their team leader Brittany. Together, they share experiences with their team of 40. Change starts with one but gains momentum through organic collaboration.

Grassroots movements inspire collective power often absent in formal employment settings. These coalitions can bolster employee self-efficacy and purpose, ultimately enhancing organizational resilience. For example, Enron's failure to heed employee opposition, discussed at the start of this chapter, highlights the potential power of grassroots movements to challenge harmful policies and prevent organizational downfall.

Sometimes, revolutionary bottom-up change emerges from an atmosphere of passivity, in which attitudes are affirming and nonchallenging. Employees become so disillusioned and disheartened by the current system that they're willing to risk everything to break free from the past and embrace the possibilities of the future. For instance, when many companies announced plans to return to in-person work postpandemic, Apple CEO Tim Cook proposed a mandatory 3-day-a-week office return without flexibility to choose the days (Hern, 2022). The employees resisted; they pushed back against lengthy commutes, unproductive open office layouts, and rigid schedules that felt restrictive. This resistance coalesced into a coalition called AppleTogether (n.d.), comprising thousands of Apple employees who shared similar grievances. Communicating via the Apple Slack channel, the group crafted letters to Cook and other company leaders to express their perspectives and to highlight the lack of recognition from leadership on the matter.

Despite the grassroots movement's efforts, Apple's leadership remained firm in their approach, and many employees departed. One individual shared on AppleTogether's (n.d.) website,

> The main reason I left was because of the RTO [return to office] policy. The hours were terrible for me, 9am–6pm, and not getting home till almost 7pm when I have a two-year-old and eight-month-old was hard. As much as I miss my team and leaders, I found a more flexible and family-friendly employer in Virginia where everyone is remote and it works fantastic. I do hope Apple can turn things around; they are losing great people.

Other times, grassroots movements can happen when a workplace isn't toxic but workers align on a critical well-being need that isn't met, such as worker bargaining rights. This alignment happened at Starbucks as workers across 400 stores sought to unionize against the notoriously anti-union multibillion-dollar corporation (Greenhouse, 2024). Beginning in 2022, workers fought with the company through walkouts, strikes, and other methods of protest and organizing. In March 2024 Starbucks and the union announced together they will resume bargaining negotiations with intentions to create a starting point for agreement. If Starbucks agrees to negotiate terms with the union, this could set a precedent for other workers seeking to unionize at Amazon and REI, creating a ripple effect of collective power that can bolster employee well-being.

Leaders must be mindful that not all grassroots organizations add value. Occasionally, a mob mentality can emerge, leading employees to target specific individuals to harm, bully, or cause reputational damage (Suskind, 2020). However, such instances are rare compared to employees' genuine efforts to create positive change in the workplace.

From Concept to Action: Four Workforce Strategies for Grassroots Change

Author James Clear (2018) discussed the significance of microsteps and the daily commitment to habits as essential components for instigating change. He noted, "Every action you take is a vote for the type of person you wish to become. No single instance will transform your beliefs, but as the votes build up, so does the evidence of your new identity. This is one reason why meaningful change does not require radical change" (p. 38).

Four strategies can serve as "single votes" toward the transformation of an organization's identity and culture. The first strategy is to build employee agency. In the ever-changing environment of organizations, it's vital for leaders to acknowledge and cultivate the power of their employees in response to grassroots movements. Employee agency—the emotional, cognitive, and material capacity individuals have to make choices that shape their lives—is frequently compromised in the workplace. Employees may find that superiors dictate their tasks, tools, schedules, and personal welfare aspects like health insurance, which may lead to feelings of disengagement, burnout, or helplessness. Traditional leadership responses to grassroots movements, such as suppression or assumption of control, can exacerbate these issues, prompting further resistance, the emergence of new movements, or employee departure.

A more nuanced approach may involve embracing the motivations that unite employees, even if they manifest through unconventional channels like grassroots coalitions. By identifying and protecting the source of the group's agency—enabling them to feel empowered and retain control—and participating in organizing events as collaborators rather than directors, leaders can foster an engaged and resilient workforce. Offering relevant information that affects the cause is also crucial, as a well-informed employee base is empowered to effect meaningful change.

Table 8.1 shows a comparison of traditional and grassroots approaches to addressing employee agency within an organization. In what areas is your organization entrenched in mainstream practices? Where might opportunities exist to embrace unconventional methods for supporting and empowering agency in the workforce?

A second strategy is to adopt a human-centered approach that prioritizes employee well-being over compliance-driven models. While discussing grassroots approaches to change may induce panic, especially if a leader fears that a grassroots approach could embolden a brazen workforce, it's helpful to keep in mind that when executed correctly, these methods can lead to innovative solutions and enhanced employee engagement. Grassroots change is an approach that involves simply trying to comprehend the needs of the workforce. That's it. However, organizations often favor top-down

TABLE 8.1. Traditional Versus Grassroots: Shaping Employee Agency

Traditional approach to employee agency	Grassroots approach to employee agency
1. Centralized decision making by top management	1. Distributed decision making, in which employees are empowered to make decisions relevant to their roles
2. Strict hierarchical structure in which directives flow downward	2. Flatter organizational structure with a focus on lateral communication and collaboration, allowing employees to take ownership of their work
3. Micromanagement to ensure adherence to established procedures	3. Trusting employees to manage their tasks and encouraging autonomy and innovation
4. Limited flexibility in job roles and responsibilities	4. Encouraging employees to explore their interests and strengths, allowing them to shape their roles within the organization
5. Performance measured solely by meeting predefined targets set by management	5. Performance evaluated based on achieved outcomes, creativity, and initiative shown by employees in pursuing organizational goals
6. Limited access to information and decision-making processes for employees	6. Openness and transparency in sharing information across the organization, enabling employees to understand the big picture and contribute effectively
7. Emphasis on conformity and following established norms and procedures	7. Cultivating a culture of diversity, inclusion, and acceptance of different perspectives, fostering creativity and out-of-the-box thinking

command and control philosophies and adopt a compliance-driven mindset that centers on ensuring employee adherence with directives.

In challenging conventional wisdom, a potent alternative emerges: a human-centered approach that prompts us to ask, "How can we empower employees to wield greater influence?" Reflecting the sentiments of business magnate Richard Branson, this approach places human well-being at the heart of organizational strategy. Branson is often credit as saying that "clients do not come first. Employees come first" (Soares, 2022). That statement underscores a paradigm shift in corporate ethos, prioritizing internal empowerment over external demands. This philosophy advocates for nurturing individual agency within roles and steering away from compliance-driven models toward a culture that prizes autonomy and impact. Embracing this mindset necessitates confronting outdated practices.

This shift in focus can be seen in the evolving practices within traditionally stringent industries, such as law. Historically, law firms have been known for their demanding, often family-unfriendly cultures. However, many of the country's largest and most influential firms are now embracing a more empathetic and inclusive approach to employee well-being. For instance, Orrick, a global law firm powerhouse, has been recognized for its comprehensive wellness programs. Ranking #2 in law firm wellness, Orrick involves both employees and leaders in shaping its wellness initiatives, which include flexible work-from-home arrangements, full pay for caregivers working at 80% capacity, enhanced training credits, and free meditation classes across all U.S. offices. Orrick's approach prioritizes employee wellness, demonstrating that addressing nuanced workforce needs leads to a more satisfied and productive team (Brafford, 2021).

Similarly, global law firm McDermott Will & Emery has adopted a unique strategy with the implementation of "happiness committees" at the office level. These committees, inspired by a talk from Dan Harris of the 10% Happier podcast, focus on creating events tailored to local cultures to foster engagement around well-being concepts and strategies. As highlighted by Hannah Fabrikant, McDermott's director of professional development, the firm's significant investment in well-being resources sends a clear message: McDermott genuinely cares about its employees. This commitment extends beyond policy creation to actively promoting well-being through meaningful initiatives (Brafford, 2021).

Consider another sector, in which the commitment to employee well-being is equally pronounced: The National Parks Conservation Association (NPCA) goes beyond the mission of protecting national parks, prioritizing values such as justice, diversity, equity, and work-life flexibility. It received recognition as a top workplace and for its "culture of excellence," with an impressive 87% employee survey response rate indicating a belief in the organization's commitment to listening to their voices (Curry-Wheat, 2023). In 2022, NPCA implemented a 4-day work week, a coveted benefit advocated for by the United Auto Workers union and grassroots organizers. CEO Theresa Pierno (2022) highlighted the move as a step toward work-life balance, emphasizing the importance of flexibility and kindness among employees while maintaining dedication to park protection.

The allure of top-down, compliance-focused policies can be strong. This approach is straightforward and centralized, and it leans heavily on the authority of leadership. However, Orrick, McDermott, and NPCA have resisted this tempting siren call, choosing instead to prioritize understanding and empowering their workforce.

Within your own organization, consider the following questions, which can help you gauge whether your approach to employee well-being is more human-centric or compliance-centric:

- Do employees shape company policies, or are decisions made by management alone?
- Is success solely target driven, or do we value employee happiness and empowerment?
- How do we encourage innovation and creativity among employees?
- How do we fuel innovation among our staff?
- What avenues exist for employees to shape their roles and outcomes?
- Do any rigid rules restrict employee agency, and if so, how can we modify them?
- What daring steps will we take to shift from top-down to an employee-empowered approach?

A third strategy is to institutionalize employee forums. Germany employs a unique work governance structure, known as "works councils," to foster employee agency (Geoghegan, 2023). For organizations with five or more full-time employees, this federally mandated program requires that decision-making bodies have equal representation from workers and owners. This approach ensures that every employee, regardless of rank, has a voice in shaping the direction of the company. For instance, if the owners of a firm aim to build another manufacturing facility, workers are in the boardroom and able to influence the company toward an employment guarantee. While this setup may pose challenges for owners seeking to implement cost-cutting measures, the upside is clear: When workers' perspectives are consistently valued, they feel a sense of agency and influence that contributes to their resilience.

Granting employees more freedom can be a tough pitch. It might seem easier to opt for virtue signaling rather than to embrace substantial changes. Just as fake wellness initiatives can leave employees feeling that their well-being isn't genuinely valued, simply paying lip service to the idea of employee influence—for example conducting surveys for ideas but never implementing any of those ideas—may lead to the same disillusionment. Instead, inviting employees to participate actively in ideation and decision-making processes in open forums has the potential to yield significant benefits. This approach may include establishing inclusive organizing bodies akin to Germany's model, hosting regular community forums, conducting focus groups, or soliciting input early and consistently when seeking change.

Research suggests that people place higher value on things they helped build or create, a principle known as "the IKEA effect" (Norton et al., 2012). After all, who doesn't cherish their Freheten sleeper sectional even more after dedicating 6 hours to assembling the hulking behemoth with nothing but a disposable 6-inch mini hex key wrench? Just as building a beloved IKEA couch brings satisfaction, involving employees in the decision-making process—where their input carries weight—fosters buy-in, validates them, and fuels grassroots movements.

Netflix has carved its own path by eschewing traditional workplace rules, like tracking workplace travel arrangements, and instead offers perks like unlimited paid time off and ample flexibility (Allyn, 2020). Moreover, the company actively encourages employee criticism, going as far as to reward it with promotions. CEO Reed Hastings attributes much of Netflix's exceptional success to this unorthodox culture, with the value of the company skyrocketing from a $1/share IPO in 2000 to $500/share in 2020. While Netflix maintains high standards for its employees, its flexibility and receptiveness to employee feedback distinguish it in the industry.

Following are a few effective programs I've observed for ensuring that employees feel heard and their feedback is given due consideration:

- **Idea incubators.** Transform employee feedback into actionable projects through a structured, supportive program that nurtures innovation and development.

- **Feedback festivals.** Create engaging events dedicated to open dialogue, where employees can share and discuss feedback in a creative and supportive environment.

- **Digital town halls with real-time polling.** Utilize digital platforms for transparent communication, allowing real-time employee input and discussions on key company issues.

- **Cross-functional feedback groups.** Establish diverse teams across departments to facilitate broad-based feedback discussions, ensuring a wide range of perspectives are considered.

- **Feedback-linked performance metrics.** Integrate feedback responsiveness into performance evaluations to incentivize managers to act on employee suggestions effectively.

Finally, a fourth strategy is to take action. With the conditions ripe for igniting grassroots change, what can a single employee do from the ground up? I outline eight key steps an employee can take to manage change effectively, from recognizing emotional dissonance in the workplace to securing corporate buy-in for transformative strategies. Each step builds on the previous one so that together they create a comprehensive and resilient process that aligns with the long-term goals and cultural values of the organization.

1. **Recognize emotional dissonance.** Sense a disconnect between your organization's words and their actions, and let emotions like fear or frustration fuel a desire for improvement.

2. **Construct a data-supported plan.** Channel your energy into crafting a meticulous plan grounded in data-driven insights to address organizational shortcomings, particularly in workforce resilience.

3. **Form a collaborative team.** Rally peers with diverse skills to develop a robust proposal for change that draws on industry best practices and empirical evidence.

4. **Secure sponsorship.** Identify a key sponsor within the organization who has positional authority to champion your proposal and offer support.

5. **Foster collaboration through communication.** Cultivate an environment conducive to collaboration and open dialogue by leveraging internal communication platforms.

6. **Persevere amidst resistance.** Remain steadfast in your commitment to driving positive change, inspiring confidence and momentum among peers despite challenges.

7. **Secure corporate buy-in.** Present a compelling case to decision makers, emphasizing the benefits and positive impact of the proposed change.

8. **Advise on change strategy.** Play a pivotal role in shaping the change strategy, ensuring alignment between proposed changes and organizational objectives through hands-on involvement in policy formulation, training initiatives, and system recalibration.

It's important to understand that there isn't a one-size-fits-all blueprint for grassroots change. Although this guide can provide valuable insights, it may not be entirely applicable to all scenarios. For instance, the cases of Apple and Starbucks suggest that sponsorship isn't always a prerequisite for initiating change. Alternatively, employees can harness their influence through digital communication platforms such as social media, effectively amplifying their voices and their impact. While each workplace is distinct, the central message remains: Every employee has the potential to influence. The decision on whether and how to wield this influence lies with them.

CHAPTER SUMMARY

- Disregarding ethical red flags or seemingly innocent warning signs can not only impede change but potentially trigger an organizational catastrophe.

- The primal instinct of self-preservation makes humans resist change, often favoring the familiar status quo over the risky unknown.

- Transformative leadership during change requires humility, transparency, and the audacity to defy the status quo to foster innovation and growth.

- Every individual has the potential to instigate and steer change within the organization, regardless of their rank.

- A shift toward a culture that values feedback, champions employee autonomy, and views change as an ongoing process rather than a series of disjointed events is indispensable.

- Single individuals can ignite mighty grassroots movements, which reshape and fortify organizational resilience with their collective strength.

- The embrace of unconventional work models, such as Convictional's async work model, prioritize deep work and employee well-being over traditional efficiency metrics and signify a notable alteration in work culture.

- In environments of passivity, revolutionary change can unexpectedly erupt from the seemingly placid surface of employee dissatisfaction, as evidenced by movements like AppleTogether.

- By creating platforms for employees to voice their opinions and contribute to decision making, organizations not only validate their workforce but also fuel grassroots efforts.

CHAPTER QUESTION

- What is creating my resistance to change? Is it self-preservation, loss of control, lack of information, emotional distress like anxiety or fear, fear of how I will be perceived, loss aversion, or something else? What steps will I take to confront this obstacle?

- What could make me reluctant to challenge the established norms? To what extent do factors such as control, perfectionism, approval seeking, and the need to demonstrate competence influence any reluctance I might have?

- How can I, regardless of my position, contribute to cultivating a culture that embraces innovation and change this week? As a first step, when can I begin initiating feedback sessions?

- Have I ever received a warning from an employee that raised concerns similar to the Enron incident? Did I take action? Why or why not?

- Am I participating in any employee-led initiatives to instigate change in my organization? How successful are these initiatives, and are they bringing about the desired changes? If not, why?

- This week, what questions could I pose to my team to strike a balance between the necessity for organizational change and the human instinct for stability and familiarity?

- How can I enhance employee agency within my team or organization? What actions could I take this week, and what results do I anticipate?

9

PUTTING IT ALL TOGETHER

Practical Use Cases

The best way to predict the future is to create it.

—often attributed to Abraham Lincoln

Throughout the exploration of rethinking resilience in this book, we've covered diverse ground. This chapter serves as a synthesis, bringing together the insights gained throughout the journey and offering a series of practical use cases that integrate these collective insights.

Here's a recap of what we've covered so far. We began with a simple yet potent concept: Questioning conventional wisdom helps reveal the mental shortcuts and biases that inadvertently keep us tethered to the status quo and hinder innovation (Chapter 1). The pervasive one-size-fits-all narrative surrounding burnout, entrenched in organizations and propagated by the self-help industry, suggests that individual responsibility alone cannot address the burden of burnout. When this myth persists, it downplays the risks of burnout, shifts organizational accountability, and inadvertently harms the workforce by overemphasizing employee engagement (Chapters 2 through 4). Next, we

https://doi.org/10.1037/0000454-010
Rethinking Employee Resilience: Why Our Current Approach to Worker Burnout Is Failing, and How to Fix It, by D. Pelton

explored systemic workforce solutions, adopting a nuanced approach to resilience that incorporates evidence-based practices. Balancing job demands and resources, we navigated through four "organizational fulcrums"—influential levers encompassing performance management, analytics, job crafting, and strategic communications—to advocate for a culture conducive to workforce resilience (Chapter 5). We then turned the focus to leadership and examined the essential qualities and strategies that drive organizational change (Chapter 6). Following that, we considered a series of case studies showcasing organizations that are mindful of both job demands and resources and carefully craft resilience within their workforce (Chapter 7). This journey revealed the intricacies of shaping organizational culture, a narrative applicable to leaders at all levels, from the top tier to the most junior members (Chapter 8). So, where do we go from here? And more important, how can these ideas be applied to organizations of all sizes?

To answer this question, let's briefly discuss organizational change theory. Amidst the myriad theories, a colleague once distilled it for me simply and linearly: An organization requires four elements to change—motivation, talent (affectionally known as "change makers"), strategic planning, and resilience. Imagine navigating a ship through turbulent waters. You need a clear vision (motivation), a skilled crew (change makers), a meticulously charted course (strategic planning), and the ability to weather storms (resilience).

Reflecting on this analysis over the years, I've often questioned whether the resilience aspect is oversimplified, for two distinct reasons. First, it is based on the belief that motivation automatically translates into action. Have you ever felt motivated to exercise, eat well, or reduce screen time yet struggled to follow through? If so, you're not alone. Many Americans share this experience; motivation alone often fails to change behavior. Perhaps what's missing is a clear vision of your goals and their associations. As Clear (2018) suggested, habits are more likely to stick when they're tied to positive feelings. He recommended creating a motivation ritual by engaging in something enjoyable before tackling a challenging habit. If tasks like exercise or healthy eating feel burdensome, we are unlikely to succeed in forming habits until we change our relationship with them. In other words, reframing our relationships with our goals is essential. In this context, reframing adversity associated with resilient behaviors can be transformative. It may be more appropriate to view adversity and suffering as opportunities to build courage and shed unrealistic self-regard, rather than as entirely negative experiences. Changing our relationship with adversity in this way can strip away ego and motivate more authentic connections with others.

Second, the metaphor reduces resilience to merely the sum of its parts. From a workforce perspective, a dash of motivation coupled with an eager army of well-being wizards and seasoned with a splash of strategic planning will create a culture of resilience. But what about starting with resilience? Consider the ripple effect of this approach. Shifting toward a resilience-centric culture not only energizes change makers to engage actively but also motivates individuals to contribute and inspires leaders to craft strategies with depth. There's a well-cited adage suggesting that if we wait for motivation, it never happens; action creates motivation. In this context, action toward workforce resilience becomes the catalyst for organizational transformation.

USE CASES

Let's consider several use cases, two instances of employee-driven (bottom-up) change and two of leadership-driven (top-down) change. Each case study sheds light on the size of the organization, diverse roles, and key change makers and addresses groups as well as individuals, from senior as well as junior levels. Each case study highlights the four cultural levers essential for workforce resilience and provides a before-and-after snapshot of the organization. It's crucial to emphasize that these examples are purely hypothetical, though each has elements drawn from my 10+ years of experience bridging psychology and business. My aim is to offer insights that you may find applicable to your own circumstances.

Bottom-Up Change: Empowering Communication and Performance Management in a Small Boutique Business With 15 Employees and No Budget

Radiant Glow Essentials, a boutique skincare company located in Rochester, NY, was established and is currently owned by individuals hailing from marginalized communities, a demographic the company is dedicated to empowering. The team, under the leadership of Zara, the owner, comprises 15 members specializing in roles including formulating skincare products, selling, and managing product promotion.

Amidst weekly all-hands meetings, a shadow of disconnection has crept into the team dynamics. Maya, one of the newest team members, recognizes the importance of a cohesive culture in maintaining employee engagement and warding off burnout. She believes that fostering stronger bonds among her teammates is essential. Taking her concerns to Zara, Maya offers suggestions for revitalizing the company culture. In the face of budget constraints and competing priorities, resources for such initiatives are limited, but Zara encourages Maya to take the reins to drive improvements in team dynamics as a personal project without additional expenditure, so long as it doesn't impede her regular duties. Despite the challenges, Radiant Glow Essentials remains resolute in its pursuit of empowerment and unity within its ranks.

Maya conducts a mini assessment to explore cultural strategies for fostering a positive workplace culture. Table 9.1 shows her findings across the four domains of workforce resilience, along with her personal comments and ratings. Based on her results, Maya pledges to dedicate a few hours per week for the next 4 weeks to devising innovative, cost-free activities that address each area. She plans to use part of the time to engage in discussion with her colleagues. The activities she is considering include the following:

- **Performance management.** Goal: increase engagement to impact performance positively.

  1. **Virtual coffee chats.** Have a random drawing each week to pair employees to discuss professional goals, challenges, and aspirations over coffee.

  2. **Peer partners.** Pair employees with "buddies" from different workstreams to foster cross-departmental collaboration, for example engaging in a skill-swapping session in which each employee teaches their buddy a skill or technique relevant to their own workstream.

  3. **Growth challenges.** Organize monthly or quarterly challenges, such as wellness or learning challenges, in which employees set personal growth goals and share progress updates with each other.

TABLE 9.1. Radiant Glow Essentials Mini-Assessment Prior to Implementing Changes

Domains	Performance management	Strategic communications	Job crafting	Analytics
Rating	👎	👋	👋	👎
Comments	"We don't do anything for performance management."	"We have weekly all-hands meetings, and then occasional team meetings. We have a robust website that highlights our mission, value, and brand."	"Since we are such a small company, everyone has to be prepared to support other roles. We are well cross-trained in case someone is out."	"We don't have any sorts of surveys. We track customer data closely, but not as much with our own staff."

4. **Gamified goal setting.** Implement a gamified system featuring a visible leaderboard in the breakroom, incentivizing employees with points or rewards for reaching their goals and milestones. For instance, Sarah sets an ambitious target of boosting client satisfaction ratings by 10%, earning 50 points for her effort. Upon achieving a 5% increase in ratings, she unlocks a reward—an additional day of paid time off.

5. **Appreciation board.** Encourage ongoing recognition on special occasions by allowing anyone to leave notes of encouragement or praise for colleagues, for example by placing sticky notes on a designated whiteboard under a "Celebrations" section.

- **Strategic communication.** Goal: foster transparent communication to promote collaboration.

  1. **Employee podcasts.** Empower employees to host and produce their own podcasts discussing industry trends, workplace initiatives, and personal experiences.

  2. **Vision boards.** Encourage employees to create vision boards representing their career aspirations, displayed in a shared physical or online space for inspiration.

  3. **Storytelling workshops.** Host storytelling workshops in which employees learn how to craft and share personal narratives related to their work experiences and goals.

  4. **Open Q&A sessions.** Schedule open question-and-answer sessions during which employees can anonymously submit questions for leadership to address transparently.

  5. **Feedback circles.** Organize feedback sessions for employees to provide constructive input in a supportive environment, using the situation-behavior-impact (Center for Creative Leadership, 2022) method for critical feedback, which focuses on specific situations, observed behaviors, and their impacts to ensure objectivity and actionability. This process keeps feedback objective, constructive, and actionable because it focuses on observable actions and their consequences rather than subjective opinions or character judgments.

- **Job crafting.** Goal: promote skill development and innovation to help empower each employee.

  1. **Skill swap days.** Designate days for employees to temporarily swap roles to gain firsthand experience in different areas of the business.

2. **Passion projects.** Allocate time for employees to work on passion projects aligned with their interests, whether related to their role or to personal hobbies.

3. **Reverse mentoring.** Establish a reverse mentoring program in which junior employees mentor senior leaders on topics such as new technologies, social media trends, or diversity and inclusion.

4. **Job rotation roulette.** Implement a randomized job rotation system in which employees are assigned to new roles or projects based on chance, fostering adaptability and cross-functional collaboration.

- **Analytics.** Goal: extract valuable data insights to drive informed decision making.

  1. **Emoji feedback.** Implement an emoji-based feedback system in which employees express their mood, workload, and job satisfaction through sticker packs. Employees can use physical stickers on a chart to indicate their feelings, providing managers with insights into the team's well-being.

  2. **Analog data tracking.** Design simple charts or graphs on paper to track relevant metrics manually over time. Employees can update these charts regularly to visualize trends and patterns.

  3. **Paper surveys.** Create paper-based surveys to collect data from customers, clients, or colleagues. Employees can distribute these surveys in person or via mail and then manually compile and analyze the responses.

  4. **Decision trees.** Develop decision trees on paper to help employees systematically analyze different options and potential outcomes for decision-making processes.

  5. **Data visualization workshops.** Host workshops on data visualization techniques, teaching employees how to create visually engaging charts and graphs to communicate complex information effectively.

Let's diverge for a moment as I make two quick observations. First, Maya's approach differs from creating a new performance management system or incorporating advanced technology. Instead, she's focusing on catalyzing cultural change in each aspect. While achieving a complete overhaul of performance management may not be feasible within the first year, she's laying the groundwork for the development of a structured system in the near future. This brings us to my second point: The primary mechanism involved in creating a culture of workforce resilience is through engaging employees and addressing burnout risks. Notably, the term "burnout" is conspicuously absent in Maya's activities. This absence doesn't mean that burnout is no longer a concern, nor does it mean she is straying too far afield. Rather, it simply implies that she acknowledges moderating variables that influence the severity of burnout. For instance, while the overarching goal of analytics is to facilitate informed decision making, this process may involve methods such as exit surveys (analytics) that explicitly probe burnout concerns. Thus, analytics indirectly touch on burnout concerns, but given the early stage of the process for Radiant Glow Essentials, the term "burnout" may not be explicitly emphasized.

With that said, let's revisit Maya's initiatives. Maya initially presents the list of activities to the group, and together, they collectively decide to pursue eight of them within the upcoming year. Collaboratively, the team allocates specific tasks to individual members based on their respective skills and interests, ensuring that everyone is actively involved and has a meaningful role to play in the implementation process. For the virtual coffee chats and peer partners programs, Carmen creates a sign-up sheet so that her colleagues can indicate their availability and preferences. She then pairs employees and schedules the initial meetings. Mariam designs and prints out physical materials, including challenge trackers for the growth challenges and stickers for the emoji feedback system. Alessia sets up dedicated spaces in the office for the appreciation board and vision boards and provides everyone with sticky notes, markers, and poster boards. Nyla schedules times for the storytelling workshops and feedback circles, and she invites guest speakers or facilitators to lead the sessions.

Throughout the implementation process, Maya consistently seeks feedback from her colleagues to gather insights and address any concerns or obstacles that may arise. She also regularly communicates with Zara, providing updates and debriefing her on the progress of the initiatives. Maya's efforts have helped promote open communication and transparency, creating a collaborative environment in which everyone feels empowered to contribute and share their thoughts.

The initiatives are perceived very positively by everyone at Radiant Glow Essentials; they appreciate Maya's leadership in helping to improve team dynamics and morale. The virtual coffee chats and peer partners programs are hits, fostering stronger relationships across departments and promoting increased collaboration and knowledge exchange. The growth challenges and passion projects offer valuable opportunities for people to grow personally and professionally. The vision boards and emoji feedback help employees to feel that they are being heard and have a voice contributing to the company. As a result of the initiatives, employees experience a strengthened sense of community, belonging, and inclusion. Particularly noteworthy is the heightened intention among employees. Employees express a much stronger connection and shared commitment both to each other and to Radiant Glow Essentials. Remarkably, over the next 12 months, Radiant Glow Essentials retains all of its employees.

To close out this task, Maya conducts a reassessment of progress across the four domains, as shown in Table 9.2.

Top-Down Change: Local Church Allocates $5K to Lean Heavy on Analytics

Harbor View Church has been a cornerstone of the local community for the past 15 years. In a bustling metropolitan area, the church is dedicated to the mission of disseminating its message throughout the local community. At its core, the church cherishes values such as community, servant leadership, and a commitment to nurturing the next generation. As a community church, Harbor View operates under a congregational governance model in which major decisions are made collectively by the congregation. The senior pastor and a leadership council work collaboratively to foster an inclusive approach that empowers members to contribute to the church's vision and direction.

Bolstered by a dedicated staff of 50, Harbor View Church has progressively intensified its focus on staff investment. A rapidly escalating staff

TABLE 9.2. Radiant Glow Essentials Mini-Assessment After Implementing Changes

Domains	Performance management (PM)	Strategic communications	Job crafting	Analytics
Rating	🤏	👍	🤏	🤚
Comments	"We've seen a notable rise in workforce engagement. While a formal PM system isn't in place yet, it's a Year 2 initiative building on our positive Year 1 progress."	"I'd say the most significant Year 1 improvement has been communication, particularly transparency across all levels."	"While it wasn't a primary focus in Year 1, it will be a major area of emphasis for us in Year 2."	"The emoji feedback was well received. Additionally, we've started developing employee surveys as part of our Year 2 launch."

turnover rate serves as a catalyst, prompting Harbor View to embark on a thorough reevaluation of its internal culture. Through its governance process, the church allocates $5,000 to help address some of the challenges. The Director of Student Ministries, Tammy, volunteers to lead this effort.

From a workforce resilience perspective, Harbor View initially assesses their performance management system, job crafting capabilities, strategic communications, and analytics to gauge their status and plan for the future. As outlined in Table 9.3, Tammy assigns ratings and offers personal comments.

Harbor View Church demonstrates commendable communication practices, especially fitting for its role as a church community. However, they have room for improvement in explicitly defining norms related to performance management and job crafting, as they currently seem more compliance driven than value-centric and are possibly operating on implicit assumptions. While the church manually tracks essential metrics such as performance management, turnover, salaries, and meetings, they do not use comprehensive analytics beyond these aspects.

With these insights, Tammy focuses on how to allocate time and resources to optimize investments and benefit her church staff the most. She initially considers the church's existing infrastructure, including its connections to other churches in the community and particularly the churches that attend an annual conference including approximately 200 similar churches from

TABLE 9.3. Harbor View Church Mini-Assessment Prior to Implementing Changes

Domains	Performance management	Strategic communications	Job crafting	Analytics
Rating	✍	👍	✍	🖐
Comments	"We have an annual paper-and-pencil evaluation system that we haven't updated in many years. It may not be measuring the right things and the impact is unclear."	"Our pastor is very open and transparent with staff. We have weekly all staff meetings, and he has biweekly 1-1 meetings with each team lead."	"There's a fair amount of flexibility to 'make jobs our own.' People just don't seem know what to do."	"We don't have any technology, if that's what we mean by analytics. We track turnover, and some other things, but we don't have employee surveys or anything like that."

across the nation. Her plan is straightforward and cost-effective: She and the church leadership will conduct a benchmarking analysis and invite all 200 churches to participate. The aim is to understand the workforce resilience practices at the other churches.

Tammy reaches out to the conference management for contact information of the main representatives from each church, and she decides that those who agree to participate will receive the results of the analysis. She considers free survey software, but church leadership agrees to invest in a $2,000 subscription fee for a cloud-based survey platform. The only additional cost will be the time of her church staff. Fortunately, one staff member is proficient in data analytics and is willing to provide support.

After consulting with church staff and leadership, Tammy devises 11 questions for the survey. She ensures that the questions are concise, do not consume too much time, and are approachable for the recipients:

1. How satisfied are you with the current performance evaluation processes within the church?
2. To what extent are church roles and responsibilities clearly and transparently defined?
3. How frequently does the church use data analytics or insights to inform decision making?
4. How satisfied are you with the level of communication and transparency regarding the church's strategies and objectives?
5. To what extent do you feel supported in your professional development and career advancement opportunities within the church?
6. How well do you believe job roles could be optimized or restructured for better efficiency and effectiveness within the church?
7. To what extent do you feel empowered to voice your opinions or concerns regarding church decisions or changes?
8. How clear and consistent do you find communication channels and messaging within the church?
9. To what extent do you feel the church has ongoing efforts to improve workplace culture?
10. Do employees have sufficient resources and support from the organization to manage work-related stress?
11. How would you rate the overall burnout level of church staff?

She asks two qualitative questions and leaves space for responses:

1. Please list what's working well or what you could consider to be "best practices" your church is doing in performance management, strategic communications, job crafting, and analytics.

2. Are there any areas for improvement or challenges you've encountered in performance management, strategic communications, job crafting, and analytics that you would like to address?

The results are received and tabulated, and Tammy and her church have new insight into their standing in these areas relative to other churches across the nation. Tammy then devises a plan to allocate the remaining $3,000, partly informed by the survey results. Harbor View ranks in the bottom third in analytics, and this ranking comes as no surprise to Tammy. In response, she proposes leveraging the cloud-based survey platform to develop a series of pulse surveys for real-time insights into Harbor View staff morale. This service incurs an additional fee of $1,000. The church also agrees to hire an independent consultant to overhaul their performance management system. With the remaining $2,000, the church receives a guide outlining how to implement the following recommendations:

- Update the performance management system to align with both corporate and mission values, encompassing staff's day-to-day responsibilities.

- Create behavior rubrics for assessing performance and providing clear expectations.

- Host routine performance management check-ins to emphasize the importance of performance communication.

- Explore training sessions or workshops to educate staff on the revised performance management process.

After one year, Tammy conducts a reassessment of each domain and offers comments to provide rationale for any changes or observations. The results of this reassessment are outlined in Table 9.4. While the effort was aimed at improving the internal employee experience, it also helped Harbor Live Church better and more effectively meet the mission of the church. Through better meeting their mission, they brought more people to the church to hear their message.

Top-Down Change: Large City Police Department Identifies and Intervenes in Officer Well-Being Hot Spots

The Springfield Police Department (SPD) is among the largest city police departments in the country, boasting nearly 10,000 sworn police officers. The department has a hierarchical structure. It is led by the chief of police, who oversees deputy chiefs and various bureaus responsible for functions such as administration, special operations, and support services. Patrol and

TABLE 9.4. Harbor View Church Mini-Assessment After Implementing Changes

Domains	Performance management	Strategic communications	Job crafting	Analytics
Rating	👍	👍	🖐	🖐
Comments	"We are measuring what we value; staff input was used for our new system; there is a direct tie between job roles and performance criteria; we've begun to introduce incentives!"	"If anything, the head pastor's communication with staff has improved because of the insights gained from the various surveys. And, retention has improved."	"Even though we didn't explicitly address job crafting, roles and feasibilities are much clearer. But still a lot to do in this space."	"I would rate this as good, but the survey platform we had was just for a year. We are looking into other cost-effective ways to collect data ultimately to help benefit staff well-being."

detective divisions are organized by geographical areas, and specialized units play crucial roles in law enforcement across the city.

Within SPD, the Office of Employee Services handles personnel mental health and wellness initiatives, including mental health resources, counseling services, and wellness programs aimed at supporting officers' emotional and mental well-being. Additionally, SPD houses an in-house psychological services bureau staffed with psychologists specializing in law enforcement psychology. These psychologists are integrated into precincts so that they can provide immediate support for critical incidents and day-to-day needs, fostering trust among officers.

Due to a high rate of mental health challenges and recent officer suicides, SPD prioritizes resilience initiatives to help officers cope with stress and adversity. The chief of police, personally affected by suicide in his own family, is dedicated to fostering a culture of help-seeking and is breaking down stigma and barriers to care within the department. He is equally committed to prioritizing operational readiness, recognizing that a destigmatized approach to mental health ensures officers are performing at their peak while on duty.

While SPD has a substantial budget for personnel matters, the chief aims for a judicious approach in addressing mental health challenges and, in particular, suicide. Requesting an assessment of drivers of well-being, the chief seeks insights to develop effective strategies for supporting officer mental health and reducing further incidents of suicide. Table 9.5 shows the results of his first assessment.

With a commitment to proactive measures, the chief of police prioritizes a data-driven approach to address officer mental health, particularly focusing on upstream prevention. His approach involves designing a solution to identify and quantify pressing resiliency challenges by collecting critical data, visualizing it for different workforce segments, and pinpointing geographic hotspots, common activities, and historical trends. His team gathers all relevant data, including insights into historical challenges, current data collection practices, information gaps, risk identification processes, and critical incident tracking. His team then devises a real-time data visualization implementation plan to integrate desired metrics into an SPD-wide well-being dashboard. This dashboard is developed based on various data sources, including support codes for depersonalized chaplain support services, HR data such as work hours and leave utilization, and operational data such as officer activity logs and arrest records.

All collected data are integrated into a comprehensive SPD-wide well-being dashboard, customized to offer tailored views for key leaders at headquarters and various precincts. For instance, while the department's overall well-being score is positive, 75/100, there are stark differences at the

TABLE 9.5. Springfield Police Department (SPD) Mini-Assessment Prior to Implementing Changes

Domains	Performance management	Strategic communications	Job crafting	Analytics
Rating	👆	👍	👍	👎
Comments	"While the annual competency and proficiency-based assessment process is satisfactory, there are limited opportunities for innovation in the upcoming cycle."	"The communication structures, both central and peripheral, are robust and well-established. However, there are often variations in communication practices between bureaus."	"Cross-training is a central tenet within SPD, and SPD has a strong training program and infrastructure to support it. This ensures our personnel are versatile and ready to handle diverse tasks effectively."	"SPD lacks a robust data governance strategy despite having a wealth of data, resulting in under-utilization of available information."

enterprise level, with Liberty Heights field office scoring significantly lower at 42/100. Analysis reveals that Liberty Heights officers are overstretched, with chaplain visits for stress management exceeding capacity and operational tempo as a particular challenge.

Upon viewing this real-time data, the chief of police collaborates with the Liberty Heights captain to deploy support resources and considers reallocating officers from other precincts to address the identified needs. The chief observed similar, albeit less overt, trends at Oakwood Park field office, prompting proactive collaboration with the captain and resource allocation to avert potential escalations. Effectively using available data, aggregated at enterprise, precinct, and field office levels, the Oakwood Park field office captain identifies and addresses issues before they affect officer duties.

Over the course of a year, the chief of police monitored well-being scores and devised improvements based on trends. As this process becomes more sophisticated, the chief of police empowers his staff to devise change management strategies, training programs, user guides, tutorials, tabletop exercises, and ongoing feedback mechanisms to refine the approach.

Subsequently, the dashboard becomes accessible to department leaders, accompanied by pioneering gamified strategies aimed at inspiring field offices to compete with their peers. When SPD implements incentives and constructive competition to bolster motivation, positive outcomes associated with the dashboard emerge, including real-time identification of mental health hot spots requiring attention, easier access to mental health and peer support services, increased willingness to seek services, and more trust and transparency regarding mental health within the workforce. The assessment data from after the annual review are shown in Table 9.6.

Bottom-Up Change: John's Grassroots Campaign to Integrate Workforce Resilience Into Workplace Culture at Giant Technology Company

As the tech landscape continues to evolve at lightning speed, John, an invested software engineer at Giant Technology Company, has become increasingly troubled by the prevalence of burnout among his coworkers. His friends are leaving, disillusioned, because they don't buy into the wellness gospel of the company. John, however, is committed to the company and resolves to initiate a grassroots movement for change. Even if he fails, he is determined to exhaust every effort to institutionalize meaningful change at Giant Technology Company.

John delves into extensive research on supporting wellness in the workforce. Although Giant Technology Company is known for its commitment to

TABLE 9.6. Springfield Police Department (SPD) Mini-Assessment After Implementing Changes

Domains	Performance management	Strategic communications	Job crafting	Analytics
Rating	👎	👍	👍	👍
Comments	Not addressed	Not addressed	Not addressed	"Integrating desired metrics into an SPD-wide resiliency dashboard resulted in improved morale and well-being as indicated by upward trends in sentiment surveys."

employee well-being, John senses a deep issue within the corporate culture that unsettles him. Despite the company's substantial investment in wellness initiatives such as flexible work hours, gym memberships reimbursement, and wellness stipends, John can't shake off a sense of discrepancy between the company's stated value that "our core value is our employees' well-being" and its actual rewards and recognition system. This dissonance triggers an emotional response in John, leading to confusion, frustration, and disbelief. These feelings prompt him to delve back into the literature to focus on workplace wellness and performance management, aiming to understand the best practices for integrating wellness metrics into existing systems.

Armed with newfound knowledge and a sense of purpose, John begins rallying support for his cause. He recruits colleagues from across Giant Technology Company, including data analysts, performance experts, and change strategists to institute systemic change. The team then works together to develop a comprehensive proposal outlining their vision for integrating wellness into the company's performance management system.

Their meticulously crafted business case is supported by industry data and draws inspiration from successful models at rival companies. It highlights the numerous benefits of incorporating wellness into the performance management system. From enhanced employee engagement and morale to reduced absenteeism and turnover, the potential advantages are vast and compelling, and the data are very persuasive.

John and his coalition then embark on a campaign to engage leadership and raise awareness among their peers. Through persuasive arguments and evidence-backed research, they present their case for change, emphasizing both the financial benefits and the positive impact on employee well-being by instituting this change. As momentum grows, John leverages internal communication channels to amplify their message, fostering a culture of collaboration and engagement. Through town hall sessions, departmental discussions, and employee forums, he encourages open dialogue and feedback, ensuring that everyone has a voice in the process. John faces some resistance along the way—cultural inertia, skepticism from some peers, leadership hesitation, resource constraints—but he remains persistent, addressing objections with empathy and understanding while remaining steadfast in his belief that change is both necessary and achievable.

Ultimately, John's grassroots approach proves successful. With the support of his coalition and the employee community, Giant Technology Company embraces the idea of integrating wellness into its performance management system. As changes are implemented, John monitors their effectiveness, ensuring ongoing improvement and refinement.

However, Giant Technology Company's journey toward institutionalizing change is not yet complete. Formalizing such a significant shift requires careful planning and execution. John continues to play a pivotal role, advising on a change strategy that encompassed policy and procedure formation, training and development initiatives, and reassessing recognition and reward systems within the performance management framework.

In summary, driven by his passion, dedication, and unwavering commitment, John successfully moves the needle on institutionalization of change by investing considerable time

- galvanizing a coalition of like-minded colleagues dedicated to employee well-being (100 hours);

- conducting extensive research and crafting a compelling business case (450 hours);

- advocating to leadership and key stakeholders with persuasive arguments and evidence-based research (50 hours);

- leveraging internal communication channels to amplify the importance of integrating wellness into the performance management system (100 hours); and

- building sufficient momentum to garner executive support and implementation of John's recommendations (400 hours).

A word of encouragement: If you're skeptical about the feasibility of these types of large-scale change—perhaps you believe they are oversimplified or impractical, or you question the potential for grassroots efforts to drive institutional change—I offer two considerations. First, note that John and his team dedicated more than 1,000 hours of their spare time to the initiative. Implementing change is complex and multifaceted and demands concerted effort, with individuals like John (or like you) weighing whether the upfront time investment outweighs the eventual benefits. It certainly did for John. With unwavering conviction and determination like John's, meaningful change can indeed be realized. Second, recognize the numerous examples of successful bottom-up organizational change, including Google's response to sexual harassment (Elias, 2020), whistleblowers challenging corporate ethics (e.g., Nurhidayat & Kusumasari, 2019), and Starbucks' initiatives on racial bias (Gabbatt, 2018).

Eyrich et al. (2019) highlighted Dr. Tadataka Yamada's influential leadership at Glaxo SmithKline (GSK), showcasing how a single individual can transform an organization's ethical compass. Dr. Yamada's pivotal moment came upon discovering GSK's involvement in a lawsuit against Nelson Mandela and the South African government regarding HIV/AIDS drug accessibility. He engaged his research team, emphasizing GSK's moral obligation to alleviate human suffering. Through his unwavering conviction, he persuaded GSK to drop the lawsuit and slash prices of antiretroviral drugs. Dr. Yamada's persistent dedication catalyzed a cultural shift within GSK, elevating global health initiatives as organizational priorities. Notably, his impact underscores the profound influence of an individual with moral clarity and a resolute voice advocating for change.

CHAPTER SUMMARY

- The Case Study on Radiant Glow Essentials shows that
  - Empowerment and active engagement are critical in small businesses, even without a budget.
  - Creative, cost-effective cultural strategies can significantly enhance team dynamics and employee satisfaction.
  - Personal projects and leadership initiatives, like those undertaken by Maya, can drive cultural change and improve performance management through grassroots efforts.
- The Case Study on Harbor View Church shows that
  - Strategic investments in analytics and performance management systems can lead to positive organizational outcomes.

- Benchmarking against similar organizations can provide valuable insights and drive targeted improvements.
- Allocating funds judiciously toward technology and consultancy can enhance data-driven decision making and performance evaluations.

- The Case Study on Springfield Police Department shows that
  - Proactive, data-driven approaches to resilience can identify and address departmental and individual stress points effectively.
  - Implementing a well-being dashboard allows for real-time monitoring and management of employee resilience.
  - Collaboration between different levels of leadership is essential to successfully address and mitigate mental health challenges.

- The Case Study on Giant Technology Company shows that
  - Grassroots movements, led by dedicated individuals like John, can institutionalize significant changes in large organizations.
  - Integrating wellness into performance management systems aligns corporate values with actual practices, enhancing employee well-being.
  - Persistent advocacy and leveraging internal communication channels are key to overcoming resistance and implementing new strategies.

CHAPTER QUESTIONS

- Which strategic levers should I focus on to enhance resilience and reduce turnover within my team?

- Am I equipping my leaders with the necessary tools and training to effectively drive and sustain organizational change?

- How can I better leverage data and analytics to inform my strategic decisions and improve employee well-being?

- In what ways can I foster a more inclusive and engaging culture that empowers all employees to contribute to change?

- Is our current performance management system aligned with our organizational values and equipped to support employee growth and well-being?

- What proactive steps can I take to ensure that our resilience initiatives effectively prepare us to handle future challenges?

EPILOGUE

Challenge and adversity are intrinsic to the human experience, deeply ingrained in the fabric of our existence. Rather than catching us off guard, they offer opportunities for growth when met with courage and grace. These principles extend seamlessly to organizations. When confronted with challenges such as overwork, heightened cognitive load, emotional exhaustion, and lack of transparency, the very core of our essence, and the workforce by extension, can be tested. Inevitable as they are, these challenges can either fortify or fracture us. However, one thing is certain: After confronting adversity, we are not the same. So why not harness adversity to cultivate a culture of resilience?

What follows is not just a summary; it is also a call to action presented as rules to live by. While "rules" may sound authoritarian, the essence of these 10 rules of resilience lies in foundational values. These are not just abstract ideals. They are practical guidelines designed for daily life, and they can foster personal resilience and aid in cascading these practices across the workforce.

https://doi.org/10.1037/0000454-011

RULE 1: EMBRACE ADVERSITY FOR FOUNDATIONAL RESILIENCE

We must accept adversity as a prerequisite for resilience. In U.S. culture, the age-old debate between confronting adversity head-on and avoiding suffering altogether has long been a point of contention. Traditional mindsets advocate for a stiff-upper-lip approach, urging individuals to weather life's storms with unwavering resilience, whereas modern Western society tends to favor a comfortable, pain-free existence. Yet nestled within the realm of clinical psychology lies a revolutionary perspective: acceptance and commitment therapy (ACT). Unlike conventional wisdom that seeks to suppress negative thoughts and emotions, ACT is based on the idea of psychological flexibility; individuals learn to embrace the present moment, fully engage with life's challenges, and navigate them with grace and resilience. It's a paradigm shift that invites us to rethink our relationship with discomfort and recognize it as an integral part of the human experience. I urge you to explore this concept further. ACT is easily accessible to the general public, thanks in part to an extensive collection of workbooks and resources tailored for everyday readers.

RULE 2: QUESTION AND RETHINK ESTABLISHED NORMS

To drive innovation and progress, we must bravely question conventional wisdom and established truths. This principle applies across various domains, from rethinking beliefs about burnout and mental health stigma to reevaluating workforce engagement strategies. The first step in this process is to understand and label any resistance we might have to challenging the status quo. This resistance could be rooted in a desire for control, perfectionism, a need for approval, or a fear of change. It could also stem from emotional distress such as anxiety or fear, a concern about perceptions, or an aversion to loss. Once we've identified these barriers, we can take steps to confront and overcome them. In doing so, we move beyond passive acceptance and boldly question widely accepted beliefs, leading to true advancement.

RULE 3: STAY VIGILANT OF BURNOUT OR RISK THE FROG'S SLOW BOIL

Burnout is a stealthy adversary, mirroring the fable of the frog in the kettle: The temperature rises incrementally, and the frog, unaware, finds itself in peril too late. This fable strikingly parallels the modern workplace, where factors like overwhelming workloads, perceived injustices, and a lack of autonomy subtly embed themselves into the fabric of daily routines. These elements, though insidious, become normalized to the point at which workers overlook warning signs until the burden becomes unbearable. Recognizing and addressing these early indicators of burnout is crucial to maintaining not just individual well-being but also the health of the organizational culture.

RULE 4: PRIORITIZE BREAKS FROM WORK—YOUR LIFE MAY DEPEND ON IT

Ignoring burnout can lead to catastrophic outcomes, making work-related stress the fifth leading cause of death in the United States (Schulte, 2018, 2022; see also Chapter 2). The emergence of American karoshi, echoing Japan's fatal overwork syndrome, signals a grave health crisis with job stress implicated in a 29% surge in heart disease and stroke deaths since 2000 (Pega et al., 2021). This stark reality underscores the lethal risks of burnout, which diminishes brain function, impairing decision making and emotional regulation, and significantly increases mortality rates (Loh & Kanai, 2014; Pega et al., 2021). The convergence of individual avoidance strategies and organizational practices that intensify stress has created a toxic environment, driving employees to seek workplaces that prioritize well-being to escape the potential of dying from overwork. Fortunately, regular breaks stand out as a critical defense, markedly reducing stress and cognitive strain while boosting focus and engagement (Microsoft WorkLab, 2021). Remember, taking a break isn't just beneficial; your life may very well depend on it.

RULE 5: CUSTOMIZE YOUR DEFENSE AGAINST BURNOUT

While organizations bear responsibility for fostering fair and resilient work environments, it's essential to recognize that susceptibility to burnout may be related to temperament. For instance, if you find yourself higher on the neuroticism scale—characterized by a tendency to experience more negative emotions—you are at increased risk for burnout (Bianchi, 2018). Unsure if you're neurotic? Consider evaluating your levels of frequent worry, emotional reactivity, stress sensitivity, and mood fluctuations as indicators. Taking proactive measures to fortify yourself against burnout is paramount. Develop self-awareness, prioritize stress management, establish boundaries, engage in ACT practices, and cultivate self-compassion.

RULE 6: BE ON GUARD–BURNOUT IS CONTAGIOUS

Burnout is the kryptonite of workforce resilience. Just as kryptonite weakens Superman, burnout undermines the collective strength of an organization's workforce. Furthermore, negative emotions tend to spread more rapidly and potently than positive ones, compounding the detrimental effects of burnout (National Research Council, 1994). The heartbeat of burnout pulsates with negativity, depleting energy through emotional exhaustion, optimism through cynicism, and productivity through apathy. Enhance your emotional awareness by engaging in practices that boost emotional intelligence, actively seek feedback on your interactions, remain attuned to the emotional states of your colleagues, and adapt your behavior to support a positive environment. Protect yourself from burnout contagion by prioritizing self-care, developing your emotional literacy, and proactively building resilience.

RULE 7: SEEK DEPTH BEYOND ENGAGEMENT

Engagement and burnout, surprisingly, can exist simultaneously, creating a perilous mix. As discussed in Chapter 4, a pivotal study (Moeller et al., 2018) revealed that individuals classified as "engaged–exhausted," had high levels of engagement but also suffered from severe burnout; they were likely to consider leaving their jobs. This finding highlights the critical need for balance to avoid the dangers of excessive engagement. The question then arises: How do we optimize employee potential without crossing into burnout territory? Arianna Huffington's collapse from exhaustion and sleep deprivation in 2007 (Huffington, 2017) starkly illustrates the dangers of overwork and the neglect of self-care and serves as a real-life example that too much engagement, while seemingly beneficial, can become harmful if not kept in check. This scenario underlines the "too-much-of-a good thing" principle, highlighting the thin boundary between healthy engagement and harmful exhaustion. It serves as a caution that even the most dedicated individuals face the risk of burnout if they do not maintain a balanced approach.

RULE 8: DRIVE RESILIENCE (AND PROFIT) THROUGH CULTURE

Workforce resilience balances conditions that lead toward engagement and away from burnout. Among these conditions are a series of cultural levers that serve as conduits for company values and play a pivotal role in shaping organizational culture. These levers include performance management, analytics, strategic communications, and job crafting. Each lever is supported by a robust empirical foundation. Embracing these practices is not merely an ethical choice; it's a strategic imperative with tangible financial implications for the company.

RULE 9: EMBODY RESILIENCE DAILY

Certain leadership qualities stand up above others, as discussed in Chapter 6. Think of leaders like Indra Nooyi, whose consciousness, dependability, and diligence drove transformative change at PepsiCo. Then there's Oprah Winfrey, whose optimism and ability to navigate adversity inspired millions. And let's not forget Jose Salvador Alvarenga, whose emotional endurance during harrowing survival at sea speaks volumes about resilience in the face of unimaginable challenges. Such leadership qualities, buoyed by social relationships, not only bolster individual resilience but also cascade to teams and shape organizational culture. The good news is that these traits can be nurtured, but amidst cultivating these positive traits, we must also be vigilant of the toxic quadruplets: self-pity, self-righteousness, self-absorption, and self-sufficiency, which are infectious and will corrode any culture. It's about challenging our thinking—not just nurturing the positive but intentionally buffering from the negative—for the sake of employee culture and, ultimately, progress.

RULE 10: WIELD YOUR INFLUENCE TO ALTER YOUR ORGANIZATION'S DNA

A grassroots approach has the power to significantly alter an organization's direction. Often, the desire for change is sparked by existing norms that no longer serve the organization's best interests. Whether driven by a commitment to principles like environmental stewardship, diversity and inclusion, and employee well-being or perhaps by a dissatisfaction with the current way of doing things, individuals (like you!) can create substantial shifts in the architecture of an organization. Your personal conviction and advocacy can create a domino effect, transforming the very core of your organization. It doesn't matter if you're the first employee or the 10,000th—your voice is crucial. Use it wisely. Change doesn't require rebellion but rather a dedicated effort to improve the culture of the organization from within.

In navigating the implementation of these 10 steps, courage emerges as a critical yet elusive factor. Famed economist John Maynard Keynes emphasized this sentiment, suggesting a deep-seated psychological attachment to our existing beliefs and ideas. Keynes (1936) famously remarked, "The difficulty lies, not in the new ideas, but in escaping from the old ones" (p. 4). Thus, while the path forward seems clear, it's the courage to challenge or break away from entrenched beliefs that presents the primary obstacle to innovation. So, here is your commission: With courage, dare to be bold, reevaluate your established beliefs, and be willing to stand out from the crowd. This pioneering approach sparks innovation, something sorely lacking but with vast potential, in the field of workforce resilience.

References

Acosta, J. D., Becker, A., Cerully, J. L., Fisher, M. P., Martin, L. T., Vardavas, R., Slaughter, M. E., & Schell, T. L. (2014, September 30). *Mental health stigma in the military*. RAND Corporation. https://www.rand.org/pubs/research_reports/RR426.html https://doi.org/10.7249/RR426

Adobe. (n.d.). *Check-in*. Retrieved January 6, 2024, from https://www.adobe.com/check-in.html

Aflac. (n.d.). *Aflac workforces report: An employee benefits survey*. Retrieved September 15, 2023, from https://www.aflac.com/business/resources/aflac-workforces-report/default.aspx

Agbelusi, S. (2020). *3 key areas leaders should focus on to succeed in the modern workplace*. Medium. https://sopeagbelusi.medium.com/3-key-areas-leaders-should-focus-on-to-succeed-in-the-modern-workplace-a50d0220ccf6

Agence France-Presse. (2016, October 8). Japan: One fifth of employees at risk of death from overwork—Report. *The Guardian*. https://www.theguardian.com/world/2016/oct/08/japan-one-fifth-of-employees-at-risk-of-death-from-overwork-report

Alarcon, G. M. (2011). A meta-analysis of burnout with job demands, resources, and attitudes. *Journal of Vocational Behavior, 79*(2), 549–562. https://doi.org/10.1016/j.jvb.2011.03.007

Albulescu, P., Macsinga, I., Rusu, A., Sulea, C., Bodnaru, A., & Tulbure, B. T. (2022). "Give me a break!" A systematic review and meta-analysis on the efficacy of micro-breaks for increasing well-being and performance. *PLoS One, 17*(8), Article e0272460. https://doi.org/10.1371/journal.pone.0272460

Ali, H., & Subah, N. (2022, June 1). *DEI is foundational to workforce resilience*. Center for Strategic & International Studies. https://www.csis.org/analysis/dei-foundational-workforce-resilience

Allyn, B. (2020, September 15). *Netflix CEO embraces 'no rules,' but work is anything but chill*. NPR. https://www.npr.org/2020/09/15/912917612/netflix-ceo-embraces-no-rules-but-work-is-anything-but-chill

American Psychological Association. (2006, March 20). *Multitasking: Switching costs.* https://www.apa.org/topics/research/multitasking

American Psychological Association. (2023, May 12). *Employers need to focus on workplace burnout: Here's why.* https://www.apa.org/topics/healthy-workplaces/workplace-burnout

Anderson, K., & Looi, J. C. (2020). Chronic Zoom syndrome: Emergence of an insidious and debilitating mental health disorder during COVID-19. *Australasian Psychiatry, 28*(6), 669. https://doi.org/10.1177/1039856220960380

Anderson, P. (2018, May 7). *Physicians experience highest suicide rate of any profession.* Medscape. https://www.medscape.com/viewarticle/896257?scode=msp&st=fpf&socialSite=google&form=login#vp_1

Angelini, G. (2023, February 19). Big five model personality traits and job burnout: A systematic literature review. *BMC Psychology, 11*(1), Article 49. https://doi.org/10.1186/s40359-023-01056-y

Aon. (2022). *A guide to workforce resilience.* https://insights-north-america.aon.com/enhancing-wellbeing/aon-a-guide-to-workforce-resilience-ebook

AppleTogether. (n.d.). *Goodbye messages from former Apple employees.* Retrieved March 25, 2024, from https://appletogether.org/goodbye-apple.html

Armstrong, D. (2019, February 21). *Sackler embraced plan to conceal OxyContin's strength from doctors, sealed testimony shows.* ProPublica. https://www.propublica.org/article/richard-sackler-oxycontin-oxycodone-strength-conceal-from-doctors-sealed-testimony

Asch, S. E. (1955). Opinions and social pressure. *Journal of Personality and Social Psychology, 24*(2), 23–32. https://www.jstor.org/stable/24943779

Associated Press. (2024, January 16). *Nearly half of CEOs fear their companies won't survive 10 years due to AI and climate change.* Fast Company. https://www.fastcompany.com/91011371/nearly-half-ceos-fear-their-companies-wont-survive-10-years-as-ai-climate-challenges-grow

Attenberg, J. (2020, August 19). Is resilience overrated? *The New York Times.* https://www.nytimes.com/2020/08/19/health/resilience-overrated.html

Attorney General Press Office. (2022, March 3). *Attorney General Bonta announces details of $6 billion settlement with Purdue Pharma and Sackler family.* State of California Department of Justice. https://oag.ca.gov/news/press-releases/attorney-general-bonta-announces-details-6-billion-settlement-purdue-pharma-and

Auxier, B., Westcott, K., & Bucaille, A. (2021, December 1). *Mental health goes mobile: The mental health app market will keep on growing.* Deloitte. https://www2.deloitte.com/us/en/insights/industry/technology/technology-media-and-telecom-predictions/2022/mental-health-app-market.html

A-Z Quotes. (n.d.). *Merry go round quotes.* Retrieved September 15, 2023, from https://www.azquotes.com/quotes/topics/merry-go-round.html

Bailenson, J. (2021). Nonverbal overload: A theoretical argument for the causes of Zoom fatigue. *Technology, Mind, and Behavior, 2*(1). https://doi.org/10.1037/tmb0000030

Baker, M. (2020, October 14). *Change fatigue is rising; first tackle small everyday changes*. Gartner. https://www.gartner.com/smarterwithgartner/how-to-reduce-the-risk-of-employee-change-fatigue

Bakker, A. B., Demerouti, E., & Sanz-Vergel, A. I. (2014, March 21). Burnout and work engagement: The JD–R approach. *Annual Review of Organizational Psychology and Organizational Behavior, 1*(1), 389–411. https://doi.org/10.1146/annurev-orgpsych-031413-091235

Bakker, A. B., Hakanen, J. J., Demerouti, E., & Xanthopoulou, D. (2007). Job resources boost work engagement particularly when job demands are high. *Journal of Educational Psychology, 99*(2), 274–284. https://doi.org/10.1037/0022-0663.99.2.274

Bakker, A. B., Le Blanc, P. M., & Schaufeli, W. B. (2005). Burnout contagion among intensive care nurses. *Journal of Advanced Nursing, 51*(3), 276–287. https://doi.org/10.1111/j.1365-2648.2005.03494.x

Bakker, A. B., & Schaufeli, W. B. (2000). Burnout contagion processes among teachers. *Journal of Applied Social Psychology, 30*(11), 2289–2308. https://doi.org/10.1111/j.1559-1816.2000.tb02437.x

Barrick, R. F., & Mount, M. K. (1991). The Big Five personality dimensions and job performance: A meta-analysis. *Personnel Psychology, 44*(1), 1–26. https://doi.org/10.1111/j.1744-6570.1991.tb00688.x

Baumeister, R. F., Vohs, K. D., & Tice, D. M. (2007). The strength model of self-control. *Current Directions in Psychological Science, 16*(6), 351–355. https://doi.org/10.1111/j.1467-8721.2007.00534.x

Beck, J., Loretz, E., & Rasch, B. (2022). Stress dynamically reduces sleep depth: Temporal proximity to the stressor is crucial. *Cerebral Cortex, 33*(1), 96–113. https://doi.org/10.1093/cercor/bhac055

Berg, S. (2017, September 11). *Family doctors spend 86 minutes of "pajama time" with EHRs nightly*. American Medical Association. https://www.ama-assn.org/practice-management/digital/family-doctors-spend-86-minutes-pajama-time-ehrs-nightly

Bernier, D. (1998). A study of coping: Successful recovery from severe burnout and other reactions to severe work-related stress. *Work & Stress, 12*(1), 50–65. https://doi.org/10.1080/02678379808256848

Bersin, J. (n.d.). *The definitive guide to pay equity*. Retrieved October 1, 2023, from https://joshbersin.com/the-definitive-guide-to-pay-equity-increasing-productivity-innovation-and-sustainability/

Bersin, J. (2023a, March 14). *How to fulfill the dream of equal pay for equal work*. https://joshbersin.com/2023/03/how-to-fulfill-the-dream-of-equal-pay-for-equal-work/

Bersin, J. (2023b, May 4). *Why do corporate pay practices feel broken? Because they are*. https://joshbersin.com/2023/05/why-do-corporate-pay-practices-feel-broken-because-they-are/

Bianchi, R. (2018). Burnout is more strongly linked to neuroticism than to work-contextualized factors. *Psychiatry Research, 270*, 901–905. https://doi.org/10.1016/j.psychres.2018.11.015

Biondi, F. N., Cacanindin, A., Douglas, C., & Cort, J. (2021, August). Overloaded and at work: Investigating the effect of cognitive workload on assembly task performance. *Human Factors, 63*(5), 813–820. https://doi.org/10.1177/0018720820929928

Bogg, T., & Roberts, B. W. (2004). Conscientiousness and health-related behaviors: A meta-analysis of the leading behavioral contributors to mortality. *Psychological Bulletin, 130*(6), 887–919. https://doi.org/10.1037/0033-2909.130.6.887

Bookey. (n.d.). *30 best Tristan Harris quotes with image.* Retrieved January 13, 2024, from https://www.bookey.app/quote-author/tristan-harris

Brafford, A. M. (2021, May). *What's working well in law firm well-being programs.* https://lawyerwellbeing.net/wp-content/uploads/2021/05/Well-Being-Firm-Profiles_4-2021.pdf

Brewerton, P. (2022, October 10). *Top 4 strategies for avoiding the strengths in overdrive trap* [Audio podcast]. Strengthscope. https://www.strengthscope.com/podcasts/top-4-strategies-for-avoiding-the-strengths-in-overdrive-trap

Brief, A. (1998). *Attitudes in and around organizations.* Sage Publications.

Bruggen, A. (2015). An empirical investigation of the relationship between workload and performance. *Management Decision, 53*(10), 2377–2389. https://doi.org/10.1108/MD-02-2015-0063

Buckingham, M., & Goodall, A. (2019, March 1). *The feedback fallacy.* Harvard Business Review. https://hbr.org/2019/03/the-feedback-fallacy

Buffer. (n.d.). *Transparent salaries.* https://buffer.com/salaries

Burkus, D. (2017, July 20). *How Adobe structures feedback conversations.* Harvard Business Review. https://hbr.org/2017/07/how-adobe-structures-feedback-conversations

Burton, A. (2023, June 26). *Genpact is using A.I. to flag employee dissatisfaction and tying leaders' bonuses to the results.* Fortune. https://fortune.com/2023/06/26/genpact-ai-employees-satisfaction-engagement-retention-bonuses/

Caloyeras, J. P., Liu, H., Exum, E., Broderick, M., & Mattke, S. (2014). Managing manifest diseases, but not health risks, saved PepsiCo money over seven years. *Health Affairs, 33*(1), 124–131. https://doi.org/10.1377/hlthaff.2013.0625

Cameron, L., & Hafenbrack, A. (2022, December 12). *Research: When mindfulness does—And doesn't—Help at work.* Harvard Business Review. https://hbr.org/2022/12/research-when-mindfulness-does-and-doesnt-help-at-work

Carnegie, M. (2023, July 23). *The creepy rise of bossware.* Wired UK. https://www.wired.co.uk/article/creepy-rise-bossware

Carney, M. (2015). *Karoshi: Stroke, heart attacks and suicide attributed to overwork killing hundreds of Japanese employees.* ABC News. https://www.abc.net.au/news/2015-06-11/epidemic-of-overwork-killing-hundreds-of-japanese-each-year/6536860

Carroll, L. (1865). *Alice's adventures in wonderland.* Macmillan.

Cavanaugh, M. A., Boswell, W. R., Roehling, M. V., & Boudreau, J. W. (2000). An empirical examination of self-reported work stress among U.S. managers.

Journal of Applied Psychology, 85(1), 65–74. https://doi.org/10.1037/0021-9010.85.1.65

CB Staff. (2023, July 7). *"We could have lost half our workforce": How Purolator worked to curb employee attrition.* Canadian Business. https://canadianbusiness.com/ideas/how-to-reduce-employee-attrition/

Center for Creative Leadership. (2022). *Use Situation-Behavior-Impact (SBI) to understand intent.* https://www.ccl.org/articles/leading-effectively-articles/closing-the-gap-between-intent-vs-impact-sbii/

Chaiken, S., & Eagly, A. H. (1983). Communication modality as a determinant of persuasion: The role of communicator salience. *Journal of Personality and Social Psychology, 45*(2), 241–256. https://doi.org/10.1037/0022-3514.45.2.241

Chamorro-Premuzic, T. (2022, June). *Are successful people more neurotic?* Forbes. https://www.forbes.com/sites/tomaspremuzic/2022/06/07/are-successful-people-more-neurotic/#:~:text=Besides%2C%20around%2030%25%20of%20the,%2C%20and%20be%20self%2Dcritical

Chouinard, Y. (2006). *Let my people go surfing: The education of a reluctant businessman.* Penguin Books.

Chowdhury, M. R. (2019, April 9). *The neuroscience of gratitude and effects on the brain.* PositivePsychology.com. https://positivepsychology.com/neuroscience-of-gratitude/

Clarida, M. (2013). *"There is no such thing as failure," Oprah tells Harvard graduates.* The Harvard Crimson. https://www.thecrimson.com/article/2013/5/31/oprah-commencement-2013-speech/

Clark, S. (2022, April 14). *The critical role technology plays in company culture.* reworked.co. https://www.reworked.co/digital-workplace/the-critical-role-technology-plays-to-support-company-culture/

Clarke, S. (2020). *The 4 surprising benefits of burnout.* Medium. https://salcla.medium.com/the-4-surprising-benefits-of-burnout-1748b5cc35ed

Clear, J. (2018). *Atomic habits: An easy & proven way to build good habits & break bad ones.* Avery.

Clifford, C. (2018, June 26). *How Starbucks' Howard Schultz went from the projects to building a $3 billion fortune.* CNBC. https://www.cnbc.com/2018/06/04/rags-to-riches-story-of-starbucks-howard-schultz.html

Conversano, C., Rotondo, A., Lensi, E., Della Vista, O., Arpone, F., & Reda, M. A. (2010). Optimism and its impact on mental and physical well-being. *Clinical Practice and Epidemiology in Mental Health, 6*(1), 25–29. https://doi.org/10.2174/1745017901006010025

Cook, B. (2022, September 19). *How Oprah Winfrey grew up.* Clever Tykes. https://clevertykes.com/how-oprah-winfrey-grew-up/

Crane, M. (2021). The multisystem approach to resilience in the context of organizations. In M. Ungar (Ed.), *Multisystemic resilience: Adaptation and transformation in contexts of change* (pp. 455–476). Oxford University Press. https://doi.org/10.1093/oso/9780190095888.003.0024

Croes, E. A. J., Antheunis, M. L., Schouten, A. P., & Krahmer, E. J. (2019). Social attraction in video-mediated communication: The role of nonverbal affiliative behavior. *Journal of Social and Personal Relationships, 36*(4), 1210–1232. https://doi.org/10.1177/0265407518757382

Cross, R., Rebele, R., & Grant, A. (2016, January 1). *Collaborative overload.* Harvard Business Review. https://hbr.org/2016/01/collaborative-overload

Crowley, D. (2014, February 6). *Castaway was a soldier trained in guerrilla warfare says best friend.* Daily Mail. https://www.dailymail.co.uk/news/article-2552838/Castaway-soldier-trained-guerrilla-warfare-used-drink-turtle-juice-wasn-t-sea-s-no-surprise-survived-says-best-friend.html

Crutchfield, R. S. (1955). Conformity and character. *American Psychologist, 10*(5), 191–198. https://doi.org/10.1037/h0040237

Cuijpers, P., Smit, F., Penninx, B. W., de Graaf, R., ten Have, M., & Beekman, A. T. (2010, October). Economic costs of neuroticism: A population-based study. *Archives of General Psychiatry, 67*(10), 1086–1093. https://doi.org/10.1001/archgenpsychiatry.2010.130

Curry-Wheat, C. (2023, May 9). *NPCA's work culture, values prove award-winning.* National Parks Conservation Association. https://www.npca.org/articles/3481-npca-s-work-culture-values-prove-award-winning

Deci, E. L., & Ryan, R. M. (2000). The "what" and "why" of goal pursuits: Human needs and the self-determination of behavior. *Psychological Inquiry, 11*(4), 227–268. https://doi.org/10.1207/S15327965PLI1104_01

Deloitte. (2015). *Workplace burnout survey.* https://www2.deloitte.com/us/en/pages/about-deloitte/articles/burnout-survey.html

Deloitte. (2020). *2020 global human capital trends report.* https://www2.deloitte.com/cn/en/pages/human-capital/articles/global-human-capital-trends-2020.html

Demerouti, E., Bakker, A. B., Nachreiner, F., & Schaufeli, W. B. (2001). The job demands–resources model of burnout. *Journal of Applied Psychology, 86*(3), 499–512. https://doi.org/10.1037/0021-9010.86.3.499

Di Fabio, A., Palazzeschi, L., & Bucci, O. (2017). Gratitude in organizations: A contribution for healthy organizational contexts. *Frontiers in Psychology, 8,* Article 2025. https://doi.org/10.3389/fpsyg.2017.02025

Dick, P. K. (1956). The minority report. *Fantastic Universe, 4*(6), 4–26.

Dickinson, K. (2023, January 24). *We must learn from karoshi, Japan's overwork epidemic.* Big Think. https://bigthink.com/the-learning-curve/karoshi/

Dishman, L. (2015, July 10). Show me the money: The businesses opting for salary transparency. *The Guardian.* https://www.theguardian.com/business/2015/jul/10/salary-wage-glassdoor-payscale-buffer-sumall

Donnellan, M. B., Larsen-Rife, D., & Conger, R. D. (2005). Personality, family history, and competence in early adult romantic relationships. *Journal of Personality and Social Psychology, 88*(3), 562–576. https://doi.org/10.1037/0022-3514.88.3.562

Eagle Hill Consulting. (2018). *The business case for culture: How organizational culture impacts business performance.* https://www.eaglehillconsulting.com/insights/organizational-culture-impacts-performance/

Elias, J. (2020). *Google's $310 million sexual harassment settlement aims to set new industry standards.* CNBC. https://www.cnbc.com/2020/09/29/googles-310-million-sexual-misconduct-settlement-details.html

Entrepreneur Life. (2023, July 16). *Howard Schultz biography—How he created Starbucks coffee.* Medium. https://medium.com/@EntrepreneurLife_yt/howard-schultz-biography-how-he-created-starbucks-coffee-2904d21e9c93

Eurich, T. (2018, January 4). *What self-awareness really is (and how to cultivate it).* Harvard Business Review. https://hbr.org/2018/01/what-self-awareness-really-is-and-how-to-cultivate-it

Evans, R. (Host). (2022, October). *Outside-in—How the healthcare industry transformed Purolator* [Audio podcast]. CAATPension. https://podcasts.apple.com/us/podcast/outside-in-how-the-healthcare-industry-transformed/id1587239838?i=1000583104876

Eyrich, N. W., Quinn, R. E., & Fessell, D. P. (2019, December 27). *How one person can change the conscience of an organization.* Harvard Business Review. https://hbr.org/2019/12/how-one-person-can-change-the-conscience-of-an-organization

Fagan, M. (2021, June 9). *Innovation week—Atlassian Security Team's 20% time ritual.* Atlassian Community. https://community.atlassian.com/t5/Trust-Security-articles/Innovation-Week-Atlassian-Security-Team-s-20-Time-Ritual/ba-p/1714481

Fan, J., & Smith, A. P. (2017). The impact of workload and fatigue on performance. In L. Longo & M. C. Leva (Eds.), *Human mental workload: Models and applications* (pp. 90–105). Springer International Publishing. https://doi.org/10.1007/978-3-319-61061-0_6

FasterCapital. (2024, June 17). *Navigating the comeback: Lessons from successful second chance business ventures.* FasterCapital. https://fastercapital.com/content/Navigating-the-Comeback--Lessons-from-Successful-Second-Chance-Business-Ventures.html

Feld, B. (2010, October 10). *Quarterly week off the grid* [Video]. TEDxBoulder. https://www.youtube.com/watch?v=Hp-rF9Qr7KU

Feldscher, K. (2022, February 9). *What led to the opioid crisis—And how to fix it.* Harvard T. H. Chan School of Public Health. https://www.hsph.harvard.edu/news/features/what-led-to-the-opioid-crisis-and-how-to-fix-it/

Felicia, F., Satiadarma, M. P., & Subroto, U. (2022). The relationship between locus of control and resilience in adolescents whose parents are divorced. In T. A. Ping, H. K. Tunjungsari, & W. P. Sari (Eds.), *Proceedings of the 3rd Tarumanagara International Conference on the Applications of Social Sciences and Humanities (TICASH 2021), Part 1* (pp. 1426–1431). Atlantis Press. https://doi.org/10.2991/assehr.k.220404.228

Ferran, C., & Watts, S. (2008). Videoconferencing in the field: A heuristic processing model. *Management Science, 54*(9), 1565–1578. https://doi.org/10.1287/mnsc.1080.0879

Fletcher, E. (2015). *The neuroscience of gratitude*. HuffPost. https://www.huffpost.com/entry/the-neuroscience-of-gratitude_b_8631392

Forbes. (2013, June 6). *Enron the incredible.* https://www.forbes.com/2002/01/15/0115enron.html

Forsdick, S. (2022, May 10). *Buffer's salary policy takes transparency to another level*. Raconteur. https://www.raconteur.net/talent-culture/buffer-transparent-salary-pay

Forsyth, D. R. (2014). How do leaders lead? Through social influence. In G. R. Goethals, S. T. Allison, R. M. Kramer, & D. M. Messick (Eds.), *Conceptions of leadership: Enduring ideas and emerging insights* (pp. 185–200). Palgrave MacMillan. https://doi.org/10.1057/9781137472038_11

Frankl, V. E. (1959). *Man's search for meaning: An introduction to logotherapy.* Beacon Press.

Franklin, J. (2015). *438 days: An extraordinary true story of survival at sea.* Atria Books.

Freudenberger, H. J. (1974). Staff burn-out. *Journal of Social Issues, 30*(1), 159–165. https://doi.org/10.1111/j.1540-4560.1974.tb00706.x

FullContact. (2012, July 10). *Paid vacation? That's not cool. You know what's cool? Paid, PAID vacation.* https://www.fullcontact.com/blog/2012/07/10/paid-paid-vacation-2/

Gabbatt, A. (2018). Starbucks closes more than 8,000 US cafes for racial bias training. *The Guardian.* https://www.theguardian.com/business/2018/may/29/starbucks-coffee-shops-racial-bias-training

Gale, C. R., Hagenaars, S. P., Davies, G., Hill, W. D., Liewald, D. C., Cullen, B., Penninx, B. W., Boomsma, D. I., Pell, J., McIntosh, A. M., Smith, D. J., Deary, I. J., Harris, S. E., & the International Consortium for Blood Pressure GWAS, CHARGE Consortium Aging and Longevity Group. (2016, April). Pleiotropy between neuroticism and physical and mental health: Findings from 108,038 men and women in UK Biobank. *Translational Psychiatry, 6*(4), Article e791. https://doi.org/10.1038/tp.2016.56

Gallo, C. (2022, October 18). *4 communication skills Indra Nooyi used that helped her become CEO of PepsiCo*. Inc.com. https://www.inc.com/carmine-gallo/indra-nooyi-communication-skills-pepsico-ceo.html

Gamble, K. R., Cassenti, D. N., & Buchler, N. (2018, July 4). Effects of information accuracy and volume on decision making. *Military Psychology, 30*(4), 311–320. https://doi.org/10.1080/08995605.2018.1425586

Geoghegan, T. (2023). *Consider the Germans: Co-determination and works councils.* COTO Report. https://coto2.wordpress.com/2010/03/23/consider-the-germans-co-determination-and-works-councils/

Gerhart, B., & Fang, M. (2014). Pay, intrinsic motivation, extrinsic motivation, performance, and creativity in the workplace: Revisiting long-held beliefs.

Annual Review of Organizational Psychology and Organizational Behavior, 1(1), 489–521. https://doi.org/10.1146/annurev-orgpsych-031413-091304

Gerwig, G. (Director). (2023). *Barbie* [Film]. Warner Brothers.

Global Wellness Institute. (n.d.). *Wellness economy statistics & facts*. Retrieved January 26, 2024, from https://globalwellnessinstitute.org/press-room/statistics-and-facts/

Goethe, J. W. v. (2012). *The sorrows of young Werther*. Oxford University Press. (Original work published 1774)

Goetz, K. (2011, February 1). *How 3M gave everyone days off and created an innovation dynamo*. Fast Company. https://www.fastcompany.com/1663137/how-3m-gave-everyone-days-off-and-created-an-innovation-dynamo

Goffman, E. (1961). *Encounters: Two studies in the sociology of interaction*. Bobbs-Merrill Co.

Goldenberg, S. (2010). BP oil spill blamed on management and communication failures. *The Guardian*. https://www.theguardian.com/business/2010/dec/02/bp-oil-spill-failures

Goldenberg, S., & Kollewe, J. (2010, October 29). BP and Halliburton knew of Gulf Oil well cement flaws. *The Guardian*. https://www.theguardian.com/environment/2010/oct/29/bp-oil-spill-bp

Golkar, A., Johansson, E., Kasahara, M., Osika, W., Perski, A., & Savic, I. (2014). The influence of work-related chronic stress on the regulation of emotion and on functional connectivity in the brain. *PLOS ONE, 9*(9), Article e104550. https://doi.org/10.1371/journal.pone.0104550

Gordon, A. M., & Mendes, W. B. (2021). A large-scale study of stress, emotions, and blood pressure in daily life using a digital platform. *Proceedings of the National Academy of Sciences of the United States of America, 118*(31), Article e2105573118. https://doi.org/10.1073/pnas.2105573118

Grassi, L., McFarland, D., & Riba, M. B. (Eds.). (2021). *Depression, burnout and suicide in physicians: Insights from oncology and other medical professions*. Springer. https://doi.org/10.1007/978-3-030-84785-2

Greenhouse, S. (2024, March 22). "Huge breakthrough" in Starbucks union talks—Which other US firms will follow? *The Guardian*. https://www.theguardian.com/us-news/2024/mar/22/starbucks-union-talks-trader-joes-amazon-rei

Greeven, M. J., Xin, K., & Yip, G. S. (2023, March 1). *How Chinese companies are reinventing management*. Harvard Business Review. https://hbr.org/2023/03/how-chinese-companies-are-reinventing-management

Gröschke, D., Hofmann, E., Müller, N. D., & Wolf, J. (2022). Individual and organizational resilience—Insights from healthcare providers in Germany during the COVID-19 pandemic. *Frontiers in Psychology, 13*, Article 965380. https://doi.org/10.3389/fpsyg.2022.965380

Hakanen, J. J., & Bakker, A. B. (2017). Born and bred to burn out: A life-course view and reflections on job burnout. *Journal of Occupational Health Psychology, 22*(3), 354–364. https://doi.org/10.1037/ocp0000053

Hall, E. T. (1966). *The hidden dimension*. Knopf Doubleday Publishing Group.

Hanssen, M. M., Vancleef, L. M. G., Vlaeyen, J. W. S., Hayes, A. F., Schouten, E. G. W., & Peters, M. L. (2015). Optimism, motivational coping and well-being: Evidence supporting the importance of flexible goal adjustment. *Journal of Happiness Studies, 16*(6), 1525–1537. https://doi.org/10.1007/s10902-014-9572-x

Hatfield, E., Cacioppo, J. T., & Rapson, R. L. (1994). *Emotional contagion.* Cambridge University Press.

Hatfield, S., Fischer, J., & Silverglate, P. (2022, June 22). *The C-suite's role in well-being.* Deloitte Insights. https://www2.deloitte.com/us/en/insights/topics/leadership/employee-wellness-in-the-corporate-workplace.html

Haumer, F., Schlicker, L., Murschetz, P. C., & Kolo, C. (2021). Tailor the message and change will happen? An experimental study of message tailoring as an effective communication strategy for organizational change. *Journal of Strategy and Management, 14*(4), 426–443. https://doi.org/10.1108/JSMA-08-2020-0207

Heljala, H. (2016, August 22). *How Typeform uses Bonusly and Merit Money for motivation.* Management 3.0. https://management30.com/blog/typeform-merit-money/

Hern, A. (2022, August 16). Apple tells staff to come into the office for at least three days a week. *The Guardian.* https://www.theguardian.com/technology/2022/aug/16/apple-tells-staff-to-come-into-the-office-for-at-least-three-days-a-week

Herzberg, F., Mausner, B., & Snyderman, B. B. (1959). *The motivation to work* (2nd ed.). John Wiley & Sons.

History.com Editors. (2019, June 19). *Could the Titanic disaster have been avoided?* [Video]. A&E Television Networks. https://www.history.com/topics/early-20th-century-us/titanics-achilles-heel-attempt-to-avoid-disaster-video

Hobfoll, S. E. (1989). Conservation of resources: A new attempt at conceptualizing stress. *American Psychologist, 44*, 513–524.

Holt-Lunstad, J., Smith, T. B., & Layton, J. B. (2010, July 27). Social relationships and mortality risk: A meta-analytic review. *PLOS Medicine, 7*(7), Article e1000316. https://doi.org/10.1371/journal.pmed.1000316

Houlis, A. (2019). *Not everyone is buying the 'millennial burnout' fad—Including these millennials.* Fairygodboss. https://fairygodboss.com/career-topics/not-everyone-is-buying-the-millennial-burnout-fad--including-these-millennials

HRMorning. (2023, September 1). *The state of pay equity in 2023: How HR can move the needle.* https://www.hrmorning.com/articles/the-state-of-pay-equity-in-2023/

Huffington, A. (2017). *10 years ago I collapsed from burnout and exhaustion, and it's the best thing that could have happened to me.* Medium. https://medium.com/thrive-global/10-years-ago-i-collapsed-from-burnout-and-exhaustion-and-its-the-best-thing-that-could-have-b1409f16585d

Hunter, E. M., & Wu, C. (2016). Give me a better break: Choosing workday break activities to maximize resource recovery. *Journal of Applied Psychology, 101*(2), 302–311. https://doi.org/10.1037/apl0000045

Ignatius, A. (2021, November 5). *Indra Nooyi, former CEO of PepsiCo, on nurturing talent in turbulent times* [Video]. Harvard Business Review. https://hbr.org/2021/11/indra-nooyi-former-ceo-of-pepsico-on-nurturing-talent-in-turbulent-times

Jerome, J. (1975, June 9). The Jaggers. *People Weekly*. https://people.com/archive/cover-story-the-jaggers-vol-3-no-22/

Jiang, M. (2020). *The reason Zoom calls drain your energy*. BBC. https://www.bbc.com/worklife/article/20200421-why-zoom-video-chats-are-so-exhausting

Jomuad, P. D., Antiquina, L. M. M., Cericos, E. U., Bacus, J. A., Vallejo, J. H., Dionio, B. B., Bazar, J. S., Cocolan, J. V., & Clarin, A. S. (2021). Teachers' workload in relation to burnout and work performance. *International Journal of Educational Policy Research and Review, 8*(2), 48–53. https://doi.org/10.15739/IJEPRR.21.007

Jones, L. (2021, April 29). *Microsoft patent points to stress monitoring and advice tool for workers*. WinBuzzer. https://winbuzzer.com/2021/04/29/microsoft-patent-points-to-stress-monitoring-and-advice-tool-for-workers-xcxwbn/

Kahn, W. A. (1990). Psychological conditions of personal engagement and disengagement at work. *Academy of Management Journal, 33*(4), 692–724. https://doi.org/10.2307/256287

Kalisch, R., Baker, D. G., Basten, U., Boks, M. P., Bonanno, G. A., Brummelman, E., Chmitorz, A., Fernàndez, G., Fiebach, C. J., Galatzer-Levy, I., Geuze, E., Groppa, S., Helmreich, I., Hendler, T., Hermans, E. J., Jovanovic, T., Kubiak, T., Lieb, K., Lutz, B., . . . Kleim, B. (2017, November). The resilience framework as a strategy to combat stress-related disorders. *Nature Human Behaviour, 1*(11), 784–790. https://doi.org/10.1038/s41562-017-0200-8

Kantor, J., & Streitfeld, D. (2015, August 15). Inside Amazon: Wrestling big ideas in a bruising workplace. *The New York Times*. https://archive.nytimes.com/www.nytimes.com/2015/08/16/technology/inside-amazon-wrestling-big-ideas-in-a-bruising-workplace.html

Keller, T. (2013). *Walking with God through pain and suffering*. Redeemer, Dutton.

Keng, S.-L., Smoski, M. J., & Robins, C. J. (2011, August). Effects of mindfulness on psychological health: A review of empirical studies. *Clinical Psychology Review, 31*(6), 1041–1056. https://doi.org/10.1016/j.cpr.2011.04.006

Keynes, J. M. (1936). *The general theory of employment, interest, and money*. Palgrave Macmillan.

Khullar, D. (2023, February 27). Can A. I. treat mental illness? *The New Yorker*. https://www.newyorker.com/magazine/2023/03/06/can-ai-treat-mental-illness

Klein, L. K., Earl, E., & Cundick, D. (2023, May 1). *Reducing information overload in your organization*. Harvard Business Review. https://hbr.org/2023/05/reducing-information-overload-in-your-organization

Kotler, S. (2021, January 20). *Why a free afternoon each week can boost employees' sense of autonomy*. Fast Company. https://www.fastcompany.com/90595295/why-a-free-afternoon-each-week-can-boost-employees-sense-of-autonomy

Ladley, D., Wilkinson, I., & Young, L. (2015). The impact of individual versus group rewards on work group performance and cooperation: A computational social science approach. *Journal of Business Research, 68*(11), 2412–2425. https://doi.org/10.1016/j.jbusres.2015.02.020

Lah, K. (2016). *Real-life castaway survived 438 days lost at sea*. CNN World. https://www.cnn.com/2016/01/08/world/rewind-real-life-castaway/index.html

Lahey, B. B. (2009). Public health significance of neuroticism. *American Psychologist, 64*(4), 241–256. https://doi.org/10.1037/a0015309

Lam, L., Hayden Cheng, B., Bamberger, P., & Wong, M.-N. (2022, August 12). *Research: The unintended consequences of pay transparency*. Harvard Business Review. https://hbr.org/2022/08/research-the-unintended-consequences-of-pay-transparency

Lee, K. (2018, October 29). *Why business transparency matters (and how to get started)*. Buffer Resources. https://buffer.com/resources/transparency-in-business/

Lee, R. T., & Ashforth, B. E. (1996). A meta-analytic examination of the correlates of the three dimensions of job burnout. *Journal of Applied Psychology, 81*(2), 123–133. https://doi.org/10.1037/0021-9010.81.2.123

Leiter, M. P., & Maslach, C. (1999). Six areas of worklife: A model of the organizational context of burnout. *Journal of Health and Human Services Administration, 21*(4), 472–489.

Lench, H. C., Levine, L. J., Dang, V., Kaiser, K. A., Carpenter, Z. K., Carlson, S. J., Flynn, E., Perez, K. A., & Winckler, B. (2021). Optimistic expectations have benefits for effort and emotion with little cost. *Emotion, 21*(6), 1213–1223. https://doi.org/10.1037/emo0000957

Lengnick-Hall, C. A., Beck, T. E., & Lengnick-Hall, M. L. (2011, September 1). Developing a capacity for organizational resilience through strategic human resource management. *Human Resource Management Review, 21*(3), 243–255. https://doi.org/10.1016/j.hrmr.2010.07.001

Leon, M. R., Halbesleben, J. R. B., & Paustian-Underdahl, S. C. (2015). A dialectical perspective on burnout and engagement. *Burnout Research, 2*(2–3), 87–96. https://doi.org/10.1016/j.burn.2015.06.002

Lewis, R. (2021, March 11). *From fashion to suicide: Why we imitate each other*. Psychology Today. https://www.psychologytoday.com/us/blog/finding-purpose/202103/fashion-suicide-why-we-imitate-each-other

Libby, T., & Thorne, L. (2009). The influence of incentive structure on group performance in assembly lines and teams. *Behavioral Research in Accounting, 21*(2), 57–72. https://doi.org/10.2308/bria.2009.21.2.57

Limeade. (2020, July 15). *New Limeade research reveals "communicating with care" is critical for organizations*. https://www.limeade.com/company/newsroom/new-limeade-research-reveals-communicating-with-care-is-critical-for-organizations/

Liu, Q., Liu, Y., Leng, X., Han, J., Xia, F., & Chen, H. (2020, November). Impact of chronic stress on attention control: Evidence from behavioral and event-related potential analyses. *Neuroscience Bulletin, 36*(11), 1395–1410. https://doi.org/10.1007/s12264-020-00549-9

Loh, K. K., & Kanai, R. (2014, September 24). Higher media multi-tasking activity is associated with smaller gray-matter density in the anterior cingulate cortex. *PLOS ONE, 9*(9), Article e106698. https://doi.org/10.1371/journal.pone.0106698

Maddi, S. (2006). Hardiness: The courage to grow from stresses. *The Journal of Positive Psychology, 1*(3), 160–168. https://doi.org/10.1080/17439760600619609

Mann, J., & Varanasi, L. (2023, October 28). *Surf breaks, yacht trips, and digital detox cabins, here are some of the top perks at companies outside of big tech.* Business Insider. https://www.businessinsider.com/cool-perks-offered-companies-employees-airbnb-patagonia-adobe-2023-9

Mardell, S. (n.d.). *Creating more clarity for your employees around growth, compensation, and promotions.* Button. https://www.usebutton.com/post/creating-more-clarity-for-your-employees-around-growth-compensation-and-promotions

Martin, R. (2015, December 6). *How "resilience" is misunderstood when talking about racism.* NPR. https://www.npr.org/2015/12/06/458662021/how-resilience-is-misunderstood-when-talking-about-racism

Maslach, C. (1993). Burnout: A multidimensional perspective. In W. B. Schaufeli, C. Maslach, & T. Marek (Eds.), *Professional burnout: Recent developments in theory and research* (pp. 19–32). https://doi.org/10.4324/9781315227979-3

Matheson, J. (n.d.). *Physician suicide.* American College of Emergency Physicians. https://www.acep.org/life-as-a-physician/wellness/wellness/wellness-week-articles/physician-suicide

Mattke, S., Liu, H. H., Caloyeras, J. P., Huang, C. Y., Van Busum, K. R., Khodyakov, D., & Shier, V. (2013, May 30). *Workplace wellness programs study: Final report.* RAND Corporation. https://www.rand.org/pubs/research_reports/RR254.html

Mauno, S., Kinnunen, U., & Ruokolainen, M. (2007). Job demands and resources as antecedents of work engagement: A longitudinal study. *Journal of Vocational Behavior, 70*(1), 149–171. https://doi.org/10.1016/j.jvb.2006.09.002

McCrae, R. R., & Costa, P. T., Jr. (1987). Validation of the five-factor model of personality across instruments and observers. *Journal of Personality and Social Psychology, 52*(1), 81–90. https://doi.org/10.1037/0022-3514.52.1.81

McGonigal, J. (2012, October 1). *Building resilience by wasting time.* Harvard Business Review. https://hbr.org/2012/10/building-resilience-by-wasting-time

McGonigal, J. (2015). *SuperBetter: A revolutionary approach to getting stronger, happier, braver and more resilient.* Penguin Press.

McGregor, J. (2018, March 22). This professor says the workplace is the fifth leading cause of death in the U.S. *The Washington Post.* https://www.washingtonpost.com/news/on-leadership/wp/2018/03/22/this-professor-says-the-workplace-is-the-fifth-leading-cause-of-death-in-the-u-s/

Medscape. (2022, March 4). *Physician suicide report 2022.* https://www.medscape.com/register?client=205502&scode=msp&action=complete&lang=en&register=true&form=about&urlCache=aHR0cHM6Ly93d3cubWVkc2NhcGUuY29tL3NsaWRlc2hvdy8yMDIyLXBoeXNpY2lhbi1zdWljaWRlLXJlcG9ydC02MDEyMDE3LCwP3JlZz0x

Medscape. (2023). *Doctors' burden: Medscape physician suicide report 2023*. https://www.medscape.com/slideshow/2023-physician-suicide-report-6016243

Melamed, S., Ugarten, U., Shirom, A., Kahana, L., Lerman, Y., & Froom, P. (1999). Chronic burnout, somatic arousal and elevated salivary cortisol levels. *Journal of Psychosomatic Research, 46*(6), 591–598. https://doi.org/10.1016/s0022-3999(99)00007-0

Mercom Capital Group. (2024, March 31). *Mental health apps raised $1.2 billion in 2020*. https://mercomcapital.com/mental-health-apps-raised/

Microsoft WorkLab. (2021, April 20). *Research proves your brain needs breaks*. https://www.microsoft.com/en-us/worklab/work-trend-index/brain-research

Miller, S. (2010, January 20). *Wellness programs as an employee retention tool*. SHRM. https://www.shrm.org/resourcesandtools/hr-topics/benefits/pages/wellness_employeeretention.aspx

Minnick, J. (2023). *How psychological safety affects employee productivity*. Ragan. https://www.ragan.com/how-psychological-safety-affects-employee-productivity/

Mischel, W., Ayduk, O., Berman, M. G., Casey, B. J., Gotlib, I. H., Jonides, J., Kross, E., Teslovich, T., Wilson, N. L., Zayas, V., & Shoda, Y. (2011, April). "Willpower" over the life span: Decomposing self-regulation. *Social Cognitive and Affective Neuroscience, 6*(2), 252–256. https://doi.org/10.1093/scan/nsq081

Moeller, J., Ivcevic, Z., White, A. E., Menges, J., & Brackett, M. A. (2018, January 25). *Highly engaged but burned out: Intra-individual profiles in the US workforce* [Preprint]. Open Science Framework. https://doi.org/10.31219/osf.io/h6qnf

Moss, J. (2021). *The burnout epidemic: The rise of chronic stress and how we can fix it*. Harvard Business Review Press.

Murphy, B., Jr. (2020, November 1). *Google says it still swears by the 20 percent rule to find big ideas, and you should totally copy it*. Inc.com. https://www.inc.com/bill-murphy-jr/google-says-it-still-uses-20-percent-rule-you-should-totally-copy-it.html

Murty, R., Dadlani, S., & Das, R. (2022, August 29). *How much time and energy do we waste toggling between applications?* Harvard Business Review. https://hbr.org/2022/08/how-much-time-and-energy-do-we-waste-toggling-between-applications

National Institute of Mental Health. (2023). *Major depression*. Retrieved October 17, 2023, from https://www.nimh.nih.gov/health/statistics/major-depression

National Research Council. (1994). *Learning, remembering, believing: Enhancing human performance*. National Academies Press. https://doi.org/10.17226/2303

Nerstad, C. G. L., Wong, S. I., & Richardsen, A. M. (2019). Can engagement go awry and lead to burnout? The moderating role of the perceived motivational climate. *International Journal of Environmental Research and Public Health, 16*(11), 1979. https://doi.org/10.3390/ijerph16111979

Nestler, E. J. (2016). Transgenerational epigenetic contributions to stress responses: Fact or fiction? *PLOS Biology, 14*(3), Article e1002426. https://doi.org/10.1371/journal.pbio.1002426

Neuroscience News. (2023, July 28). *AI traces emotional contagion.* https://neurosciencenews.com/emotional-contagion-ai-23715/

Niederkrotenthaler, T., Herberth, A., & Sonneck, G. (2007). "Werther-Effekt": Mythos oder Realität? [The "Werther-effect": Legend or reality?]. *Neuropsychiatrie, 21*(4), 284–290.

Nooyi, I. K. (2021). *My life in full.* Penguin Random House.

Nooyi, I. K., & Govindarajan, V. (2020, March 1). *Becoming a better corporate citizen.* Harvard Business Review. https://hbr.org/2020/03/becoming-a-better-corporate-citizen

Norton, M. I., Mochon, D., & Ariely, D. (2012). The IKEA effect: When labor leads to love. *Journal of Consumer Psychology, 22*(3), 453–460. https://doi.org/10.1016/j.jcps.2011.08.002

Nurhidayat, I., & Kusumasari, B. (2019). Why would whistleblowers dare to reveal wrongdoings? An ethical challenge and dilemma for organisations. *International Journal of Law and Management, 61*(3–4), 505–515. https://doi.org/10.1108/IJLMA-03-2018-0055

Office of the Commissioner. (2020, June 17). *FDA permits marketing of first game-based digital therapeutic to improve attention function in children with ADHD* [Press release]. U.S. Food & Drug Administration. https://www.fda.gov/news-events/press-announcements/fda-permits-marketing-first-game-based-digital-therapeutic-improve-attention-function-children-adhd

Ofri, D. (2019, June 8). The business of health care depends on exploiting doctors and nurses. *The New York Times.* https://www.nytimes.com/2019/06/08/opinion/sunday/hospitals-doctors-nurses-burnout.html

Oliver, D. (2023, January 19). New Zealand prime minister Jacinda Ardern resigned. What that says about privilege, burnout. *USA TODAY.* https://www.usatoday.com/story/life/health-wellness/2023/01/19/jacinda-ardern-resignation-burnout-privilege/11080849002/

Online Etymology Dictionary. (n.d.). *analytics (n.).* https://www.etymonline.com/word/analytics

Oprah Winfrey Charitable Foundation. (n.d.). *Oprah Winfrey Leadership Academy For Girls.* https://www.oprahfoundation.org/portfolio-item/oprah-leadership-academy

Oshinsky, D. (2023, July 21). It's time to bring back asylums. *The Wall Street Journal.* https://www.wsj.com/articles/its-time-to-bring-back-the-asylum-ec01fb2

Owl Labs Staff. (2021, November 4). *Engaged employees are happy employees.* https://resources.owllabs.com/blog/engaged-employees

Payscale. (2018, July 15). *How your pay raise practices affect employee turnover.* https://www.payscale.com/research-and-insights/employee-turnover-pay-raises/

Pega, F., Náfrádi, B., Momen, N. C., Ujita, Y., Streicher, K. N., Prüss-Üstün, A. M., Descatha, A., Driscoll, T., Fischer, F. M., Godderis, L., Kiiver, H. M., Li, J., Magnusson Hanson, L. L., Rugulies, R., Sørensen, K., Woodruff, T. J., & the Technical Advisory Group. (2021, September). Global, regional, and national burdens of ischemic heart disease and stroke attributable to exposure to long working hours for 194 countries, 2000–2016: A systematic analysis from the WHO/ILO joint estimates of the work-related burden of disease and injury. *Environment International, 154*, Article 106595. https://doi.org/10.1016/j.envint.2021.106595

PerformYard. (n.d.-a). *Google's performance management playbook: Inspiration for your organization*. https://www.performyard.com/articles/googles-performance-management-playbook

PerformYard. (n.d.-b). *How Netflix does performance management, 360 feedback, & rewards*. https://www.performyard.com/articles/how-netflix-does-performance-management

Petitta, L., & Jiang, L. (2020). How emotional contagion relates to burnout: A moderated mediation model of job insecurity and group member proto-typicality. *International Journal of Stress Management, 27*(1), 12–22. https://doi.org/10.1037/str0000134

Pezirkianidis, C., Galanaki, E., Raftopoulou, G., Moraitou, D., & Stalikas, A. (2023). Adult friendship and wellbeing: A systematic review with practical implications. *Frontiers in Psychology, 14*, Article 1059057. https://doi.org/10.3389/fpsyg.2023.1059057

Phenom People, Inc. (2022). *How Kuehne+Nagel is empowering employees to own & grow their careers*. https://assets.phenom.com/hubfs/02_Assets/casestudy/210316-EN-CS-KuehneNagel.pdf

Phillips, D. P. (1974). The influence of suggestion on suicide: Substantive and theoretical implications of the Werther effect. *American Sociological Review, 39*(3), 340–354. https://doi.org/10.2307/2094294

Pierno, T. (2022, June 30). *The gift of time*. National Parks Conservation Association. https://www.npca.org/articles/3220-the-gift-of-time

Pink, D. H. (2009). *Drive: The surprising truth about what motivates us*. Riverhead Books.

Poulin, M. J., Brown, S. L., Dillard, A. J., & Smith, D. M. (2013). Giving to others and the association between stress and mortality. *American Journal of Public Health, 103*(9), 1649–1655. https://doi.org/10.2105/AJPH.2012.300876

PR Newswire. (2014, September 10). *Majority of workers don't aspire to leadership roles, finds new CareerBuilder survey*. CareerBuilder. https://www.prnewswire.com/news-releases/majority-of-workers-dont-aspire-to-leadership-roles-finds-new-careerbuilder-survey-274574401.html

Prieto, L., & Talukder, M. F. (2023, January). Resilient agility: A necessary condition for employee and organizational sustainability. *Sustainability, 15*(2), Article 1552. https://doi.org/10.3390/su15021552

Psico-Smart Editorial Team. (2024). *How do continuous feedback tools impact organizational culture and performance?* Vorecol. https://psico-smart.com/en/blogs/blog-how-do-continuous-feedback-tools-impact-organizational-culture-and-performance-123122

Ramesh, R. (2018, May 15). *Employee engagement: The holy grail of talent management.* TD.org. https://www.td.org/insights/employee-engagement-the-holy-grail-of-talent-management

Reclaim. (2021, November 2). *Productivity trends report: One-on-one meeting statistics.* https://reclaim.ai/blog/productivity-report-one-on-one-meetings

Reclaim. (2022, March 29). *Task management trends report: +200 stats on managers vs. individual contributors.* https://reclaim.ai/blog/task-management-trends-report

Richardson, M., & Abraham, C. (2009). Conscientiousness and achievement motivation predict performance. *European Journal of Personality, 23*(7), 589–605. https://doi.org/10.1002/per.732

Riedl, R. (2022). On the stress potential of videoconferencing: Definition and root causes of Zoom fatigue. *Electronic Markets, 32*(1), 153–177. https://doi.org/10.1007/s12525-021-00501-3

Rotenstein, J. (2009, February 19). *Atlassian's 20% time: A year in review.* Atlassian. https://www.atlassian.com/blog/archives/atlassians_20_time_a_year_in_review

Rotenstein, L. S., Brown, R., Sinsky, C., & Linzer, M. (2023). The association of work overload with burnout and intent to leave the job across the healthcare workforce during COVID-19. *Journal of General Internal Medicine, 38*(8), 1920–1927. https://doi.org/10.1007/s11606-023-08153-z

Rump, J., & Brandt, M. (2020). *Zoom fatigue.* Institute for Employment and Employability. https://www.ibe-ludwigshafen.de/fileadmin/ibe/Medien/Publikationen/EN_IBE-Studie-Zoom-Fatigue.pdf

Saner, E. (2018, January 12). Oprah Winfrey: From poverty to America's first black billionaire . . . to #Oprah2020? *The Guardian.* https://www.theguardian.com/tv-and-radio/2018/jan/12/oprah-winfrey-unlikely-to-run-for-us-president-but-could-win-if-she-did

Savic, I., Perski, A., & Osika, W. (2018). MRI shows that exhaustion syndrome due to chronic occupational stress is associated with partially reversible cerebral changes. *Cerebral Cortex, 28*(3), 894–906. https://doi.org/10.1093/cercor/bhw413

Schaufeli, W. B., & Bakker, A. B. (2004). Job demands, job resources, and their relationship with burnout and engagement: A multi-sample study. *Journal of Organizational Behavior, 25*(3), 293–315. https://doi.org/10.1002/job.248

Schaufeli, W. B., Salanova, M., Gonzalez-Roma, V., & Bakker, A. B. (2002). The measurement of engagement and burnout: A two-sample confirmatory factor analytic approach. *Journal of Happiness Studies, 3*(1), 71–92. https://doi.org/10.1023/A:1015630930326

Scheier, M. F., Weintraub, J. K., & Carver, C. S. (1986). Coping with stress: Divergent strategies of optimists and pessimists. *Journal of Personality and Social Psychology, 51*(6), 1257–1264. https://doi.org/10.1037/0022-3514.51.6.1257

Schrage, M. (2013, August 20). *Just how valuable is Google's "20% time"?* Harvard Business Review. https://hbr.org/2013/08/just-how-valuable-is-googles-2-1

Schulte, B. (Host). (2018, June 15). *Your work may be killing you* [Audio podcast]. Better Life Lab, Apple. https://podcasts.apple.com/us/podcast/your-work-may-be-killing-you/id1386944144?i=1000413852857

Schulte, B. (2022, April 11). *Working ourselves to death: What is American karoshi?* New America. https://newamerica.org/better-life-lab/blog/working-ourselves-to-death-what-is-american-karoshi/

Schwartz, L., Levy, J., Endevelt-Shapira, Y., Djalovski, A., Hayut, O., Dumas, G., & Feldman, R. (2022). Technologically-assisted communication attenuates interbrain synchrony. *NeuroImage, 264*, Article 119677. https://doi.org/10.1016/j.neuroimage.2022.119677

Schwartz, T. (2011, April 4). *Why I appreciate Starbucks.* Harvard Business Review. https://hbr.org/2011/04/why-i-appreciate-starbucks

Schweyer, A. (2021). *Academic research in action: Individual or team-based incentives?* Incentive Research Foundation. https://theirf.org/research_post/academic-research-in-action-individual-or-team-based-incentives

Scott, K. (2012, December 7). *The LinkedIn [in]Cubator.* https://www.linkedin.com/blog/member/archive/linkedin-incubator

Sellnow, T. (2010, August 1). *BP's crisis communication: Finding redemption through renewal.* National Communication Association. https://www.natcom.org/communication-currents/bps-crisis-communication-finding-redemption-through-renewal

Silverman, R. E. (2016, June 8). GE re-engineers performance reviews, pay practices. *The Wall Street Journal.* https://www.wsj.com/articles/ge-re-engineers-performance-reviews-pay-practices-1465358463

Simester, D., & Knez, M. (2000, March 20). *Firm-wide incentives and mutual monitoring at Continental Airlines.* SSRN. https://doi.org/10.2139/ssrn.207208

Singer-Velush, N., Sherman, K., & Anderson, E. (2020, July 15). *Microsoft analyzed data on its newly remote workforce.* Harvard Business Review. https://hbr.org/2020/07/microsoft-analyzed-data-on-its-newly-remote-workforce

Smallfield, J., & Kluemper, D. H. (2022, April). An explanation of personality change in organizational science: Personality as an outcome of workplace stress. *Journal of Management, 48*(4), 851–877. https://doi.org/10.1177/0149206321998429

Smith, S. (2011, October 10). *Deepwater Horizon: Production rewarded, safety ignored.* EHS Today. https://www.ehstoday.com/safety/article/21904043/deepwater-horizon-production-rewarded-safety-ignored

Smith, T. (2020, October 29). *This startup's employees thank each other—With real cash.* Sifted. https://sifted.eu/articles/typeform-culture/

Soares, J. (2022). *Does your team or client come first? Well, which came first: The chicken or the egg?* Forbes. https://www.forbes.com/councils/

forbeshumanresourcescouncil/2022/11/28/does-your-team-or-client-come-first-well-which-came-first-the-chicken-or-the-egg/

Song, Z., & Baicker, K. (2019, April 16). Effect of a workplace wellness program on employee health and economic outcomes: A randomized clinical trial. *JAMA: Journal of the American Medical Association, 321*(15), 1491–1501. https://doi.org/10.1001/jama.2019.3307

Spector, P. E. (1997). *Job satisfaction: Applications, assessment, causes, and consequences.* Sage. https://doi.org/10.4135/9781452231549

Stambor, Z. (2006). Optimists have longer, more satisfying relationships, study suggests. *Monitor on Psychology, 37*(8), 15. https://www.apa.org/monitor/sep06/optimists

Statista. (n.d.). *Wellness industry—Statistics & facts.* Retrieved August 27, 2024, from https://www.statista.com/topics/1336/wellness-and-spa/#topicOverview

Stolzoff, S. (2019, February 1). *How do you turn around the culture of a 130,000-person company? Ask Satya Nadella.* Quartz. https://qz.com/work/1539071/how-microsoft-ceo-satya-nadella-rebuilt-the-company-culture

Strengthscope. (n.d.). *Transforming talent acquisition at Siemens.* https://www.strengthscope.com/case-studies/siemens-2

Sugawara, S. K., Tanaka, S., Okazaki, S., Watanabe, K., & Sadato, N. (2012). Social rewards enhance offline improvements in motor skill. *PLOS ONE, 7*(11), Article e48174. https://doi.org/10.1371/journal.pone.0048174

Suskind, D. (2020, December 31). *Are you being mobbed at work?* Psychology Today. https://www.psychologytoday.com/us/blog/bully-wise/202012/are-you-being-mobbed-at-work

Tainaka, T., Miyoshi, T., & Mori, K. (2014). Conformity of witnesses with low self-esteem to their co witnesses. *Psychology, 5*(15), 1695–1701. https://doi.org/10.4236/psych.2014.515177

TechCentral.ie. (2021, April 19). *Microsoft patents tech to combat employee stress.* https://www.techcentral.ie/microsoft-patents-tech-to-combat-employee-stress/

Thiel, P., & Masters, B. (2014). *Zero to one: Notes on startups, or how to build the future* [NO-VALUE edition]. Crown Currency.

Threlkeld, K. (2021). *A piece of the pie: Understanding the importance of fair pay.* Indeed. https://www.indeed.com/lead/the-importance-of-fair-pay-and-salary-transparency

Tims, M., & Bakker, A. B. (2010). Job crafting: Towards a new model of individual job redesign. *South African Journal of Industrial Psychology, 36,* 1–9. https://doi.org/10.4102/sajip.v36i2.841

Tims, M., Bakker, A. B., & Derks, D. (2013). The impact of job crafting on job demands, job resources, and well-being. *Journal of Occupational Health Psychology, 18*(2), 230–240. https://doi.org/10.1037/a0032141

Tims, M., Derks, D., & Bakker, A. B. (2016, February). Job crafting and its relationships with person–job fit and meaningfulness: A three-wave study. *Journal of Vocational Behavior, 92,* 44–53. https://doi.org/10.1016/j.jvb.2015.11.007

Tosti, D. T., & Jackson, S. F. (1994). Organizational alignment: How it works and why it matters. *Training Magazine, 5,* 8–64.

Transparency Market Research. (n.d.). *Global corporate wellness market outlook 2031*. https://www.transparencymarketresearch.com/corporate-wellness-market.html

Tyagarajan, T. (2020). *Genpact's CEO Tiger Tyagarajan discusses using Amber to remotely engage employees during COVID-19, 2020* [Video]. YouTube. https://www.youtube.com/watch?v=g8v4RFveRpI

UNC Kenan-Flagler Business School. (2015, November 25). *Enron whistleblower shares lessons on corporate integrity*. https://www.kenan-flagler.unc.edu/news/enron-whistleblower-shares-lessons-on-corporate-integrity/

U.S. Bureau of Labor Statistics. (2023, September 6). *Data scientists*. https://www.bls.gov/ooh/math/data-scientists.htm

U.S. Department of Health and Human Services. (2023, May 3). *New surgeon general advisory raises alarm about the devastating impact of the epidemic of loneliness and isolation in the United States*. https://www.hhs.gov/about/news/2023/05/03/new-surgeon-general-advisory-raises-alarm-about-devastating-impact-epidemic-loneliness-isolation-united-states.html

Uţă, I.-C. (2019, June 27). *The self-improvement industry is estimated to grow to $13.2 billion by 2022*. Brand Minds Blog. https://brandminds.com/the-self-improvement-industry-is-estimated-to-grow-to-13-2-billion-by-2022/

Valcour, M. (2016). *Beating burnout*. Harvard Business Review. https://hbr.org/2016/11/beating-burnout

Varley, T., & Glaser, J. (2023, November 10). *Using data to improve employee health and wellness*. Harvard Business Review. https://hbr.org/2023/11/using-data-to-improve-employee-health-and-wellness

Venkatesa, N. (2022, November 15). *How Convictional's async culture works*. Retrieved March 25, 2024, from https://web.archive.org/web/20240227004658/https://www.convictional.com/blog/async-culture-roundtable

Wainwright, M. (2005, April 22). Emails 'pose threat to IQ.' *The Guardian*. https://www.theguardian.com/technology/2005/apr/22/money.workandcareers

Wang, H.-J., Demerouti, E., Blanc, P. L., & Lu, C.-Q. (2018, March 13). Crafting a job in "tough times": When being proactive is positively related to work attachment. *Journal of Occupational and Organizational Psychology, 91*(3), 569–590. https://doi.org/10.1111/joop.12218

Washington Psychological Wellness. (n.d.). *Self-care tips to fight burnout & compassion fatigue*. https://washington-psychwellness.com/therapy/self-care-tips-to-fight-burnout-and-compassion-fatigue/

Watson, J. M., & Strayer, D. L. (2010, August). Supertaskers: Profiles in extraordinary multitasking ability. *Psychonomic Bulletin & Review, 17*(4), 479–485. https://doi.org/10.3758/PBR.17.4.479

Weinberg, G. M. (1991). *Quality software management: Systems thinking*. Dorset House.

Whiteman, H. (2023, January 19). *Jacinda Ardern's resignation shows burnout is real—And it's nothing to be ashamed of*. CNN. https://www.cnn.com/2023/01/19/world/new-zealand-jacinda-ardern-leadership-intl-hnk/index.html

Wible, P. (2016). *Why doctors kill themselves* [Video]. YouTube. https://www.youtube.com/watch?v=qyVAtZ9VZ4Q

Williams, T. A., Gruber, D. A., Sutcliffe, K. M., Shepherd, D. A., & Zhao, E. Y. (2017). Organizational response to adversity: Fusing crisis management and resilience research streams. *Academy of Management Annals, 11*(2), 733–769. https://doi.org/10.5465/annals.2015.0134

Wilson, J. M., Boyer O'Leary, M., Metiu, A., & Jett, Q. R. (2008, July). Perceived proximity in virtual work: Explaining the paradox of far-but-close. *Organization Studies, 29*(7), 979–1002. https://doi.org/10.1177/0170840607083105

Winfrey, O. (n.d.-a). *Oprah on why your mind defines your life.* Oprah.com. https://www.oprah.com/spirit/oprah-on-why-your-mind-defines-your-life

Winfrey, O. (n.d.-b). *Oprah's top 20 moments.* Oprah.com. https://www.oprah.com/oprahshow/oprahs-top-20-moments

Woo, E., Sansing, L. H., Arnsten, A. F. T., & Datta, D. (2021, August 29). Chronic stress weakens connectivity in the prefrontal cortex: Architectural and molecular changes. *Chronic Stress, 5*, Article 24705470211029254. https://doi.org/10.1177/24705470211029254

World Health Organization. (2021). *Long working hours increasing deaths from heart disease and stroke: WHO, ILO.* https://www.who.int/news/item/17-05-2021-long-working-hours-increasing-deaths-from-heart-disease-and-stroke-who-ilo

World Health Organization. (2024). *Burn-out an "occupational phenomenon."* https://www.who.int/standards/classifications/frequently-asked-questions/burn-out-an-occupational-phenomenon

Wright, T. A., & Bonett, D. G. (1993). The role of employee coping and performance in voluntary employee withdrawal: A research refinement and elaboration. *Journal of Management, 19*(1), 147–161. https://doi.org/10.1177/014920639301900110

Wright, T. A., & Bonett, D. G. (1997). The role of pleasantness and activation-based well-being in performance prediction. *Journal of Occupational Health Psychology, 2*(3), 212–219. https://doi.org/10.1037/1076-8998.2.3.212

Wright, T. A., & Cropanzano, R. (2000). Psychological well-being and job satisfaction as predictors of job performance. *Journal of Occupational Health Psychology, 5*(1), 84–94. https://doi.org/10.1037/1076-8998.5.1.84

Wrzesniewski, A., & Dutton, J. E. (2001). Crafting a job: Revisioning employees as active crafters of their work. *Academy of Management Review, 26*(2), 179–201. https://doi.org/10.2307/259118

Yeo, A. (2021, April 20). *Constantly stressed at work? It might actually be changing your personality.* Mashable. https://mashable.com/article/work-stress-personality-change

Yerkes, R. M., & Dodson, J. D. (1908). The relation of strength of stimulus to rapidity of habit-formation. *Journal of Comparative Neurology and Psychology, 18*(5), 459–482. https://doi.org/10.1002/cne.920180503

Zavvy. (n.d.). *Run employee performance reviews and feedback like Cisco with data-driven processes.* https://www.zavvy.io/hr-examples/employee-performance-reviews-at-cisco

Index

About the Author

Dan Pelton, PhD, is an author and speaker committed to advancing employee well-being and mental health. He challenges conventional wisdom in the well-being industry, advocating for research-backed truths that drive behavioral change and deliver tangible workplace improvements—boosting engagement, retention, productivity, and satisfaction. Dan's career spans both public and private sectors. As a board-certified clinical psychologist, he served the U.S. Army in Afghanistan, providing care to thousands of soldiers across multiple provinces. Over the past decade, he has spearheaded mental health initiatives in management consulting, developing strategies that not only enhance well-being but also significantly elevate business performance. Dan has spoken to large audiences globally, championing mental health awareness, promoting early intervention, and engaging in critical dialogues. Dan lives in Colorado with his wife, Courtnee, and his two girls, Elliana and Eva. Please visit his website to access the Resilient Leader self-assessment and learn more about the Companion Guide that supplements this book (https://www.danpelton.com/).